Managing Notorious Trials

Timothy R. Murphy

Paula L. Hannaford

Genevra Kay Loveland

G. Thomas Munsterman

National Center for State Courts

National Center for State Courts, 300 Newport Ave. (23185), P.O. Box 8798, Williamsburg, VA 23187-8798

Cover photo by Gina Ferazzi/*Los Angeles Times*.

Contents

Preface to the Revised Edition

A lot of notorious cases have been tried in American courts in the past six years. Some of these—*California v. O.J. Simpson, Harry Perzigian v. Carroll O'Conner, Delaware v. John E. du Pont,* and *U.S. v. Autumn Jackson*—attained their notoriety from the celebrity status of the parties, victims, and witnesses. Many of the most notorious cases involved horrendous crimes—such as international and domestic terrorism in the World Trade Center and Oklahoma City bombing trials, or serial murders by Jeffrey Dahmer and Theodore Kaczynski.

Other cases involved less sensational crimes per se, but captured public attention because of unique factual circumstances. Susan Smith, who instigated a national alert for the kidnappers of her two young children, was ultimately convicted of killing them herself to improve her prospects for attracting a suitable romantic partner. The trial of Louise Woodward, the British au pair charged with murdering one of the children under her care, sparked a national debate about the availability and quality of child care in the United States and about judicial second-guessing of jury verdicts. The notoriety of a few trials can only be explained as public fascination with the truly bizarre aspects of contemporary life—the assault trials of Lorena and John Wayne Bobbitt being a case in point.

Notoriety is usually a temporary condition, however. And the fact that new courthouses, names, and faces constantly replace old ones on the talk shows, evening news, or the morning edition of the local paper was not sufficient, by itself, to justify revising *A Manual for Managing Notorious Cases.* Despite the variety of circumstances that have pushed cases into the national spotlight, the principles of managing a notorious case have changed very little since this publication was first issued. Preparation, teamwork, common sense, and flexibility are still the hallmarks of effective trial management. Nevertheless, some changes and innovations in notorious case management were important enough that a revision of the manual was warranted.

One of the most significant changes is greater certainty about the effectiveness of the various techniques—particularly selection criteria for the trial judge and the trial venue—that were first discussed in the manual. As judges and court staff around the country have gained greater experience with notorious cases, they have confirmed the relative usefulness of some techniques that were only innovative ideas six years ago. A number of ideas, some of them highly effective, have become routine practice in notorious trials. Other ideas, which worked less well, were ultimately discarded. This revision describes the experiences, both good and bad, that courts have had with these innovations.

Each new notorious case seems to raise at least a few new problems requiring new solutions. Necessity being the mother of invention, judges and court staff have proven themselves to be highly innovative managers in notorious cases. This revision describes some situations not previously contemplated in notorious trials—handling pro se and other "difficult" litigants, dealing with bomb threats, extending court security beyond the courthouse, avoiding prolonged sequestration for the jury—and discusses some new ideas for handling them.

Changes in substantive law have also prompted revisions to the manual. One area of law that has undergone substantial revision is the role of victims in criminal proceedings. Over the past decade, both the federal government and the vast majority of the states have enacted "victim's rights" legislation that substantially increases the rights of crime victims to be informed of, participate in, and provide input in a variety of pretrial, trial, and postconviction proceedings.

Another major change is much greater appellate tolerance for attorney gag orders than previously. This change may reflect the ability of trial judges to draft orders that are narrowly tailored and supported by a written explanation for their necessity. Or it may reflect appellate recognition that trial judges should be permitted to take reasonable measures to ensure effective trial management—as much to advance the actual administration of justice as to promote the public appearance of effective management, fairness to the parties, and institutional credibility.

Finally, the emergence of new technology has a tremendous effect on all aspects of notorious trial management. Depending on its intended use, and the procedures and policies in place to govern it, most of this technology is very good. Judges and lawyers can use sophisticated computers to track large quantities of evidence and documentary exhibits. Courts can use Touch-Tone™ telephone systems and telephone-answering devices to inform prospective jurors about reporting dates and times for voir dire. Real-time transcription services can produce an official court transcript for use by all parties and the media almost instantaneously. Electronic media can broadcast court proceedings using smaller, less intrusive equipment that delivers a better quality signal. Security personnel have more sophisticated equipment available to screen court visitors and incoming mail entering the courtroom or the courthouse. Without certain safeguards, however, new technology can also be abused. The revised manual highlights potential trouble spots and suggests ways to compensate for technological limitations.

The revisions themselves are based largely on anecdotal reports from judges, court staff, lawyers, media representatives, and other participants in notorious trials. The authors have sometimes been directly involved in these trials as formal or informal consultants, but more often have been spectators themselves. We are grateful to the many people who have called or written over the years with comments, ideas, and suggestions for *Managing Notorious Trials*.

There are, however, some individuals who gave more than modestly of their time and expertise to bring this revision to press. Among these were a number of people who, at our request, reviewed the manual and offered detailed written commentary and criticism about topics that needed updating, topics that needed to be added, and topics that needed to be discarded altogether. Others graciously talked with us at length, permitting us to question them about new ideas and to clarify significant factual issues. Included in this group are Beth Bonora (National Jury Project, Oakland, California); Hon. Roger W. Boren (Court of Appeal of California, Los Angeles); Jack Chesnett (NBC News, Denver); Hon. Ronald S. Coen (Superior Court of Los Angeles County, Los Angeles); Hon. B. Michael Dann (Maricopa County Superior Court, Phoenix); Hon. Kenneth DeHart (District Court of Texas, 394th District, Alpine); Quin A. Denvir, (Office of the Federal Defender, Sacramento, California); Gloria Gomez (Superior Court of Los Angeles County, Los Angeles); David Graeven (Trial Behavior Consulting, Inc., San Francisco); LeeAnn Flynn Hall (U.S. District Court, Washington, D.C.); Jerrianne Hayslett (Superior Court of Los Angeles County, Los Angeles); Hon. John F. Keenan (U.S. District Court, New York); Jane E. Kirtley (Reporters Committee for Freedom of the Press, Arlington, Virginia); David McCormick (NBC News, Denver); Roger O'Neil (NBC News, Denver); Carl Stern (George Washington University, Washington, D.C.); and Hon. Stanley Weisberg (Superior Court of Los Angeles, Los Angeles).

We are also grateful to the ABA Resource Team on High Profile Trials, which provides unbiased advice and guidance to judges and attorneys about management issues in high-profile trials. The authors were extremely fortunate to be invited to participate in the team's regular business meetings. Discussions during those meetings prompted a host of ideas, concerns, and questions that have made their way into this revision. Team members represent a broad array of professions and perspectives—state and federal judges, prosecutors and defense attorneys, media lawyers, and academicians—that have found themselves at one time or another enmeshed in a notorious trial. Hon. William M. Hoeveler (U.S. District Court, Miami) chairs the Resource Team and its members are Bruce Collins (General Counsel, C-SPAN, Washington, D.C.); Linda Fairstein (Asst. District Attorney, New York); Prof. Geoffrey C. Hazard, Jr. (University of Pennsylvania Law School, Philadelphia); Eric Holder (U.S. Attorney, Washington, D.C.); Hon. William L. Howard (South Carolina Court of Appeals, Charleston);

E. Michael McCann (District Attorney, Milwaukee, Wisconsin); Nan R. Nolan (Law Offices of Nan R. Nolan, Chicago); Dean Burnele V. Powell (University of Missouri—Kansas City School of Law, Kansas City); Prof. Barry C. Scheck (Cardozo Law School, New York); and Neal R. Sonnett (Neal R. Sonnet, P.A., Miami). Thomas C. Smith, Director of the ABA Criminal Justice Section, is the project manager and primary contact for the Resource Team.

We owe our deepest thanks to a select group of judges and court staff that have survived the decade's most famous notorious trials—many of them more than once. These individuals sacrificed a long Saturday in a dark hotel conference room to review and critique an early version of the revision. Based on their own firsthand experience, they corrected many factual errors, clarified important points, and—most important for our morale—reassured us that revising the manual was a worthwhile endeavor and that the end result would justify the amount of time and effort required to update it. For these and other kind words, we are indebted to Gloria Gomez, Jury Manager, Jerianne Hayslett, Public Information Officer, and Judges David Perez and Stanley Weisberg of the Superior Court of Los Angeles County (Los Angeles); Judge William Howard of the South Carolina Court of Appeals (Charleston); James Manspeaker, Clerk of Court for the U.S. District Court, District of Colorado (Denver); Judge Hiller B. Zobel, Middlesex County Superior Court (East Cambridge, Massachusetts); and Timothy Murphy of the Commonwealth Attorney's Office (Hampton, Virginia).

Finally, thanks go to Susan J. Llewelyn (William and Mary Law School, Class of 1999) and Donald I. Pollock (Counsel, Florida Administrative Office of the Courts) for research assistance; to Chuck Campbell of the National Center for State Courts (Williamsburg, Virginia) for editing assistance; and to Catina Burrell, Ericka Burwell, and Tiffany Cutts for outstanding organizational and administrative assistance. This revision would not have been possible without the inspiration, expertise, and selfless dedication of all of these individuals. Any factual errors or bad advice are, of course, our responsibility alone.

Paula L. Hannaford, J.D.
Staff Attorney and Senior Research Analyst

G. Thomas Munsterman
Director, Center for Jury Studies

Introduction to the First Edition

The vast majority of cases in any trial court typically involve standard civil disputes, ordinary, if outrageous, crimes, or routine questions of commercial law. Occasionally, however, a particularly heinous crime is committed, a novel issue is raised, or a celebrated party is involved in a civil, domestic, or criminal matter that captivates public attention in a compelling way. When this happens, whether the public attention is merited or not, what might otherwise be a typical, mundane legal matter is transformed into a drama of extraordinary notoriety. Television minicams are deployed to search for ten-second sound bites, newspapers produce screaming headlines and reams of copy, all of which is focused on a single case and, eventually, on one courtroom and a solitary judge. This unsought attention and scrutiny are rarely welcome to a trial judge. The bright light of intense media scrutiny is particularly unsettling for trial judges who are accustomed to operating in quiet anonymity and who have thus far escaped the high-profile, high-publicity notorious case.

The existence of notorious cases is not a new phenomenon in American life. The Salem witch trials, the trial of Aaron Burr, the Scopes trial, the Lindberg kidnapping case, the Sacco and Vanzetti trials, as well as the trials of Alger Hiss, Dr. Sam Sheppard, the Chicago 7, Roxanne Pulitzer, and the Watergate defendants, are but a few of the memorable cases that come immediately to mind. The prominence of these trials reflects the fact that for a variety of reasons, notorious trials have fed an enormous American appetite for celebrity drama, trial theatrics, bizarre disputes, and pure, unadulterated voyeurism. American interest in notorious cases is no less voracious today. The Bensonhurst trials, as well as the trials of Bernard Goetz, John Gotti, Joel Steinberg, Leona Helmsley, Imelda Marcos, the Central Park jogger defendants, and the "preppie murder" trial, captured the attention of large audiences in New York City and throughout the country. Similarly, the McMartin Preschool case in Los Angeles, the child rape and mutilation trial in Tacoma, Washington, and the Sonoma Valley murder trial were the focus of intense public interest and media scrutiny. From the purely voyeuristic standpoint, the trial in Exeter, New Hampshire, of the high school media instructor accused of taking part in the murder of her husband riveted the attention of much of New England. The televised proceedings preempted the afternoon soap operas, while the public was invited to dial special "900" telephone numbers to express an opinion on the defendant's guilt or innocence.

Today the notorious case often attracts dozens of "eyewitness news" correspondents armed with communications arsenals, such as minicams and satellite uplinks. This coverage may be augmented by swarms of tabloid journalists of the "Current Affair," "Inside Edition," "Entertainment Tonight" genre who are capable of transforming an otherwise commonplace trial or court proceeding into a sensational media event. As the William Kennedy Smith trial attests, apparently there is no limit these days to America's insatiable appetite for the gossip and titillation that surround notorious trials.

These are not necessarily healthy developments. The courts must operate in neutral and detached environments where rational argument and dispassionate decision making are insulated from the passions of the streets. As a result of the proliferation of notorious cases and the burdens they place on trial judges and trial court administrators, the National Center for State Courts, supported by the State Justice Institute, researched and prepared this manual for *Managing Notorious Cases*.

Purpose and methodology

The purpose of this manual is to assist trial judges and court administrators in planning for and managing the notorious case. The guidance provided here has been gleaned from a series of interviews and conversations at site visits to state courts around the country. At each site, project staff from the National Center spoke at length with the essential parties involved in a particular notorious trial: the trial judge, court administrator, security personnel, sheriffs, bailiffs, the attorneys involved with the case, and media representatives who covered the trial.

The project staff visited and studied notorious criminal and civil trials at small and large jurisdictions: the McMartin Preschool trial in Los Angeles; the Paul Newman salad dressing lawsuit in Connecticut; a mass abortion trial in Pittsburgh; a series of capital murder trials in Talladega, Alabama; the Jean Harris and Brinks-Weathermen trials in Westchester County, New York; the natural parents versus the surrogate mother custody dispute in Santa Ana, California; and the white-supremacist, wrongful-death civil trial in Portland, Oregon. In addition, project staff spoke with federal judges who have presided over recent notorious federal trials: those of Oliver North, Marion Barry, Imelda Marcos, and Bess Meyerson, as well as the network legal correspondent who acted as the media liaison for the Oliver North trial.

Toward the end of the data collection portion of this project, the project staff also met over a two-day period with five New York City Supreme Court justices and two U.S. District Court judges who have handled some of the most prominent cases held in that city in recent years: those of Bernhard Goetz, the Central Park jogger, John Gotti, Joel Steinberg, the Chambers "sex-play murder" in Central Park, Imelda Marcos, Bess Meyerson, and the Westmoreland–CBS trial.

From these experienced trial judges and members of their support staff, the project staff learned what worked and what did not during these trials, extracted the lessons learned from having been in the spotlight of public and media attention, and elicited some of the tools, techniques, and approaches that other trial judges could use when they find themselves confronted with a high-profile notorious case.

Many of the lessons learned are neither profound nor complex. The primary lessons involve thinking and planning ahead, anticipating contingencies, and being prepared. Handling a notorious case may be unlike anything a trial judge and court have ever experienced before. Pitfalls, dangers, and opportunities for embarrassment abound. But notorious cases can be managed, and they can be rewarding. Good management of a notorious case provides a court and a judge with the opportunity to showcase the legal system in general, and an individual court in particular. The public has a rare opportunity to observe a court at its best, in a trial presided over by a confident and well-prepared judge, assisted by a competent and well-prepared staff, functioning efficiently and effectively in the full glare of daily public and media scrutiny.

The court officials involved in notorious cases had no automatic answers to the dilemmas posed by these notorious cases. Nor is any one course of action necessarily the best for all judges or in every type of jurisdiction. A trial judge must select from the management options available that course of action that best suits his or her temperament and outlook. For example, a method of dealing with the media that suits one judge may not necessarily work for another judge in a different time and place. A suggested course of action for managing a jury may be suitable for one court but not for another. For these reasons, this manual sets out, where applicable, alternative courses of action from which a judge or court manager may choose what best suits a particular court, a particular judge, or a particular type of case.

The wide variety of jurisdictions and different types of notorious cases confronting courts throughout the country make it difficult to recommend policies or actions that are applicable to all cases in all jurisdictions. This manual is designed to provide information and policy alternatives that should be of use to a broad range of trial courts confronting high-profile cases. The manual is geared for the trial judge in a multijudge court, which may or may not be supported by a trial court administrator. The manual should also benefit court administrators and their staffs in those courts that have such a position. In an effort to provide the broadest possible alternative courses of action, some of the guidance and recommendations contained in this volume are, by necessity, more applicable to urban courts than to small or rural courts. Be that as it may, even the one- and two-judge courts should find much of the guidance of some benefit; the issues that arise in an urban trial court often differ in degree, but not in kind, from those of smaller, rural jurisdictions.

Caveat

We were reminded of the important differences between small counties and urban areas by Judge John Mascio, of Steubenville, Ohio. He wrote to us to point out, among many things, that the two-judge rural court has no such thing as a civil, criminal, or domestic division and that it is impractical and meaningless to select the more experienced or better qualified judge to try a notorious case when there are only two judges. He also pointed out that in small county courts judges are generally without the supporting administrative staff that is repeatedly referred to throughout this manual. Moreover, Judge Mascio asserted that many of the rural courts throughout the country are "housed in old and sometimes antiquated courthouses without the facilities available to provide the amenities to which you refer." He added that "the number of notorious cases which come about are so few and far between that it would be uneconomical to train and keep on hand a staff to handle this type of case on a regular basis."[1]

Judge Mascio is, of course, absolutely correct. And we acknowledge up front that *some* of what we have written does not apply to his court or courts like his. Because of the nature of notorious cases, they tend to predominate in urban and suburban areas where courts are better equipped in terms of facilities, staff, and resources to deal with the notorious case. It is also increasingly apparent that rural areas are not immune from cases involving the mass murder, the negligent homicide in the meat-packing plant, or the local bank executive who loots the only bank in town and runs off to Cozumel with the wife of the district attorney.

At the inception of this project, the project staff solicited notorious cases from throughout the country for possible study. The compilation of these surveys revealed dramatically that notorious cases are by no means exclusively the unhappy attribute of urban living. Thus, Judge Mascio's point that rural courts are less well equipped to deal with notorious cases is certainly well taken. Nevertheless, it is our hope that these courts can find some useful suggestions in this manual and that these recommendations may form the basis for small courts to persuade their state administrative office that supplemental personnel or assistance may be required while a notorious case is pending.

Distinguishing the notorious case from the complex

Thus, while acknowledging that many of the suggestions and recommenda-

---

1 Judge John J. Mascio, Court of Common Pleas, Steubenville, Ohio, in a letter to Timothy R. Murphy, National Center for State Courts, dated August 8, 1991.

tions made throughout this manual may not be appropriate for the small or rural court, it is our hope that those courts may find some portions of the manual worthwhile and useful, if not today, perhaps when the mass murder or the 180-count child abuse case arrives on your desk and Geraldo or Al Sharpton follow close behind.

It should be noted that this manual does not provide guidance on the handling of the complex or complicated case-lawsuits such as multiparty antitrust litigation, asbestos litigation, complex commercial, class action, or products liability litigation. They are dealt with in the *Manual for Complex Litigation, Second*. Rather, this *Manual for Managing Notorious Cases* focuses on the management of those external forces and issues that arise in the course of a widely publicized case as a result of the notoriety surrounding the case. It provides general guidance and alternative courses of action to the trial judge and court manager who are confronted with the high-profile notorious case. Although a notorious case may present complex issues of fact or law, this manual focuses on those issues generated by the notoriety of the case rather than on the legal or procedural complexities that are intrinsic to the case.

Judge's point of view
Because the trial judge of a notorious case is, in a sense, the hub around which all the trial-related planning activities should rotate, this manual is written from the vantage point of the trial judge. This is not meant to diminish or overlook the role of the court administrator, the court clerk, the jury administrator, or the chief of security—all of whom have important responsibilities during a notorious trial. But because of the central role of the trial judge in the planning and management of the forces impinging on the trial, that perspective is the view adopted by this manual. We have attempted to make clear, nevertheless, that the trial judge should not micromanage the notorious trial, that collateral responsibilities should be clearly defined and delegated, and that the trial judge should allow those with the necessary expertise to do their jobs without excessive or unnecessary interference.

Although the term *court manager* may connote to some an elected court clerk or an appointed court administrator or court executive, we have chosen to use the term *court administrator* throughout this manual. Due to the more widespread understanding of the term *court administrator*, we have used it in the generic sense to refer to that whole group or class of persons involved in providing trial court services encompassing both elected court clerks and appointed court administrators.

Sequence of the manual
The four chapters of this manual—pretrial matters, dealing with the media, jury considerations, and planning for security—highlight the four areas of pri-

mary concern for the trial judge and the court administrator in the course of handling a notorious case. Security, dealing with the media, and the various management concerns relating to both areas permeate each chapter of the manual and are not easily categorized within a particular chapter. As a result, there is much overlap between chapters. Nevertheless, we have sought to address and highlight the most important topics and issues that will most likely confront a court, a trial judge, and a court administrator in preparing for and trying a notorious case.

The pretrial chapter deals with a variety of issues in a broad manner. Some of these issues are then dealt with in more detail in the subsequent chapters. Each chapter begins with a series of lessons learned, which reflect the most prominent issues within the chapter and recommendations concerning those issues. The lessons learned are those recommended policies or courses of action that were derived from the conversations with the primary actors recently involved in trying notorious cases—judges, court administrators, security personnel, media representatives, and attorneys—at the various sites visited by the project staff. The persons interviewed throughout the country were not unanimous in their recommendations. Where differences arose, project staff have made recommendations based on their overall assessment of the issues in light of the full range of conversations and materials reviewed throughout the course of the project.

Appendix 1 contains a review of pertinent legal materials concerning issues that may arise while trying a notorious case. As the preface to that section indicates, the materials are not exhaustive. They are an initial reference on common topics faced by the courts and the media during a notorious case. The subsequent appendices contain subject-matter-specific materials provided to supplement the manual text. The various court rules, court orders, jury questionnaires and instructions, media advisories, newspaper articles, and an article by U.S. District Court Judge Gerhard Gesell provide a range of information or sample procedures, which might not otherwise be available in most jurisdictions.

In conclusion, this manual is designed to be a practical guide for trial judges, trial court administrators, and state court administrators who may be confronted for the first time with a criminal or civil case that attracts widespread media and public attention. The manual raises issues and provides alternative courses of action in circumstances that can be expected to arise in the course of a notorious case. We hope that this manual assists judges and courts trying those difficult cases involving significant notoriety and intense media scrutiny.

A recent news commentary concerning a pending notorious case suggested that our justice system is headed in the following direction: "skip the courtroom, substitute flacks for lawyers and actually try the case in the media.

Put the proceedings on TV and let viewers call in for 1-900-CONVICT or 1-900-NO-GUILT. It would be quicker, cheaper—and make for great television. And would it be so different from what we already have?"[2] The authors here hope that this manual will, in some measure, assist judges and courts in avoiding aspects of notorious trials that might lead to the above eventuality.

2 Kaplan, *In Florida, Trial by Media Fine*, NEWSWEEK 34 (August 5, 1991).

SANTA MONI
COUNTY
BUILDING

pretrial matters

plan ahead

Pretrial Matters

Lessons Learned

1. A trial judge for a notorious case should not be selected randomly. Whenever possible, the judge should be purposefully selected on the basis of his or her training, experience, and judicial temperament.

2. The trial judge of a notorious case should be well regarded in the legal community, should be composed under stress and media scrutiny, and should be prepared to manage the case from its inception.

3. The hallmark of a well-managed notorious case is extensive preparation. Communication, coordination, and teamwork between the judge, court, and security staff cannot be overemphasized. Hold regular planning meetings, anticipate problems, and prepare for the unexpected.

4. Notorious trials make extraordinary time demands on the trial judge. Consider getting assistance from a special master or a judicial colleague.

5. The supervisory (administrative) judge, the trial judge, the court administrator, and all supporting court staff should develop explicit plans for managing a notorious case.

6. The supervisory (administrative) judge and the trial judge must control both the preparation and trial of the case, as well as the immediate environment surrounding the trial.

7. In seeking to deter attorneys for the parties from trying the case in the media, the trial judge should first seek voluntary compliance with the ABA Fair Trial and Free Press Standards and the local disciplinary rules. Gag orders, sanctions, or other means to force compliance should be used sparingly.

8. Gag orders that are narrowly tailored and supported by a written explanation for their necessity are easier to enforce and are more likely to survive appellate scrutiny.

9. Although the selection of a jury that has never heard the facts of a case is unlikely, alternatives to granting a full-scale change of venue, such as a continuance, selection of an out-of-county jury, or even jury sequestration, should be explored first.

10. The trial judge should define how the courtroom will operate during the notorious trial with reference to media arrangements, seating, security, and media access to exhibits.

11. Once a notorious trial begins, the trial judge's active trial and motion calendar responsibilities should be transferred to other judges whenever possible.

12. The trial judge should employ effective caseflow management techniques, such as requiring strict adherence to discovery deadlines and dates for motion hearings and enforcing firm continuance policies, throughout the pretrial phase of the notorious case.

Pretrial Matters

DEFINITION AND RECOGNITION

The term notorious case *often connotes a trial involving scandalous issues or people, prominent litigants, unusual settings, or some other noteworthy trait. Many notorious cases are criminal cases involving extensive negative pretrial publicity about the accused and the crime. The authors here prefer the dictionary definition of notorious: "generally known and talked of."*

Defining the notorious case

Perhaps the term is better defined by a paraphrase of Justice Potter Stewart's oft-quoted remark on obscenity: one may not be able to define a notorious case, but one knows it when one sees it. In this manual, a notorious case is one that, because of the celebrated nature of the parties involved, the crime committed, or the issues presented, becomes widely known and discussed. Because of this notoriety, the case presents the court and the trial judge with unique or unusual management concerns, primarily in the areas of pretrial publicity, security, jury selection and management, courtroom configuration, media management, and the management of the trial itself.

Recognizing a notorious case is usually not difficult. In criminal cases, crime scene publicity is often sufficient to alert prosecutors, defense attorneys, and the court to the imminent arrival of a high-profile case once a suspect is arrested. In public corruption cases, inevitable leaks to the press will alert the public to impending indictments and arrests. In civil cases, publicity and attention may evolve more slowly as the unique nature of the lawsuit becomes more apparent and the notoriety builds.

The court and the individual trial judge should recognize the signs of a notorious case early and take immediate steps to deal with the management issues and the attendant publicity. Failure to do so can have serious consequences later. Some cases can become notorious overnight—sometimes even in midtrial—and for no apparent reason. The trial judge and court staff may have little or no time to prepare in advance, but they should still be aware of the issues associated with notorious trial management and make adjustments accordingly.

Trial judge selection

Selecting the trial judge for a notorious case is a critical decision that can affect the ease and efficiency with which the case is handled or managed. For a variety of reasons, not all judges are equally qualified to handle a notorious case.

The trial judge in a notorious case must be perceived as fair and impartial by all parties. If the jurisdiction has an elected judiciary, the trial judge should not be up for reelection in the immediate future. Preferably, the judge should be experienced, have recognized stature in the legal community, and have a reputation for giving each party to the lawsuit a full and fair hearing. The trial judge should assume full command of the courtroom, articulate the court's expectations, and see that they are carried out.

The trial judge should be, to the extent humanly possible in this sort of situation, temperate in demeanor, calm under pressure, and largely unflappable. He or she should have a solid understanding of the application of First Amendment caselaw concerning the freedom of the press. Other indispensable traits are the judge's facility for dealing with the media in an orderly and sensible manner and the self-discipline to adhere to his or her own standards for appropriate judicial interaction with the media. This judge should have solid knowledge of procedural and evidentiary law so that repeated breaks to ascertain the proper legal ruling during what is often an extended trial can be avoided. The judge should also have the good management skills and judgment to convene and direct appropriate court staff to serve as an effective "trial team." Because of the physical demands of an extended trial, the judge should be in good health and without distractions stemming from family illnesses or concerns. Finally, an astute judge of character and personality can bring valuable talents and insights to bear on many questions and can defuse potentially volatile situations.

The importance of managing a notorious case at the earliest possible stage cannot be emphasized enough. The early designation of the trial judge is critical to ensuring that a notorious case is well managed from the moment it is recognized. In the vast majority of both civil and criminal cases, assignments are rotated or made randomly. **In a notorious case, however, the selection of the trial judge should be a delicate, deliberate decision that should not be left to pure chance.**

Judges who have tried notorious cases have repeatedly said that it is "insane" to select a trial judge for a notorious case at random. That approach invites disaster. These judges felt that the notorious-case trial judge should be individually selected for the reasons and characteristics discussed above. Legal background, though obviously important, is not necessarily the prime consideration for the judge of a notorious case. Stature, experience, regard among the legal community, and composure under stress are often as important as legal acumen. The selection of the trial judge should ensure that, under the microscope of daily attention, the trial will be intelligently and competently managed and that the decisions relating to the mechanics of the trial will be made thoughtfully and rationally.

Most trial judges with whom we spoke said that, ideally, the presiding or administrative judge should select the trial judge. The selection should be made only after the concurrence of the trial judge. A notorious case should not be thrust upon anyone who, for personal or professional reasons, is unwilling to accept the assignment.

Individual selection has many distinct advantages. Most court rules give discretion to the presiding judge, or the local administrative judge, to bypass the normal assignment procedures in assigning or reassigning cases. The individual selection and assignment of the trial judge to handle a notorious case often raises questions or generates complaints from other judges and court staff, the attorneys, the legal community, the media, or disgruntled bystanders. These criticisms can often be answered by explaining some of the very legitimate reasons for the exercise of the court's discretion to make a nonroutine assignment in an extraordinary situation. Trial time availability, manageable caseloads, speedy trial considerations, or a judge's willingness to expend significantly greater than usual time and attention to the trial are valid reasons for exercising the court's legitimate legal discretion to make an individual case assignment.

An alternative, of course, is to be absolutely straightforward and say, "Judge X has the needed skills and he or she has been chosen for those skills."

The court should, however, consider not assigning a notorious case to a judge who is perceived, whether fairly or unfairly, as a state's judge, a plaintiff's judge, or a defendant's judge. Any perception of a predisposition or a particular orientation on the part of a judge, in a situation where that judge is individually selected, compounds the potential for criticism and creates a difficult atmosphere in what is already a difficult case. Be assured that the media will thoroughly explore the judge's background—professional and personal—and will readily publicize rumors of bias.

Alternatives to individual selection

While individual selection of the trial judge to preside over a notorious case is preferable, there are two workable alternatives. The first is random selection of the trial judge from a small pool of experienced judges who are all deemed capable of handling a notorious case. By partially reintroducing randomness into the selection process, this technique avoids some of the criticism directed at individual selection. In using this process, however, the presiding judge must ensure that each judge in the pool can handle a notorious case, because the least suitable judge for the case could be the name randomly selected. For this reason, and because it is a compromise, the court may be less satisfied with this process.

Smaller courts (e.g., one- or two-judge jurisdictions) are obviously at a disadvantage with respect to the pool of potential judges for a notorious trial as well as the resources needed to manage such trials. To the extent that they can be employed, the selection criteria should still be followed. The presiding judge, in consultation with the judges in a smaller jurisdiction, should decide whether assignment of an out-of-jurisdiction judge or a change of venue are appropriate.

The second alternative is a "tandem" approach that combines random and individual selection of a two-judge trial team. One judge presides over the trial itself. The other, based on his or her experience, temperament, and working relationship with the trial judge, manages the logistical and public affairs aspects of the trial. Both judges should carefully define their respective roles in the trial, both to promote cooperation and confidence in one another and to prevent any opportunities for the parties or the media to engage in "divide-and-conquer" strategies. A tandem approach does not necessarily require the full-time attention of two judicial officers. Depending on the distribution of the workload between the two judges, the responsibilities might only require a quarter to a half of the second judge's schedule. The improved organization and management of the trial—not to mention the mental health of everyone involved—often far surpasses the costs of assigning a second judge to the case.

The tandem approach has three distinct advantages. First, it distributes the work associated with notorious trials into significantly more manageable amounts and insulates the trial judge from direct involvement with the media. Second, the tandem approach provides an opportunity to reflect on critical decisions and weigh the attendant consequences with a trusted colleague. The adage that "two heads are better than one" is never more true than in a notorious trial, both for the wisdom and experience that two judges can bring to bear on case management and for the emotional support they can give one another during the trial. Many judges who have presided in notorious cases have remarked that they were surprised by their reactions to the intensity of the media attention and unprepared for the sense of isolation they felt during the trial. The tandem approach relieves some of the psychological pressure on the presiding judge.

Finally, this technique is a form of natural mentoring that expands the knowledge and experience base of the court. Fortunately, notorious trials are unusual and infrequent events. By implication, however, they offer few opportunities for judges to become adept at handling them. By pairing a randomly selected trial judge with an experienced "management" judge, the trial judge has an opportunity to learn the logistical and public relations aspects of notorious trials firsthand. He or she can then serve as the management judge if lightning strikes twice and that court becomes the venue for future notorious cases. The Los Angeles County Superior Court, which has seen its fair share of notorious cases in recent years, first developed this approach for the O.J. Simpson civil trial and found it very successful.

Before the judge says yes

Before agreeing to try a notorious case, every judge should examine his or her motives and understand clearly what is involved in the case. The pressures of being the focus of daily television and newspaper coverage are intense and can exact an incredible physical and psychological toll. A notorious case can disrupt not only the judge's professional life but also the judge's home and family life for months on end.

One judge cautioned judges in notorious cases to be prepared for a constant barrage of media attention. "The press has a unique perspective on the First Amendment," he quipped, "in that they believe that it protects a constitutional 'right to pester.'" Another judge could not emphasize enough "the pressures on a judge." He pointed out, "Television, interviews, requests for seats, social approaches—these are intense and persistent. To give in once is to put the judge in a position that he must continue. He must not speak except in court."

For those who enjoy the public eye, the judge added a cautionary note: "There is sometimes a temptation to string the case out because of the notoriety it gives the judge. But a sharp, clean, and short trial under the control of the trial judge will gain the greatest respect, particularly if he doesn't get trapped into off-bench matters by the media."

The trial of a notorious case is not a healthy forum for judicial egos or grandstanding. It is a forum that requires a well-prepared trial with a competent judge who is in control of the courtroom by virtue of painstaking preparation and planning.

Developing a management philosophy

Trying a notorious case is an extremely demanding ordeal for the trial judge, the court administrator, and the entire courtroom staff. To be ready for the trial requires thought, reflection, and detailed preparation. To say that a trial judge is going to treat a notorious case "just like any other case" is to confuse means with ends. In court, ideally, the trial of a notorious case should be indistinguishable from any other criminal case or civil lawsuit. The goal of the trial judge, the court administrator, and the supporting staff should be to achieve an air of normalcy in the courtroom. To achieve that objective, however, the trial judge should institute detailed and painstaking planning measures to control and manage the forces and events occurring both inside and outside the courtroom. This must be done to ensure that when the trial begins, the case proceeds in court "just like any other case."

The trial judge cannot anticipate *every* contingency or occurrence in a high-profile case. The judge and court staff should, however, attempt to anticipate as many of the problems or concerns as possible. These issues may include handling media requests; planning courtroom and courthouse logistics for handling crowds, the media, and security; transporting the defendants or litigants; protecting the interests of the litigants and witnesses; managing the jury in a high-publicity environment; and managing the court's staff and its docket of existing cases.

To deal with potential problems effectively, a trial judge, in concert with the court administrator, must establish and articulate to the court staff, litigants, media, and perhaps the public the objectives and priorities that the court's policies and procedures are designed to achieve. Among these objectives are the following:

- to ensure fairness and due process for the parties involved in the case and provide the appearance and the reality of dignity and fairness in the courtroom
- to shield jurors, the judge, and the trial process from improper extraneous influences
- to provide for security and order for all witnesses and trial participants in the courtroom, the courthouse, and in the area surrounding the courthouse
- to give the public access to the trial—both in person and via media coverage—to the greatest extent possible given fair trial considerations
- to establish control of the pretrial process and the trial
- to provide for the needs and comfort of jurors
- to convey to the community the reality of a competently run, well-managed court
- to provide an adequate record for any retrial or appellate review
- to maximize trial efficiency by minimizing delay and costs in an atmosphere of fairness and justice
- to minimize disruptions of ongoing operations in other divisions of the court

In short, the trial judge must establish and maintain control not only of the trial but also of the immediate environment surrounding the courtroom, the courthouse, the jurisdiction, and beyond. The trial must provide for constitutional due process and fundamental fairness to all of the parties. Distracting or improper extraneous influences must be kept to an absolute minimum with respect to both the notorious case and all other business con-ducted in that courthouse. The trial judge is responsible for all this, but should not try to do it alone. The trial judge must enlist the enthusiastic support and assistance of the trial court administrator, the administrative and courtroom staff, security personnel, the jury manager, and the clerk's office—in short, of everyone who can help ensure that the case is handled efficiently.

Clearly, the court's staff is the trial judge's lifeline during a notorious case. The impact of a notorious case on both the courtroom and the courthouse staff is easy to underestimate. The story of a California court administrator whose office was used by Cary Grant when he appeared in connection with his divorce case is illustrative. Grant waited for his appearance in court by sit-ting at the court administrator's desk. For weeks after the hearing, members of the courthouse staff made a pilgrimage to the court administrator's office to view "the chair that Cary Grant sat in." That reaction indicates the degree to which court staff can be caught up in the celebrity aspect of notorious cases. Without appropriate supervision and very clear guidelines concerning com-munication with the media and the public, court clerks, administrative staff, and security officers often become the source of unauthorized, and frequent-ly inaccurate, information. Beyond that, the intense public and media atten-tion to all aspects of high-profile cases often places unanticipated demands on staff time and energy over and above the existing responsibilities of court personnel.

Some judges have found it advantageous to convene a "trial team" of key court staff to coordinate logistical, security, and media relations for the dura-tion of the trial. The judge's management style with the trial team is, of course, up to the trial judge. If the judge generally prefers to delegate to a sin-gle trusted assistant, he or she should continue to do so; likewise, if the judge prefers a hands-on approach with several members of the trial team. **The occasion of a notorious trial is not the time for the trial judge to start changing his or her method of dealing with court staff. He or she should continue to manage the trial in the style that is most comfortable.**

According to those who have tried a trial team approach, the key is for the judge to select people in whom he or she has the utmost confidence. They should be highly competent at their respective jobs and should have sufficient self-assurance and composure to assume responsibility for managing their respective duties without seeking the judge's approval for minor details. They should, however, have immediate access to the trial judge when necessary. **Once selected, the trial team should be given sufficient authority— through written court orders, as necessary—to carry out its responsi-bilities.** Investing these individuals with the authority to implement their decisions will prevent unnecessary "appeals" to the trial judge by those who are unhappy with the decisions of the trial team.

Even if a trial team approach is deemed unnecessary or impractical in a particular case, court staff should be consulted, kept apprised of the status of the case, trained, and trusted to do their jobs without unwarranted micromanagement. For example, once a security plan has been developed, discussed, and agreed upon, security staff should be given the discretion to carry out their responsibilities without the trial judge looking over their shoulders. The degree of staff autonomy will depend to a great extent on the trial judge's confidence in the court's personnel. Establishing a good relationship early on with the entire support staff can prevent major headaches during the trial and allow the trial judge to focus his or her energies more fully on the actual case.

Media scrutiny focuses a spotlight on all aspects of a court's operations during a notorious case. The trial judge is in a pivotal position, refereeing two battles: the maneuverings of the litigants in court and the inevitable out-of-court interactions with the news media. In addition, and sometimes of equal importance, the trial judge must (1) exercise some control over the mechanics of the courtroom, (2) supervise that portion of the court building adjacent to the courtroom, and (3) provide for unimpeded litigant and jury access to and egress from the court building. This is not an easy job, and the support of a competent, well-prepared court manager and support staff is essential.

For many people, a notorious case is a rare opportunity to see how the legal system functions and how well, or how poorly, the local court operates. This is true not only of Americans—many of whom have learned a great deal about the American justice system from past notorious trials—but also of the international community who often watches these trials with as rapt attention as American audiences. If the court is mismanaged, if security is haphazard, if jurors are treated indifferently, if sheriffs and bailiffs are seen lolling around the courtroom, the disarray and juror discontent will quickly become apparent. But if a court is well managed, anticipating and dealing with the inevitable problems that arise during a notorious trial, that image will be transmitted to both the observers of the trial and the community at large.[1]

The role of the court administrator[2]

Not every trial court has a trial court administrator or a court administrator's office. In some courts, staff from the court clerk's office carry out the duties

---

[1] Some experienced observers would find this an overly idealistic assertion. They believe that the way in which the media cover cases rarely allows the image of a well-managed court to be projected.

[2] We use the term *Court Administrator* to describe the person responsible for the administrative management of the court (personnel, budget and finance, security, etc.). In some jurisdictions, this position is called the *Clerk of Court, Court Manager,* or *Executive Officer.*

normally associated with a court administrator's office. In any case, courts supported by a trial court administrator or court manager should use the resources and expertise of that office.

If the court administrator is not working directly with the trial judge on the notorious case, he or she should designate an individual to act as the liaison between the judge and the administrator's office. If a specific individual normally handles court-media relations, that person may be well suited for working with the judge on the case. The individual should be someone of experience and stature who can work effectively with the judge in dealing with the various agencies and entities involved with the management of the notorious case: media, courthouse security, local police, physical plant and equipment management, and jury management.

The trial judge should not attempt to micromanage the myriad details involving the media, security, and jury management associated with a notorious case. While retaining full responsibility and accountability for all aspects of the trial, the judge needs to delegate as many of the duties associated with the trial as possible to competent subordinates, particularly the court's administrative staff. The members of the trial team, in turn, should keep the trial judge apprised of details concerning their respective assignments. The value of competent staff support through the court administrator's office cannot be overstated. The trial judge should get to know the court administrator, his or her staff, and their particular areas of expertise.

Trying the case in the media

Early in a notorious case, the lawyers on either side may comment on the merits of the case, the righteousness of the prosecution or the innocence of the defendant, and generally the unfairness of the opposing party. Once the war of words has begun, it matters little who the instigator was because reaching the public is often the primary objective of both parties. Generally, the media are all too happy to facilitate the exchange through instantaneous electronic transmission, sound bites, and gavel-to-gavel coverage.

The ABA Model Rules of Professional Conduct, Rule 3.6, "Trial Publicity" (1989), address the issue of extrajudicial statements by attorneys. Model Rule 3.6 provides that:

(a) A lawyer who is participating or has participated in the investigation or litigation of a matter shall not make an extrajudicial statement that a reasonable person would expect to be disseminated by means of public communication if the lawyer knows or reasonably should know that it will have a substantial likelihood of materially prejudicing an adjudicative proceeding in the matter.

(b) Notwithstanding paragraph (a), a lawyer may state:
  (1) the claim, offense or defense involved and, except when prohibited by law, the identity of the persons involved;
  (2) information contained in a public record;
  (3) that an investigation of a matter is in progress;
  (4) the scheduling or result of any step in litigation;
  (5) a request for assistance in obtaining evidence and information necessary thereto;
  (6) a warning of danger concerning the behavior of a person involved, when there is reason to believe that there exists the likelihood of substantial harm to an individual or to the public interest; and
  (7) in a criminal case, in addition to subparagraphs (1) through (6):
    (i) The identity, residence, occupation and family status of the accused;
    (ii) If the accused has not been apprehended, information necessary to aid in apprehension of that person;
    (iii) The fact, time and place of arrest; and
    (iv) The identity of investigating and arresting officers or agencies and the length of the investigation.
(c) Notwithstanding paragraph (a), a lawyer may make a statement that a reasonable lawyer would believe is required to protect a client from the substantial undue prejudicial effect of recent publicity not initiated by the lawyer or the lawyer's client. A statement made pursuant to this paragraph shall be limited to such information as is necessary to mitigate the recent adverse publicity.
(d) No lawyer associated in a firm or government agency with a lawyer subject to paragraph (a) shall make a statement prohibited by paragraph (a).

Currently, thirty-two states have adopted Rule 3.6, either verbatim or with insignificant variation. The key provision in evaluating attorney speech is whether the attorney knew or reasonably should have known that the speech in question "will have a substantial likelihood of materially prejudicing an adjudicative proceeding."

The constitutionality of this standard was upheld by the Supreme Court in *Gentile v. State Bar of Nevada*.[3] (A more-detailed discussion of *Gentile* is offered in Appendix 1.) *Gentile*, which revealed a divided court on the issue of attorney speech, has been criticized for failing to articulate clearly what lawyers can and cannot say about their case or their client.

So where does this leave a trial court? Model Rule 3.6 or the equivalent state rule should be the starting point in any conversation with trial attorneys.

[3] Gentile v. State Bar of Nevada, 111 S. Ct. 2720 (1991).

"Since you have already been convicted by the media,
I imagine we can wrap this up pretty quickly."

The trial court should indicate that it expects the parties and their attorneys to abide by the rule and to look to the *Gentile* decision for guidance as necessary. **A strong admonition to this effect, given in the privacy of a pretrial conference, can go a long way toward securing voluntary compliance with the rule without having to resort to gag orders or the threat of contempt sanctions.**

The trial judge should sit down with the lawyers, express the court's concerns about comments to the media, and indicate specifically his or her expectations concerning press contacts by the attorneys, including press conferences. Reaching an understanding and agreement voluntarily is far preferable to the difficulties inherent in enforcing protective orders. To secure voluntary compliance, the judge may (1) elicit an informal agreement from the participants to limit extrajudicial statements or (2) remind counsel of the local disciplinary rules and admonish counsel to restrain themselves in their comments to the press based on ABA Rule 3.6 and the *Gentile* decision. This admonition may carry with it the implicit threat that noncompliance will seriously offend the trial judge. The judge should threaten a disciplinary referral to the bar or a contempt charge only as a last resort.

To facilitate this compliance, the judge might also consider providing some protection, such as a secured entrance to the courthouse, to the attorneys and litigants. Even the most restrained of attorneys may find it difficult to avoid making statements to the press if they must pass daily through a gauntlet of reporters—many of whom are friends—to make their way up the courthouse steps.

Attorney gag orders

Protective orders (often called *gag orders* or *restrictive orders*) prohibit attorneys, parties, and court staff (including security) from discussing the case with the media.[4] Before the *Gentile* decision, appellate courts rarely viewed protective orders with favor. Because of the uncertainty surrounding their validity, judges were reluctant to issue them. In recent years, trial courts have been somewhat more successful in drafting protective orders that will survive appellate scrutiny. Some cynics suggest that appellate courts, alarmed over the inflammatory tenor of some out-of-court statements, have deliberately narrowed the scope of permissible attorney speech under the First Amendment. A more plausible explanation for the recent success of restrictive orders is that trial courts have become more adept at issuing orders that are narrowly tailored to protect the integrity of the judicial system and the defendant's right to a fair trial. The order issued by Judge Richard Maitsch in *U.S. v. McVeigh* barred the attorneys from commenting publicly on the evidence or making statements that might affect the fairness of the proceedings, but did permit them to quote or make reference to matters of public record in the case. A well-substantiated, narrowly drawn protective order directed toward attorney comments on the evidence or statements that might affect the ultimate outcome of the case is more likely to survive appellate review than a blanket prohibition on all attorney statements about any and all aspects of the case. The key elements necessary for an appellate court to uphold a protective order are

- that the order be based on a clearly articulated finding of fact
- that it be made after an evidentiary hearing at which all of the interested parties, including the media, have an opportunity to be heard
- that it be narrowly drawn to address a particular problem, which, if not addressed, poses a substantial likelihood of materially prejudicing the trial
- that alternative avenues for eliminating the prejudice are unavailable

---

[4] First Amendment considerations preclude the applicability of protective orders to witnesses testifying in the case. As a practical matter, the media liaison, even if employed by the court, is generally exempted from protective orders.

Alternatives to protective orders normally include such traditional prejudice-mitigating procedures as extensive voir dire, sequestration, or a continuance. These must be found inadequate to remedy the prejudice to the trial process before considering a protective order.[5]

Use of the contempt power is often the court's only remedy for enforcing protective orders. If necessary to address a violation, however, contempt should be used evenly and with fair notice to avoid creating an unfortunate atmosphere of animosity and bitterness between the judge and the attorneys. Although filing a complaint with the attorney disciplinary system does not provide an immediate remedy for a violation of the protective order, it should be pursued for repeated violations.

Media gag orders

Gag orders on the media are rarely imposed and are almost never successful. Once the media are in possession of information, it becomes a matter of prior restraint to prevent or delay its publication. *Nebraska Press Association v. Stuart* indicated that there are some limited circumstances in which a gag order might be upheld.[6] However, those circumstances have proven to be few and far between. (See discussion in Appendix 1.) *Procter & Gamble Co. v. Bankers Trust Co.* provides a review of the law governing gag orders on the media.[7]

As with attorney speech, the judge should seek voluntary compliance through an informal agreement with the media. Before issuing any formal orders affecting media access to the trial, the judge should give the media notice of any related proceedings and an opportunity to be heard in those matters. Several jurisdictions have found that Bench-Bar-News Committees of local or state bar associations can provide valuable assistance in negotiating acceptable parameters of media coverage about sensitive or potentially prejudicial aspects of notorious cases. By developing rapport and an understanding of one another's needs and requirements, a judge can expect a certain amount of deference. This may not always be the case, but the consensus appears to favor pursuing accommodation rather than confrontation.

Pro Se **litigants**

Some judges believe that if a litigant is foolish enough to proceed *pro se*, it is his or her responsibility to learn the applicable law and procedure without any assistance from the court. In a notorious case, however, this can be counterproductive given the confusion and disruptions likely to occur at trial. **If possible, appoint an advisory attorney to serve as a reference for the**

---

[5] As a practical matter, many remedies may be ineffective at eliminating the impact of pretrial publicity. *See generally* Norbert L. Kerr, *The Effects of Pretrial Publicity on Jurors*, 78 JUDICATURE 120 (November/December, 1994).
[6] Nebraska Press Association v. Stuart, 96 S. Ct. 2791 (1976).
[7] Procter & Gamble Co. v. Bankers Trust Co., 78 F.3d 219 (6th Cir. 1996).

"I don't mind your acting as your own attorney, but would
you please stop hopping on and off that damned chair?"

pro se **litigant on evidentiary and procedural matters.** Even if the litigant
insists on self-representation, providing access to a reliable source of legal
information and advice can alleviate many potential problems without com-
promising the appearance of judicial impartiality. Moreover, from a public
relations perspective, failure to make reasonable allowances for the *pro se* litigant fuels perceptions of a justice system that is inaccessible and unresponsive
to the needs of "ordinary citizens." Most people agree with the adage that a
person who represents himself has a fool for a client, and they will not blame
the court for the litigant's misfortunes unless it appears that he or she is being
punished for refusing the assistance of a court-appointed lawyer. If questions
or problems arise during trial, the judge can order a recess and suggest that the
litigant consult with the advisory attorney.

If the appointment of an advisory attorney is not feasible, or if the defendant declines the offer, the judge must still ensure a fair and orderly trial while avoiding the appearance of giving the litigant special treatment. Trying any case with a *pro se* litigant is a challenge. Notorious cases make this task even more difficult. Judges who have done so successfully offer the following tips:

- The judge must hold the *pro se* litigant to applicable rules of evidence and procedure.
- The judge should treat the *pro se* litigant with the same respect and seriousness as he or she would an experienced trial attorney. As a matter of due process, the *pro se* litigant has a right to present his or her case.
- The judge should give the litigant ample opportunity to make legal arguments before ruling on motions and objections.
- All objections and arguments should be preserved for the record.

Not all *pro se* litigants are unsophisticated concerning legal matters. Some, in fact, are quite adept at manipulating the justice system for their own purposes. **Do not tolerate abusive trial tactics from *pro se* litigants.** If litigants are unable or unwilling to comport themselves acceptably in court, use sanctions as necessary. In the trial of Texas separatist Richard McLaren, the defendant continually disrupted the prosecution's direct examination of witnesses. Judge DeHart had him removed to an adjacent courtroom where he was permitted to watch the trial proceedings via remote video. McLaren was returned to the courtroom to conduct his cross-examination of witnesses.

"Difficult litigants"

Fortunately, *pro se* litigants are the exception, not the rule, in criminal trials. Usually, litigants are represented by competent trial attorneys who not only understand evidentiary and procedural law but also appreciate and respect the need for appropriate behavior in the courtroom. For the most part, clients and witnesses follow the lead of their attorneys and comport themselves appropriately. A small minority of litigants, however, will insist on disrupting the trial proceedings to the greatest extent possible regardless of the admonitions of their attorneys. Indeed, some litigants who insist on representing themselves pose a substantial challenge for the court (and the attorney representing the opposing party) with respect to maintaining the appearance of impartiality, ensuring a fair trial, and maintaining control of the courtroom. The existence of media and public interest in notorious cases intensifies the difficulty of these tasks.

Several cases involving difficult litigants have attained notoriety in recent years. Theodore Kaczynski, the "Unabomber," ultimately pled guilty to murder and attempted murder in exchange for an agreement by federal prosecutors not to seek the death penalty. Kaczynski's refusal to submit to an examination by government psychiatrists or to permit his attorneys from raising mental illness as a mitigating factor in his defense contributed to multiple delays in the opening of the trial. In a last-minute bid to prevent attorneys from characterizing him as a "sickie," Kaczynski submitted a motion to represent himself. Although the motion was denied, the defendant's attorneys and federal prosecutors quickly agreed on an acceptable plea arrangement, ostensibly to avoid the trial disruptions that would likely occur in the prosecution of an obviously mentally disturbed individual.

The judge and prosecutors of *New York v. Ferguson*, the 1995 murder trial of Colin Ferguson for the shooting deaths of six commuters on the Long Island Railroad, were not as lucky. Ferguson, who chose to defend himself rather than agree to the insanity defense proposed by his lawyers, engaged in a number of unusual trial tactics, including direct examination of himself— literally asking himself questions and then answering them. Texas judge Kenneth DeHart also faced multiple disruptions by the *pro se* defense of Richard McLaren on kidnapping charges related to a twelve-hour standoff between Texas separatists and police. McLaren's refusal to acknowledge the court's jurisdiction and other disruptive courtroom antics are typical of tactics used by various militias, "patriot" organizations, and "common-law court" adherents.

Judges, court staff, and attorneys with experience in those types of cases make several recommendations for handling difficult litigants. **First and foremost, make your expectations about trial procedures crystal clear to the litigants.** Some mental health disorders make it difficult for individuals to understand instructions or relate to people in a manner that "normal" people take for granted. Mental health professionals can help judges and lawyers understand the litigant's particular pathology and suggest ways to interact with the litigant to best facilitate communication and understanding. This type of assistance proved to be enormously beneficial to the defendant's attorneys in the Kaczynski trial. Although ultimately they were at odds with their client over legal strategy, the attorneys avoided the possibility of a much more serious breakdown in communication by heeding the advice of mental health experts and taking the time to develop a trusting relationship with their client. This technique can be useful regardless of whether the litigant appears *pro se* or with counsel.

Change of venue
Some notorious criminal cases will, during the pretrial proceedings, generate a motion for a change of venue. The allegation will be made that the selection

"Not <u>another</u> change of venue, Counsellor!"

of a fair and impartial jury is unlikely because of the poisoned atmosphere in the community resulting from the daily drumbeat of publicity unfavorable to the party. The motion will normally be supported by affidavits, copies of newspaper articles relating to the case and the defendant, and listings or video-tapes of televised newscasts concerning the trial. The change-of-venue determination is normally left to the discretion of the trial judge based on a factual determination, which involves the application of both U.S. constitutional and state law.[8] Although the trial judge should ensure that he or she is conversant with the specific legal criteria pertinent to change-of-venue determinations in his or her jurisdiction, the primary issue will be whether a fair and impartial jury can be impaneled in the current venue—a jury free of prejudice, bias, and preconceived opinions. The second question is whether a change of venue will cure the infirmities present in the existing venue. Before granting the motion, the trial judge must conclude that pretrial publicity has created an atmosphere in which there is a reasonable likelihood that any jury selected in this venue could not be fundamentally fair to the defendant.

The vast majority of notorious criminal cases are tried in the jurisdictions in which the charges are filed and where the offenses were alleged to have occurred. In the state courts, the John Wayne and Lorena Bobbitt, O.J. Simpson, Susan Smith, and Louise Woodward cases were tried in the venue in which the charges were filed. Similarly, in the federal courts, the World Trade Center bombing case and the Cali Cartel drug and conspiracy cases, as well as a long series of major Mafia cases, have all been tried in the jurisdictions where the crimes were alleged to have occurred. Although the preference for trying the case in its original venue is based primarily on statutory and common-law considerations of *in personam* jurisdiction, concern for the logistical and financial difficulties also play a part in decisions to retain a case.

Not every case, however, should be tried in its original venue. The Oklahoma City bombing trials of Timothy McVeigh and Terry Nichols, which were moved from Oklahoma City to the federal district court in Denver, are perhaps the most famous examples of change-of-venue cases. In addition to the amount of pretrial publicity, the large number of victims or members of their families in the Oklahoma City cases would have made it difficult or impossible to find jurors who did not personally know one or more of the victims. When a change of venue is granted, the justification is usually protection of the defendant's Sixth Amendment rights to a fair trial and an impartial jury. However, the specific circumstances supporting the change of venue may vary from excessive or inflammatory pretrial publicity to the risk of postverdict violence in the event of an acquittal.

In fact, courts have developed a serious appreciation for the possibility of violence given the extent of the riots in Los Angeles following the acquittal of four L.A. police officers in the Rodney King beating case.[9] The manslaugh-

---

[8] In New York, a motion for change of venue is decided by the appellate division of the supreme court.
[9] State v. Powell et al., No. B058842 (Sup. Ct. L.A. Cty. 1992).

ter conviction of William Lozano, a Miami police officer, was overturned on appeal because the trial judge denied the defendant's motion for change of venue, despite the substantial likelihood of postverdict violence in the event of an acquittal.[10] The Lozano retrial, originally slated to be tried in Orlando, was eventually held in Tallahassee after the new trial judge determined that the conditions that made Miami an unsuitable venue were also present in Orlando.[11]

Similarly, the 1993 murder convictions of two Detroit police officers were overturned in part because members of both juries became aware of the city's preparations, including plans to close the city's freeways, to handle riots in case of acquittals.[12] According to juror affidavits, the Budzyn jurors actually discussed the possibility that their failure to convict might provoke rioting.

In summary, the threshold for granting a change of venue has always been high; *Mu'Min* makes it that much higher. A change of venue should be granted only upon the showing that a fair and impartial jury cannot be impaneled in the current venue. **Alternatives to granting a full-scale change of venue, such as selecting an out-of-county jury, sequestering the jury, or granting a continuance, should be explored before moving the trial.**

In most jurisdictions, granting a change of venue removes the case from the pending jurisdiction and sends it to another jurisdiction and sometimes to another judge.[13]

Recent changes to the California Judicial Administration Standards address some of the administrative problems involved when a change of venue is ordered.[14] Section 4.1 states that in a criminal case when a change of venue has been ordered, it "should be tried in the court receiving the case by a judge from the court in which the case originated," unless the two courts otherwise agree. Section 4.2 contains detailed guidelines concerning the reimbursement of costs involved in a change of venue. Reimbursement of expenses that would not otherwise have been incurred by the receiving county can become an issue. If a change of venue is contemplated, these expenses will become increasingly important in times of fiscal austerity.

"Change of venire" (a.k.a., out-of-county juries)

When intense media coverage has been relatively localized, some judges have

---

[10] Lozano v. Florida, 584 So. 2d 19 (1991).

[11] Florida v. Gary, 609 So.2d 1291 (1992).

[12] Michigan v. Budzyn, 566 N.W.2d 229 (1997); Nevers v. Killinger, 1997 WL 816107 (E.D. Mich.).

[13] This is a convenient means for a judge to transform his or her problem into someone else's problem. While that may be a tempting, attractive, and expedient alternative for some when they are confronted with the many demands of a notorious case, it is not a way for judges to become popular with their fellow judges. A variation of the Golden Rule is applicable here: transfer unto others as you would have them transfer unto you.

[14] California Judicial Administration Standards §§ 4, 4.1, 4.2, effective July 1, 1989.

traveled to another location in the state to select the jury and then returned with that jury to the original jurisdiction to conduct the trial. This procedure is sometimes referred to as picking an out-of-county jury or an out-of-jurisdiction jury and is a substitute for a change of venue. It is useful in circumstances where local media coverage of the events leading up to the trial has been intense, while the media coverage in the out-of-county location has been relatively sparse. The out-of-county jury residence is normally outside the range of the television stations in the original locale and is served by different newspapers.

For example, a number of highly publicized trials in suburban St. Louis County, Missouri, began with jury selection in Boone County (Columbia), Missouri. The jurors were informed that they were being selected for trials in St. Louis County—125 miles away—and that they would be transported, sequestered, housed, and fed in St. Louis County for the duration of those trials.[15] This procedure eliminated the substantial cost and inconvenience of transporting dozens of witnesses to another location and lodging prosecution and defense counsel teams and their investigators out-of-town for the duration of the trial. It also allowed the judge's clerical and office support and the trial attorneys to operate in their normal offices.

Although inconvenient to the jurors who are removed from their families and homes, the experience is not unlike being sequestered in one's home jurisdiction and, on balance, has been found to be a workable and cost-effective solution to the change-of-venue problem. The out-of-county jury procedure has been used frequently. In the John Wayne Gacy trial, the jury was picked in Rockford, Illinois, and then brought to Cook County for the six-week trial. After the trial, the jurors commented that they had experienced no greater hardship than if they had been sequestered in Rockford.

The out-of-county or "foreign" jury is recommended by the ABA Standards for Criminal Justice, Standard 8-3.5(d), "Selecting the Jury." This standard suggests that whenever potentially prejudicial coverage of a criminal matter has been intense, "the court should . . . consider drawing jurors from other localities in that state (or district)." Given the Supreme Court's pronouncements in *Mu'Min*, which upheld limitations on the extent of voir dire questioning concerning jurors' exposure to pretrial publicity, finding jurors who are totally ignorant of the facts and issues involved in a notorious case may be less necessary.[16] Nevertheless, the trial judge must be satisfied that the jurors *can be believed* when they state that they have not formed an opinion about the case despite the widespread publicity surrounding it.

---

[15] The costs of sequestration were not a factor in the court's decision to use out-of-county juries. The juries would have been sequestered regardless of the county from which they were selected.
[16] Mu'Min v. Virginia, 111 S.Ct. 1899 (1991).

Postverdict issues to consider during pretrial planning

Victim impact statements

By 1995, the federal government and most states had enacted legislation granting crime victims a right to present evidence at the sentencing phase of criminal trials, either as part of the presentence report or through a written or oral statement at the sentencing hearing.[17] Typically, victims are permitted to present evidence and testimony of the physical, mental and emotional, and social and economic harm experienced by themselves or their families. Although a few states grant the trial judge sole discretion to decide whether a victim may testify at the hearing,[18] most states guarantee victim participation as a matter of right. In either case, the details of victim participation at sentencing are another aspect of the notorious trial that should be planned well in advance of the event.

Some judges may prefer to wait until after the guilty/not-guilty phase of the trial before considering the logistics of victim impact statements. In almost all jurisdictions, the jury determines the sentence in capital cases and generally, very little time is available between the guilty/not-guilty phase of the trial and the sentencing phase. **As a practical matter, victim participation at sentencing should be addressed as a contingency matter during the pretrial conferences.**

Issues concerning victim impact statements that should be addressed include the form of victims' statements (e.g., written or oral, freestanding or incorporated as part of the presentence report). If the statement will be presented orally, must victims submit a written statement in advance of their testimony? If so, may they deviate from the written statement in their oral presentation to the court? The trial judge should also instruct victims, either directly or through the prosecutor, about appropriate demeanor during the proceedings. In the Jeffrey Dahmer case, for example, a family member of one of the victims lunged at the defendant during the sentencing hearing and had to be restrained by court security. In the Oklahoma City bombing trial of Terry Nichols, a victim's angry outburst during her testimony nearly provoked a motion for a mistrial.

Another aspect of victim impact statements is the number of persons who will be permitted to present testimony and evidence. Evidentiary law in both state and federal courts permits the trial judge to limit or exclude evidence, including victim impact evidence, in the interest of either avoiding prejudice to the defendant or maintaining trial efficiency.[19] In the Oklahoma City

---

[17] See NATIONAL VICTIM CENTER, 1996 VICTIMS' RIGHTS SOURCEBOOK: A COMPILATION AND COMPARISON OF VICTIMS' RIGHTS LEGISLATION 231-32.

[18] See, e.g., CAL. PENAL CODE § 1191.15 (1997); GA. CODE ANN. § 17-10.1.2 (1997).

[19] FED. R. EVID. 403.

bombing cases, Judge Maitsch substantially limited the number of persons allowed to testify at the sentencing portion of the McVeigh and Nichols trials.

Although the presence or absence of a jury may influence this decision, how presentations will be made should also be discussed before the sentencing hearing. Will the victims read from a prepared statement from the well of the court, as the Eappens (the parents of the child) did in the *Massachusetts v. Woodward* trial? Or will they present their testimony under oath from the witness stand as part of direct and cross-examination by the prosecution and defense? If the latter, should any restrictions be placed on the defendant's ability to cross-examine the witnesses (e.g., present written questions through the trial judge)?[20]

Postverdict treatment of criminal defendants

Regardless of the verdict in a notorious case, the trial judge should give some thought to the defendant's treatment immediately following the verdict. If the defendant has been free on bail, will he or she be immediately incarcerated following a conviction and sentence? Will the defendant need an opportunity to gather personal belongings before going to jail? Should the defendant be given an opportunity to visit privately with family or close friends before leaving the courthouse? Following an acquittal, will the defendant be permitted to go free immediately following the trial? Or must the defendant return to jail for administrative purposes? Will the defendant be given the opportunity to participate in a press conference at the courthouse after the verdict? Will he or she be permitted to address the jury (publicly or privately) after the trial?

Trial record

A well-managed court also produces an orderly and understandable record of its proceedings. A judge managing a notorious case should not be overly concerned about appellate review and should manage and rule with confidence and appropriate discretion. Nonetheless, a trial judge should consistently strive to ensure that the record is free of vague or confusing references and that exhibits are properly marked and identified. While a trial judge should not be looking over his or her shoulder, the judge should require trial participants to render arguments, questions, and answers in a logical and understandable manner. The judge should require that the record accurately reflect the proceedings. Meaningful gestures may need verbal descriptions, and references to exhibits should be precise.

---

[20] *See* NATIONAL VICTIM CENTER, *supra* note 17.

Preparing for trial

Once a trial date becomes reasonably definite, the trial judge and court staff should assess the case's anticipated length, the extent of media coverage, the security requirements, courtroom alternatives, seating requirements, and conditions of coverage peculiar to their jurisdiction. The judge and the court staff should develop concise summaries, not exceeding two pages in length, of the duties and responsibilities of each responsible party for each of these areas. Such documents will help each department define and carry out its responsibilities. And the written protocols may provide a basis for cooperation among all the entities and clarify overlapping responsibilities.

In addition, each department may find it worthwhile to develop detailed trial plans tailored to the needs of the individual case. Regardless of the approach, each department should develop and understand its individual responsibilities in consultation with the other departments in the courthouse and each of the responsible law enforcement agencies. Cooperation and clear delineation of responsibilities, with no gaps in security or other functions, are essential.

A courthouse operation should not be reconfigured or reorganized in the relatively short time that a notorious case is pending. A trial judge must rely on the organization of the court that is in place when a notorious case is filed. The judge can build on that organization and expand its capacities, but the court must operate within the given resources of the physical plant and the existing personnel. Recognizing and using the capabilities of the court's personnel is the first step in both enlisting the support of the court staff and managing the trial itself.

The court administrator can be extremely helpful during this pretrial stage, acting on behalf of the judge in chairing planning or security meetings, taking care of media arrangements, or handling the details and arrangements for the trial. As has been stated before, the judge, although accountable for the whole range of trial preparations, cannot be personally responsible for supervising each detail. To the extent that the court administrator or his designated assistant can alleviate any of the burdens or concerns of the judge, that manager makes a worthwhile contribution to the trial preparation effort. Judges should not hesitate to delegate responsibilities to the court manager or any of his or her assistants.

Managing the courtroom

At least one incident occurs in every notorious trial that can serve as a lesson for future trial judges about the importance of having firm control of the activities and people in the courtroom. In one trial, for example, the defense attorney, who had received several death threats for representing an unpopular defendant, arrived at the courthouse with his own "personal security" force—bodyguards supplied by the Nation of Islam. In another case, a reporter used an open line on a cellular telephone to surreptitiously broadcast the trial proceedings, despite standing court orders prohibiting live broadcasts.

The trial judge handling a notorious case must define how the courtroom will function when the case is tried. Plans must be made for security while the court is in session. *Who* will sit *where* during the trial must be determined, as well as the circumstances under which persons will be allowed to enter and leave the courtroom. Press seating, reserved seating, and open seating should be delineated meticulously. The security personnel responsible for screening people before they enter the courtroom and enforcing the seating requirements should be well briefed on their duties and responsibilities.

New technology also raises questions about courtroom management. The judge should be very clear about how much and what types of equipment the parties will be permitted to bring into the courtroom. Will laptop computers be permitted? Facsimile machines? Cellular telephones? Access to Westlaw, Lexis/Nexis, or the Internet? How much physical space will be needed to accommodate these machines? Will each party need its own equipment? Or can some items be shared, with the parties splitting the operation costs?

Thus, while the trial judge must control the litigants involved in any trial, in a notorious case the trial judge and the court administrative staff must also plan for and manage the unusual outside forces that will impinge on the trial. While the trial judge has the ultimate responsibility for managing the notorious trial, he or she should not hesitate to delegate specific responsibilities to the court administrative staff. The trial judge must orchestrate staff and support personnel so as to give the public and the press reasonable access to the trial proceedings while controlling the immediate environment of the trial (media and public) to avoid jeopardizing the trial proceedings.

The trial judge's expectations, both within and outside the courtroom, should be clearly articulated. If television cameras are allowed in the courtroom, the placement and ground rules governing their operation should be clearly defined and established. Likewise, the permissible use of still cameras, microphones, and other forms of media technology should be clearly defined and understood by their respective users. The judge may, *sua sponte*, issue a series of orders spelling out the security requirements, media arrangements, access to court rules, and the court's expectations regarding in-court media and the public. Some courts organize an orientation meeting for the media during which the trial judge, media liaison, or the court administrator discusses these arrangements. Press packets with copies of relevant court orders or court policies are distributed at this time. Other judges have issued what they refer to as decorum orders. These orders lay out the day-to-day housekeeping rules and expectations for the operation of the court. Such an order might include the following:

- the prohibition of interviews being conducted at any time in the courtroom
- the prohibition of press and public in the well of the courtroom at any time
- submission to search by metal detector
- spectator-seating requirements
- spectator entry and reentry rules while court is in session
- media-seating requirements
- times when seating will commence each morning and after the noon recess
- seating rules upon the return from each recess
- the use of cellular telephones and beepers/pagers
- whether people can display messages on buttons or clothing

In addition to court decorum matters, the order should cover the logistical arrangements for dealing with media requests during the trial. These matters might include the following:

- how questions from the media will be handled
- how the media will have access to clerk's office filings
- how the media will obtain copies of documentary exhibits admitted into evidence
- how the media will have access to photographs and other tangible items admitted into evidence

The procedures for access to clerk's office filings should be established well before the trial and should be included for the benefit of out-of-town media representatives who arrive at the start of the trial. (See Chapter 2 for a discussion of media access to and copying of filings and exhibits.)

This order can be adjusted as the trial progresses, but it is worthwhile to work out these matters before the trial commences while planning for as many contingencies as possible. These decorum matters are not insignificant. Having them well in place before the start of the trial can save unnecessary misunderstandings once the trial begins. (See Chapter 4 for a detailed discussion of courtroom considerations.)

Examples of decorum orders used in the Marion Barry, Raymond Buckey, and McMartin criminal trials are provided in Appendix 3.

Controlling the notorious case

In the maelstrom of events that accompany a notorious case, it is easy to over-

look the fundamental principles of caseflow management, which should be
applied to a notorious case. While planning for and attempting to manage
those outside forces that may impinge on the trial of a notorious case, the
judge must continuously manage the time and events involved in the movement of the case to disposition.

**The trial date is the judge's most powerful tool for controlling
case management in a notorious case.** The trial date sets the parameters
for all other pretrial proceedings, including discovery schedules, hearings on
motions *in limine*, and pretrial conferences. It encourages timely preparation
by the attorneys and tends to discourage constant delays and continuances.
The trial date should be reasonable given the complexity of the case and the
expected amount of pretrial discovery.

The judge should encourage timely preparation by the attorneys, establish sufficient time intervals to allow for adequate attorney preparation, and
establish realistic schedules and deadlines between events before the trial date.
Most important, the judge in a notorious trial should schedule realistic and
credible hearing dates for motions and strictly control continuances from
those hearing dates. Motions should be heard when they are scheduled. If
these hearings are continued once, they have a tendency to be continued
repeatedly. Repeated continuances lead to loss of control of the case at an early
stage. In criminal cases, continuances often accrue to the benefit of the defendant, who rarely has incentive to push for a speedy trial. Similarly, continuances from the scheduled trial date should not be routinely granted; they
should be granted only for demonstrably verifiable good cause. When the case
is ultimately set for trial, it should start when scheduled.

Judges should avail themselves of such case management techniques as
frequent conferences with attorneys for the parties and the creation and monitoring of deadlines for completion of discovery. Serious efforts should be
made to monitor and enforce compliance with discovery schedules.

In criminal cases, motions to suppress evidence and statements are often
extremely critical, particularly with regard to confessions. These motion hearings often amount to a preview of the upcoming trial. The judge and the
court's staff should be fully prepared for these hearings and for media coverage equivalent to that of the trial. In any event, judges should not neglect
sound caseflow management techniques while preoccupied with managing
the media, dealing with security, allocating courtroom seating and camera
placement, and providing for the comfort and safety of jurors. A special master or tandem judge, as discussed earlier, can be assigned responsibility for
some or all of these tasks, thus easing the pressures on the trial judge.[21]

---

[21] For a worthwhile review of caseflow management techniques, see MAUREEN SOLOMON and DOUGLAS K.
SOMERLOT, CASEFLOW MANAGEMENT IN THE TRIAL COURT (American Bar Association, 1987).

Trial consultants

In notorious cases the parties will often retain consultants to assist in the various phases of the trial. These persons or firms help counsel with jury selection; design of prescreening questionnaires; advise on legal issues, such as establishing a jury challenge or moving for change of venue; or help prepare demonstrative evidence, such as computer-generated graphics or displays, and generally help with the presentation of the evidence.[22] They are usually knowledgeable about jury composition and venue law, as well as about the developing case law on the discriminatory use of peremptory challenges. In capital cases, trial consultants often engage in demographic analyses, which are used for challenging the jury array. Judges and jury staff should be prepared for challenges to the array. During the pretrial meetings, the role of consultants in the trial, including where they will sit, facilities, equipment or techniques (e.g., "mock" or "shadow" juries) they will use, and the records that they will request, should be covered.

Managing the existing caseload

Whether a court operates under a master calendar assignment system or assigns cases individually, a judge has other cases, other calendars, and the continual filing of new cases to deal with while a notorious case is pending. Judges in most jurisdictions, particularly in smaller courts, are normally not in a position to drop their entire caseload and devote all of their time and attention to a high-profile case.

During the early pretrial stages of a notorious case, most judges operate on the same basis as they did before the notorious case. While many judges are required to maintain their caseload during the trial of a notorious case, a persuasive argument can be made that the judge of a notorious case should be relieved of his or her normal caseload once the notorious trial begins.

Some judges have attempted to manage the existing caseload by trying their notorious case four days a week. The fifth day is devoted to other calendars involving other cases. This approach is not advisable. The trial judge will be overwhelmed by the intensive schedule in a short period of time, and the jurors will not appreciate the inefficient use of their time. One judge in this situation started the notorious trial at 10:30 in the morning and ended at 4:30 in the afternoon. Thus, the judge was available for other matters between nine and ten in the morning, and all day on Friday. This schedule proved exhausting for the trial judge and contributed to what was referred to as "a high stress level" in the courtroom during the notorious trial. When the judge in this case transferred his existing caseload, the notorious trial began to move at a

---

[22] See generally ELISSA KRAUSS & BETH BONORA, JURYWORK: SYSTEMATIC TECHNIQUES (1997). This two-volume work details the techniques, applicable case law, and statutory requirements concerning these topics.

perceptibly faster pace. This resulted in less time for the trial attorneys to prepare their case. It was difficult for the attorneys, but the change to a five-day week was the most effective step taken to shorten the trial. Trial output was estimated to have tripled. The reduction in the generation of frivolous motions may have been a significant factor.

The consensus among judges with whom we spoke is that as a matter of policy, once a notorious case begins, the active trial and motion responsibilities of the trial judge should be transferred to another judge or judges. Avoiding distractions and disruptions during the trial of a notorious case is important. Hearing motions or signing orders during recesses or at lunch can result in major distractions, resulting in a loss of focus on the case at hand. The high level of concentration and intellectual and emotional involvement required in a difficult trial cannot be maintained while attempting to deal with other matters, whether serious or routine. The odds of overlooking something or making a mistake while shifting gears from the notorious trial to other cases are compounded when a judge handles a matter from another case. The risk to the notorious trial is too great for the minimal gain achieved. The trial judge should stay with the case at trial and not get caught up in other matters.

Planning for a mass trial

A misdemeanor jury trial in Pittsburgh of sixty-eight abortion protesters illustrates the potential pitfalls of moving a trial from a standard courtroom into a 5,100-square-foot room in the downtown Pittsburgh Convention Center. The notoriety of the cases stemming from the nature of the protests, the number of defendants to be tried simultaneously, and the unique location of the trial provide some useful lessons for any court contemplating a mass trial away from the courthouse.

Initial considerations in evaluating possible locations include the size of the alternate site and its ability to accommodate a large trial and an unusually large prospective jury panel; availability of rooms to accommodate the judge's chambers, counsel for the defendants, jury assembly and deliberation rooms, witness rooms, and the clerk's office and security personnel; adequacy of parking; accessibility to public transportation; and lunchroom and press facilities. Once a site is chosen, insurance coverage and the liability of the court and its funding agency (state or local) should be clearly established with the facility's operator.

As in every aspect of "traditional" notorious cases, an off-site notorious trial of multiple defendants requires that the judge and the court administrative staff plan ahead meticulously. Because the courtroom must be built from scratch, the local court manager or staff person must work closely with facility management personnel to create a courtroom and provide it with the necessary furnishings and seating arrangements for the public and the press. Other matters that must be anticipated include

- requiring that competent staff are available throughout the trial to respond to contingencies
- ensuring that security personnel secure the necessary doors to control public access into the facility
- ensuring that the facility allows for isolation of the jury panel from the public
- providing that jury summonses indicate clearly where jurors are to report when a trial is moved from the standard courthouse location to a temporary site
- providing an area for the secure storage of evidence and court records
- ensuring that the facility personnel responsible for heating, air conditioning, lighting, and the public-address system are clearly identified and available so that immediate adjustments can be made throughout trial
- providing more security if protests or disruptions are anticipated
- providing telephones for all of the necessary support personnel, the prosecutor, and the judge
- providing accessible microphones for each defense attorney (each defense attorney need not have his or her own microphone, but each must have easy access to a microphone)

Although the need to shift court operations from the courthouse to an off-site facility is fairly rare, this response can be used to deal with the situations that civil disobedience cases generate, especially when each defendant demands a jury trial, and in other multiple-party situations, civil as well as criminal. Courts should not hesitate to take advantage of imaginative or innovative responses to these unique situations.

dealing with the media

in a notorious trial

Dealing with the Media in a Notorious Trial

Lessons Learned

1. Whatever method the judge ultimately chooses for dealing with the media, **the most important thing to remember is to be comfortable with that method.**

2. Establish an effective communication method between the court and the media about the basic procedural and legal aspects of the proceedings.

3. No matter who is assigned to deal with any particular problem, the judge will ultimately be held responsible for what happens, particularly when things go wrong. The trial judge must, therefore, think through each decision or problem before acting.

4. The judge must also be aware that he or she will be the direct focus of much of the media's attention.

5. The judge, court administrative staff, and media liaison should plan for all foreseeable contingencies in dealing with the media and the public. Well in advance of the trial, the judge should meet with key staff (the court administrator, jury administrator, sheriff, police), counsel for the parties, and news media representatives to resolve as many media concerns as possible.

6. The trial judge and court administrative staff should treat all members of the media equally and fairly and ensure each media representative the same degree of access as every other media representative.

7. The judge should be careful to avoid the charge of favoritism by not appearing excessively friendly with individual members of the media.

8. Before the trial begins, the judge should establish in writing explicit, clear, and fair ground rules for the media regarding trial procedures and access to proceedings and trial participants.

9. The court should make reasonable efforts to accommodate the media's needs and provide them with the essential information they require to do their job. The judge should ensure that members of the media obtain timely responses to their questions. Information concerning the court's schedule, timing of decisions, and other procedural matters should be provided daily.

10. There should be **a single, reliable source of information** for all of the media.

11. Anyone who communicates with the media on behalf of the judge should have the judge's full confidence and support. This person should not continually have to seek authority before speaking or acting. This person should be fully informed about all matters communicated to the media.

12. To the extent reasonably possible, the judge should avoid making rulings from the bench that can be misconstrued or taken out of context in media reports.

13. The trial judge should be careful not to say or do anything that would generate additional publicity or cause him or her to become the focus of personal attention. Choice of words and demeanor are very important.

14. The judge should avoid the appearance of unnecessarily withholding information or excluding the media from proceedings by keeping them informed and providing the reasons for the court's actions. All hearings, including pretrial hearings, should be conducted in court, rather than by telephone. Frequent sidebar and *in camera* discussions should be avoided, if at all possible.

15. The court should provide a separate media room (off-site, if possible) in which telephone lines and video feeds can be set up for the media. The costs of leasing any facilities, or making any technological arrangements or modifications for the media, should be borne by the media representatives making the request.

16. The trial judge should be aware of increased pressures on the courtroom staff caused by the intense public interest and media focus on the proceedings. If possible, court and trial staff should be trained in dealing with the media and the public for notorious cases.

Dealing with the Media in a Notorious Trial

The approaches used by judges to deal with the media during a notorious case vary widely. Judges' methods are typically a function of their own personalities, styles, and attitudes toward media coverage of the courts in general. Although different judges have different ways of handling the media, on the whole they agree that **the most important thing is to be comfortable with the approach ultimately selected.** Regardless of the approach selected, an effective method of communication between the court and the media is important in avoiding and resolving problems during a trial.

Notorious cases invariably arouse intense media scrutiny—hence our definition of a notorious case. Like it or not, courts cannot ignore the media's presence. A hostile environment adversely affects both the trial and the public's perception of the court. Both judges and media representatives stress that open communication concerning basic aspects of a case (such as the scheduling and progress of the case or the procedural and legal aspects of the proceedings) fosters cooperation between the court and the media and diminishes mutual suspicion and tension. Cooperation and accommodation are preferable to hostility.

One of the judges interviewed by project staff stated, "The most important thing to the media is that they have access. A judge either accommodates the press or fights with them. I avoided the fights, which become collateral issues in a trial, by treating the press fairly and by establishing good rapport with them early in the process." When the media are treated civilly, that respect is usually reciprocated. As another judge emphasized, "When a judge is honest with the media, they give him the benefit of the doubt."

From the perspective of the media, favoritism and unfair treatment cause the most anger and resentment. Reporters do not like to be surprised or to be kept in the dark. Even if they do not agree with the court's policies concerning media access to the trial, they are far more likely to cooperate if they have an opportunity to provide input before decisions are made and sufficient notice to make plans once policies have been established. The media are generally less contentious provided that all of them have access to or are restricted from the same information.

Many judges who have tried notorious cases, as well as reporters who have covered them, say that gaining the media's cooperation and understanding is made much easier if, at the outset of a trial, the court conveys to the media the following:

- That all members of the media will be treated equally and fairly and that each individual will have the same access or lack of access.
- That explicit, clear, and fair ground rules are established, explained clearly from the start, widely promulgated, and fairly enforced. (These ground rules may be published by court order, posted on the courthouse door, placed on bulletin boards, or distributed by and among the media.)
- That the judge will make every reasonable effort to accommodate the media and to provide them with the essential information they require for their job. Media representatives should understand, however, that (1) the judge is fully responsible for the trial and must be in full control of the courtroom; (2) the judge expects the media to operate on the court's terms as he or she has defined them; and (3) the ground rules are not negotiable nor are deviations from them acceptable.
- That lines of communication between the judge and the media will be open and that a means of obtaining responses to their questions will be established.
- That information concerning the court's schedule, timing of decisions, and other procedural matters will be readily available.

Media access to the court

Some judges have established a policy of "structured accessibility" in their dealings with the media during a notorious trial. These judges may set aside a certain time, such as the end of the trial day, when reporters can ask questions or discuss problems for ten to fifteen minutes. Or they may simply respond to such questions on an ad hoc basis. Depending on the judge's preference, these meetings may be held in open court or in chambers, and counsel for the parties may be present. This helps prevent dissemination of incorrect or misconstrued information and might include such matters as an explanation of a procedural matter or an explanation for a delay or recess. As a general rule, the judge establishes specific ground rules for these meetings— for example, that all comments are "off-the-record" or "not-for-attribution," "no direct or indirect quotations," or "no questions regarding the substance of the trial." These ground rules should be repeated at the beginning of every informal meeting with the media.

Regular availability of the trial judge decreases reporters' reliance on less knowledgeable or reliable sources, such as lawyers, court staff, or those willing to leak unauthorized information. The availability of the trial judge allows the media to rely on a source of steady, consistent, reliable information, which is disclosed in a detached and unbiased fashion. Moreover, this sort of information is important for many reporters who, because of deadline pressures, often may not have time to research the legal issues themselves or to track down another source who can supply the basic information. Indeed, notorious trials in the United States often generate interest among the international media, who may have little or no familiarity with the intricacies of the American justice system. Through such sessions, the trial judge can contribute to more complete and accurate reporting at the outset rather than trying to correct errors or misunderstandings after they have been published or broadcast.

The judge should exercise some caution when dealing directly with the media. In interactions with the media, the judge must be careful to distinguish between clarifying issues of legal process and procedure, which is permitted by the canons of ethics, and expressing views or opinions about the evidence or the merits of the case, which is strictly prohibited. The judge should also understand that providing explanations to the media will not necessarily prevent inaccurate reporting. Nor will it insulate the judge from media criticism or dissatisfaction with a particular ruling or decision.

Judges who are accessible to the media do not feel that media abuse the privilege or that making themselves available to the media is overly burdensome. In fact, they feel that accessibility has enabled them to build a relationship of trust and openness that facilitates greater accuracy and understanding of the problems and concerns of courts regarding media coverage. Moreover, judges from this school of thought believe that scheduling a regular time for such meetings obviates time-consuming inquiries from the media at other less-convenient times.

No contact policy

In contrast to an accessible approach, some judges do not feel responsible for assisting the media in reporting about a case. They avoid all contact with the media and instruct their staffs to do likewise, generally on the grounds that any comment from the court violates judicial ethics. This is an understandable approach, but may put the trial judge and media in starkly adversarial positions, which in the long run serves neither the litigants, the public, nor the interests of justice.

Liaison between the court and the media

A middle-ground position for dealing with the media is to appoint a liaison to communicate information between the court and the media. This is the course for judges who prefer to operate at arm's length from the media and to meet with the media on a limited basis, if at all. The liaison may be either a person employed by the court or a member of the media. **Regardless of his or her professional affiliation, any person who serves in this capacity should be fully informed about all court policies concerning media access during the trial and have the judge's full confidence and support.** Continually having to seek authority from the judge before speaking or acting undermines much of the liaison's usefulness.

Court liaison

In some cases, a judge may elect to meet with the media to establish ground rules before the trial begins. The judge may also permit the press to take "staged" photographs (e.g., judge on the bench) or to conduct a brief interview to gather background information (e.g., education, professional background) about the judge. Thereafter, the judge has no personal contact with the media but communicates primarily through a staff member or a designated media representative acting as a liaison between the media and the trial judge.

The judge may assign someone from the court's staff to disseminate information on scheduling, seating, court procedures, and logistics to the media. This person will act as a conduit for the media's questions directed toward the judge and will convey the judge's answers.

Rather than the judge's personal staff, the judge may use another judge within the court, a public information officer attached to the court, the clerk's office, or the state court administrator's office. In civil cases, an experienced employee attached to the police department or the district attorney's office may also be used. For obvious reasons, this is not recommended for criminal cases.

Media representative as liaison

As an alternative to direct staff contact with the media, the judge may use a designated media representative as the liaison. This arrangement, although reported as extremely successful on numerous occasions, does require the judge to define the role and responsibilities of the media liaison very carefully and to be confident that the liaison understands and agrees to abide by this definition. **The media liaison is neither a pool position nor a reporter on behalf of the media, reporting everything within his or her sight and hearing.** Rather, the media liaison acts as the conduit between the media and the judge, conveying questions on behalf of the media to the judge and relaying the answers from the judge to the media. As such, the reporter selected as the liaison is obliged to share all the information he or she receives from the judge with all of the media. However, important restrictions are put on what is covered and conveyed.

The media liaison normally has access to the judge's chambers and, presumably, is in a position to overhear conversations between the judge, his or her law clerks, and his or her secretary. Matters discussed by the judge in chambers, however, whether with the staff or on the telephone, are privileged and are, therefore, off-the-record as far as the media liaison is concerned. **The liaison between the media and the judge serves a limited purpose— to convey questions and responses between the judge and the media.**

In addition, the liaison may act as the press's representative in such matters as obtaining press passes, arranging for reserved press seating, designating pool reporters and cameras, obtaining copies of documentary exhibits admitted into evidence, and conveying media concerns to the trial judge and vice versa.

The trial judge should select the media liaison, although it may be helpful to ask the media to nominate several individuals who are able and willing to assume this role. In a particularly lengthy case, the media may recommend that two or more individuals serve as the liaison on a rotating basis. Press pool committees have also served in this capacity, for example, in the *U.S. v. McVeigh* trial. This arrangement distributes the responsibilities of the liaison position so that the burden on any one person does not affect his or her ability to report the trial. **Regardless of the number of people designated in this role, the judge should have equal confidence in their willingness to comply with the requirements of being the liaison. This includes their understanding that the media liaison is not a media representative.** Although the position furthers the interests of the press, it is not designed to enhance the position of a single reporter or to create a pool position. The position allows the press to have a dependable, consistent, reliable, and knowledgeable source of daily information about the case. In return for this valuable daily access, both the media and the media liaison must understand and abide by the guidelines for its operation.

From the media's point of view, the liaison must be a respected and trusted individual who will not derive any unfair advantage from the unique position of access. A reporter found abusing the trust and access of this position to gain some competitive advantage will destroy his or her delicate relationship both with the court and with his or her peers.

In using a media liaison, a judge should keep in mind that the appearance of favoritism or unfairness must be avoided at all times. The judge should also be aware of the sacrifices the liaison will have to make to his or her journalistic instincts (being unable to report all that is heard or observed in the judge's chambers). Moreover, the liaison, while avoiding any unfair competitive advantage, will still have to deal with other members of the media who may remain unconvinced that the liaison is not obtaining some undisclosed inside information or advantage. That, unhappily, is an occupational hazard. The usefulness of the position from both the court's and the media's point of view is so great, however, that the media liaison should be willing to endure the occasional sniping from his or her colleagues to fulfill this very important role.

Judge Gerhard A. Gesell successfully used a media liaison-Carl Stern, then of NBC News-during the trial of Oliver North in the U.S. District Court in Washington, D.C. In Wisconsin, by court rule, the media liaison position rotates among designated media personnel who have been previously approved by the court.

Principles for dealing with the media

Regardless of the judge's approach for dealing with the media, the judge should keep the following in mind:

- No matter who is assigned to deal with any particular problem, the judge will ultimately be held responsible for everything that happens, especially when things go wrong. It is important, therefore, to think through each decision or problem carefully and completely.
- A judge should avoid charges of favoritism by not appearing excessively close to any one representative of the media. To the extent possible, only one source of information should be provided for all of the media. Court staff, including security personnel or other individuals assigned to the court for the trial, should be instructed to refer all media questions to the person authorized to release information. This prevents court staff, in attempting to be helpful, from releasing incorrect or unauthorized information.
- A judge should avoid the appearance of unnecessarily withholding information or excluding the media from hearings. Instead, he or she should keep them informed of what is happening and the reasons for the court's actions. In particular, frequent bench and in-chambers discussions with counsel are likely to raise suspicions of withholding information. If such discussions must be held, the trial judge should explain to the media what their purpose is and why they are necessary. If appropriate, transcripts of the sessions may be made available to the media as soon as possible.
- At hearings on motions, a judge should avoid making rulings from the bench that can be misconstrued or taken out of context in media reports. If possible, motions should be simply granted or denied with a written opinion to follow if necessary.

- A judge should avoid generating additional publicity or becoming the focus of personal attention. For example, the judge in a notorious case should control any display of intemperate speech. A judge should not say or do anything that if reported by the media would distract from the focus on the trial. Choice of words and demeanor are very important. Throughout the proceedings, a judge should beware of the temptation to relax and should not be caught off guard. The judge should avoid inappropriate or intemperate comments or incidents that would not have occurred if the judge were fully focused.
- The court should inform the media of, and give them an opportunity to object to, motions or hearings to seal records or close judicial proceedings. If the judge holds an ex parte hearing on a motion to seal records or close proceedings, any orders granting such motions should be temporary pending a formal hearing within a reasonable period of time. In the long run, such consideration demonstrates respect for the legitimate role of the media. It also prevents needless expenditures of time and effort for the court, the media, and the parties to respond to appeals from court orders restricting public access to the trial.

One judge, when confronted with a sensitive issue and an atmosphere of distrust that had developed around it decided to deal with the issue in open court so that the media could quote the judge and parties verbatim. In some instances, judges have allowed a pool or liaison reporter to be present for proceedings held in chambers.

Many judges indicate that problems with the media are often caused by outside reporters who do not cover the court on a regular basis. This can also be true of the local television stations as well as out-of-town or national press. Local media who have an ongoing relationship with the court are frequently more understanding of court problems and are, therefore, more cooperative.

Planning for court–media interaction

In planning for media coverage of a notorious trial, a checklist of the items that must be addressed is helpful. The judge and the judge's key staff, the court administrator's office, other involved agencies (sheriff, police), attorneys for the parties, and media representatives should meet well before the start of the trial to ensure that all issues are discussed and resolved.

The media are generally more knowledgeable about the specific requirements of their respective jobs (e.g., sketch artists, wire-service reporters, television or radio reporters) than judges or court staff. Some judges have found it more efficient to promulgate general rules concerning media access and leave the details for the media to work out among themselves. For example, it may be sufficient to reserve a certain number of seats in the gallery for media, without allocating seats to specific news agencies or individual reporters. Likewise, it may be more efficient to provide a single copy of all filings to the media liaison, rather than micromanaging the process by specifying how additional copies will be distributed to all of the media. Regardless of the level of detail included in court orders concerning media access, the judge and court staff should be reasonably well acquainted with the specific needs of the media and should be kept informed of any policies that the media develop to handle these issues.

Location and size of the courtroom

If the courtroom is very small and an overflow crowd of spectators and media is expected, the trial judge may consider moving to a larger facility to accommodate spectators and the media more easily. This, of course, may not be possible, and many judges do not think it is desirable. They feel that the larger the courtroom, the more likely it is to encourage larger crowds, thereby contributing to a circus atmosphere.

The location of the courtroom should also be assessed. If it is in the middle of a hallway with other functioning courts around it, there may be significant disruption of other court business, particularly if television crews are allowed to congregate in the hallway. Moreover, a location near a jury assembly room may present even greater congestion problems. In *U.S. v. McVeigh*, the trial was held in a smaller courtroom at the end of a hallway. This arrangement not only eased traffic congestion near the courtroom, but also permitted the placement of additional security for the courtroom without obstructing other court users. The decision to move the site of the proceedings is, of course, a matter for the judge's discretion and depends upon the availability of facilities. These possibilities should not be overlooked, however, in planning for a trial that is likely to attract substantial public interest.

Seating in the courtroom

Seating arrangements and requests for reserved seat passes can become a major preoccupation for the judge in a notorious case unless a uniform policy is adopted and strictly enforced. **Even the development of a uniform seating allocation policy may possibly be the most controversial and divisive administrative decision that the trial judge will make during the trial.** There are a variety of ways to arrange media and public seating in the courtroom:

Seating allocation. Generally, one-fourth to one-half of the seats in a courtroom are reserved for the media, with the rest of the space allocated between the parties and the public. Seats are normally set aside for members of the defendant's family, victims of the crime (if not testifying as witnesses), guests of the court, or other individuals who may attend the proceedings on short notice. For obvious reasons, members of the defendant's family should be seated away from victims of the crime. For trials in which large numbers of victims are expected to attend (e.g., the Oklahoma City bombing trials), the court should consider using the services of a Victims' Assistance Coordinator to accommodate seating arrangements for victims.

Reserved seating in the spectators' gallery for court staff is generally inadvisable, but limited seating within the well of the court may be made available if necessary. In a high-security trial, some seats may have to be allocated to law enforcement officers. Most often, certain rows or sections of the seats are designated for groups of spectators. Space for media sketch artists is usually set aside on the first row. For certain hearings or proceedings, courts have on occasion allowed sketch artists or the media in general to sit in the jury box when the jury is out or the proceeding does not require a jury. Aisle seats near the rear may be assigned to wire service reporters, who must leave frequently to file stories.

The judge may allocate the seats personally. However, it is preferable that a judge, court staff, the media liaison, or other individual selected by the judge allocate the seats in accordance with the judge's instructions. Alternatively, a working committee of the press can develop criteria for allocating seat assignments, including pool assignments if the media demand for seats exceeds the number that can be assigned to them. The process may be fairly formal, with press passes assigned to specific seats issued to credentialed media. Or it may be more ad hoc, with seats occupied by the press on a first-come/first-served basis each day.

If the courtroom cannot accommodate all of the media, and seating is on a first-come/first-served basis, it is advisable to allow only one representative per news organization until all organizations are represented. For very high demand trials, a rule should specify that reserved seats that are not filled by the start of each court session (or within a specified period of time before each session) will be given on a first-come/first-served basis to the public. This prevents disruptions of late entries by media personnel and keeps seats from going empty until the next session of court.

When the demand for seating is particularly high, people excluded from the trial (both media and public) will bring it to the attention of the trial judge if seats are routinely left unoccupied during the trial. Otherwise, the media liaison or court administrative personnel can be assigned to ensure that reserved seats are being used and that pooled seats are rotated properly. Passes can be canceled if they are not used a substantial percentage of the time. Forfeited passes can be reassigned to reporters next in line on a waiting list.

The court should be sensitive to complaints concerning private-citizen access to the trial. Detailed planning and strict enforcement of the seating plan between the media, the public, and the parties may limit, but will never eliminate, public-access complaints. The public-seating dilemma has been highlighted in a number of news articles written about the "seating crunch" (see Appendix 5).

Press passes. The U.S. District Court for the District of Columbia, which deals with a large number of notorious cases, issues press passes for the duration of the trial based on a written application committing the reporter or organization to daily coverage of the trial. With the exception of the wire services, one pass is issued per organization.

For high-demand trials or those in which court security is a particular concern, the court may consider differentiated press passes. The Oklahoma City bombing trials, for example, had three levels of press passes. The highest level permitted access to the courthouse, the pressroom, and the courtroom; the second level permitted access only to the courthouse and the pressroom; and the lowest level permitted access only to the courthouse. This arrangement was useful both for crowd control and for court security. Another system involves color coding the passes (e.g., for press, family members, witnesses).

For reporters and organizations unable to commit to daily coverage, there is a fifteen-minute rule for reporters with press credentials. If the reserved press seat is not filled within fifteen minutes before the start of the morning or afternoon proceedings, it can be filled by a media representative without a permanent pass, who is entitled to that seat for the remainder of the morning or afternoon session. This is particularly effective for getting the media into the courtroom on time. Through the use of this fifteen-minute rule, the court "doesn't have a lot of stragglers trailing in, which can be disruptive."

Applications for permanent passes are invited by notices sent out over the wire services or by other means. The media liaison makes a list of those who respond to the notice and makes a recommendation to the trial judge about which reporters from that list should be admitted daily to fill the seats set aside for the media.

Passes may also be issued on a day-to-day basis. Preference is usually given to the local media and those who are covering the trial daily, but passes may occasionally be given to media organizations or reporters who can be present at the trial only for a short time. If there is room in the public section, press may be permitted to sit there without a pass. In some trials, reporters have been assigned specific seats, with the provision that those seats must be occupied every day or they will be reassigned.

Because passes are an extremely valuable commodity to the media, they can also be used in conjunction with security measures. In one court, for example, reporters were required to surrender their press passes each day in exchange for court credentials. This system gave the court much greater control over courtroom access.

First come/first served. With or without trial passes, the media may sit in the seats reserved for the press on a first-come/first-served basis. They should not, however, be permitted to occupy public seats. Although the press may be required to stand in line with the public, more often some preference is accorded reporters by either allowing them into the courtroom ahead of the public or forming a separate press line.

Once the trial or hearing starts, the judge may prohibit entry or exit by the media (and the public) until there is a break in the court session. Reentry may also be prohibited because once a seat is vacated, other waiting members of the press or public may be allowed to take it. Some courts allow the media more leeway than the public in entering and leaving and may allow them to reserve their seats by indicating that they will be returning later in the day.

Special seating arrangements may be made for events likely to attract overflow crowds, such as the testimony of a key witness or the delivery of the verdict. To accommodate the overflow, a judge may want to arrange for closed-circuit transmission of the proceeding to another room in the courthouse. If this is not feasible, the court may prepare a special seating arrangement or seating assignments for the media and other spectators based on their requests. Additional pooling of the media may also be required.

An alternative for managing overflow crowds is to establish a "seating raffle" in which numbered passes for unreserved seats are distributed to the press and public. A random drawing for seats is then held for each court session. This technique alleviates the long lines, "overnighters," and "line holders" often associated with first-come/first-served approaches.

Information on scheduling and procedures

As discussed above, the judge, a staff member, or the media liaison may provide information to the media. The media can be advised about routine matters, such as the time and place of the next significant event or where and how to obtain copies of filings and orders, with daily notices posted in the pressroom or released through the wire services. Voice mail can provide information on a continuing basis by means of a recording. If a court has a public information officer, he or she may be responsible for posting the notices or updating the recording. The important point is that some arrangement for providing daily updates of routine scheduling and case status should be provided, and instructions for using this mechanism should be given to the media at the outset.

Copying of documents and exhibits, availability of transcripts

Few courts have sufficient staff to accommodate all of the requests for copies of court documents, filings, and exhibits for a notorious trial on-site. When the media provide their own photocopying machine in a pressroom or elsewhere in the courthouse, the media liaison or another designated individual may pick up copies of documents from the courtroom clerk and arrange for their duplication.

Some courts require the parties to provide an extra copy of any documents or papers admitted into evidence so that a copy is available for copying and distribution at the next recess. If the media do not provide their own copying machine, other arrangements may be made through local copying establishments. Legal pleadings and filings are handled in the same manner with the parties providing two copies of each item filed. One copy is filed in the court file, and a duplicate file is created for the media. This preserves the integrity of the official court file while allowing the media access to documents as they are filed. Obviously, copies of sealed documents are not provided to the media, and such materials are not available for public inspection in the official court file.

Arrangements must also be made for media access to tangible evidence, such as photographs, videotapes, and physical items. In some cases, a clerk or bailiff has carried a photograph outside the courthouse, where television cameras are allowed to videotape the photograph or the item. With videotapes, the television technicians can dub copies for all of the media through patch cords. But the court must make clear that these items are not available to the media until they have been admitted into evidence and have been seen by the jury. Once the jury has seen a piece of evidence in its entirety, the media is entitled to access to it. A variation on this approach is the creation of an exhibit book for the media.

Provision can also be made for making transcripts available to the media if they do not purchase a daily transcript from the court reporter. A number of private companies have made arrangements with the court reporters in notorious trials to provide simultaneous transcriptions of testimony presented in courts for purchase by members of the press who desire instantaneous transcripts. Court reporters typically are employed by the court on a contract basis and, consequently, are allowed to provide additional copies of the official court transcript to the media on a for-profit basis.[1] The media should pay for their transcripts regardless of the source.

Technological improvements have created a number of opportunities for improved media and public access to court documents, thus easing the bur-

---

[1] The Los Angeles Superior Courts ultimately rejected, but briefly toyed with, the idea of copyrighting trial transcripts.

den on court staff to provide such access. Imaging systems or scanning technology now permit courts to file documents in an electronic format, which can then be made accessible to the media over the Internet or via a remote electronic retrieval system established especially for the notorious trial. The increased use of real-time transcription now makes it possible to create the trial transcript contemporaneously with the trial. In its computerized format, the transcript can be downloaded to the Internet within minutes of the end of each court session. Many Internet providers have the capability of creating trial-specific websites from which to make filings, transcripts, and photographs of documentary evidence and other exhibits available.

Similar arrangements can be made for motions, briefs, or other materials filed by the parties, and for court orders and opinions, by supplying a file version of the document to a competent computer operator assigned to the court. Judge Hiller Zobel made his opinion in the *Massachusetts v. Woodward* case immediately available to the public, thus preventing a media frenzy in the court clerk's office, by transmitting the document via the Internet.

Television cameras in the courtroom

The issue of television cameras in most state courtrooms today is not a question of whether they are to be permitted, but when and under what circumstances proceedings will be televised. Currently, forty-seven states permit television cameras in the courtroom under certain circumstances. Twelve states are operating under experimental rules with regard to televised trial proceedings.

All states that permit television, radio, and photographic coverage of courtroom proceedings, whether under permanent or experimental rules, have adopted guidelines governing such coverage. Most states require the approval of the presiding judge and permit the trial judge to control the coverage of the proceedings. In most states, a formal, written request to televise or record trial proceedings must be made before the trial. Many states prohibit coverage of victims of sex crimes, of domestic relations cases, and of trials concerning trade or other commercial secrets. Televising voir dire is generally prohibited, and coverage of seated jurors is usually restricted to prevent visual identification of jurors. Many states prohibit coverage of witnesses or victims who object to having their testimony televised. Bench conferences are never broadcast. Most states provide guidelines for equipment placement, lights, the number of personnel operating the equipment, and movement within the courtroom.[2]

---

[2] The current Alaska, California, and New York rules concerning electronic media coverage are provided in Appendix 6. These rules provide a sampling of the guidelines and ground rules employed throughout the country regarding the electronic media.

Although the discretion of permitting televised proceedings is often vested with the presiding judge, his or her decision will normally be based on the recommendation of the trial judge. As a result, the trial judge in a notorious case will ultimately decide whether to permit televised proceedings in a case in which there is widespread public interest. That is not an easy decision, and criteria for making that decision are not always readily available. The determination to televise or not to televise should be made independent of notoriety considerations. In other words, a judge should ask, "Is there a compelling reason not to televise?"

The New York Standards and Administrative Policies Rule §131.4 ("Determination of the Application") concerning audiovisual coverage of judicial proceedings provides some helpful criteria in deciding media applications for television coverage. The trial court should consider all relevant factors, including the following:

- the type of case involved
- whether the coverage would cause harm to any participant
- whether the coverage would interfere with the fair administration of justice, the advancement of a fair trial, or the rights of the parties
- whether the coverage would interfere with any law enforcement activity
- whether the proceedings would involve lewd or scandalous matters
- the degree to which the parties or witnesses may seek media coverage to reach the public or to influence the outcome of the trial
- the objections of any of the parties, prospective witnesses, victims, or other participants in the proceeding of which coverage is sought
- the physical structure of the courtroom and the likelihood that any equipment required to conduct coverage of proceedings can be installed and operated without disturbance to those proceedings or any other proceedings in the courthouse
- the extent to which the coverage would be barred by law in the judicial proceeding of which coverage is sought

The court must deal with the following issues if television cameras are to be allowed in the courtroom:

Number and location of cameras. If local rules do not specify the number of cameras allowed in the courtroom, the decision is left to the discretion of the trial judge. The television media may be required to form a pool so that all television outlets covering the trial can receive footage from a single camera placed in the courtroom. Detailed pooling arrangements identifying which organization will provide the camera and crew coverage each day or throughout the proceedings should be left up to the media, but approved by the trial judge.

Before the start of the trial, the ground rules for the television camera person should be spelled out in detail, delineating which proceedings and which individuals may be photographed. In many cases, limits and prohibitions are set forth in court rules—perhaps the most common being prohibitions on photographing jurors and voir dire. If not specifically provided for in the rules, the trial judge may determine that certain witnesses or parties, such as children and rape victims, may not be photographed. Restrictions may also be placed on photographing or broadcasting consultations between the parties and their counsel or bench discussions with the judge. Some courts have required that the camera remain focused only on the witness stand. Others have required that television coverage include a "delayed feed" option of ten to twelve seconds—sufficient time for a competent technician to edit out any prohibited items from the broadcast.

Because most courtrooms were not designed to allow for a television camera, it is frequently necessary to determine where the camera will be located and to make special arrangements for its placement. An effort is usually made to place it in the most unobtrusive location so that its presence will not disrupt court proceedings, cause discomfort to participants, or block the view of the courtroom or the witness stand for other spectators. The media may need to provide a special platform camera and make special arrangements for running television cables in and out of the courtroom. These cables should be placed so as not to prevent the courtroom door from closing properly and should not present a significant hazard to traffic in the hallways. Representatives of the media and the judge or the court should work out these requirements in advance so that they are clearly understood by the media representatives and their crews.

Location of television monitor. Television media operating off of a pool camera require a remote monitor to view the television feed coming from the courtroom. An alternative method is to establish a "Teles" loop with the telephone company. **The monitor serves, in a sense, as an off-site courtroom, allowing any number of the media covering a trial to view the proceedings at a remote location without entering the courtroom itself.** Both on-site and off-site media centers are, in effect, an extension of the courtroom and, therefore, are subject to the same security requirements as the courthouse.

This remote-viewing capability has important advantages. Large numbers of media representatives are kept out of the courtroom, an attractive feature for both the press and the court. The press is often more comfortable in the informal setting of a media room where they can monitor the often mundane and uneventful proceedings, provided they have a chance to observe the actual in-court proceedings periodically. Moreover, when there is a shortage of seating in the courtroom, the media room frees seats for the public that would otherwise be reserved for the media.

When there is no media room available to accommodate a television monitor, the monitor is often placed in the hallway outside the courtroom. This is not a satisfactory arrangement. The free flow of traffic in the hallway and to the other rooms and proceedings in other courtrooms on the floor may be disrupted by the large numbers of people congregating around the monitor and the noise they make. Judges who have provided for a separate media room report great satisfaction with the arrangement, even when the room has been little more than a large closet.

The media room may be located on another floor of the courthouse or even in an adjacent building. If there is a pressroom in the courthouse, this might be a suitable site. The print media, however, use pressrooms more regularly than do broadcast media. Local newspaper reporters may view the placement of a monitor in the pressroom, with the resultant commotion and congestion, as an intrusion. The media are responsible for the costs of any physical or structural alterations necessary to equip the media room. The media are responsible for all costs associated with off-site media rooms.

Finding a space that can be used as a media room for monitoring the television feed from the courtroom is probably well worth the effort. If such a space cannot be provided, one alternative is a courtroom at the end of a corridor, or in a relatively isolated area of the court building, where a TV monitor in the hallway is less likely to disrupt other courtrooms. This, however, is clearly a less-desirable alternative.

Closed-circuit transmission. Trial judges in notorious cases may want to consider whether closed-circuit transmission of the proceedings into another courtroom or other location in the courthouse is feasible at those times of peak public and media interest. The testimony of the victim, a key witness, or the defendant; when the jury returns its verdict; or when the judge renders a critical ruling are moments of peak interest in any case, and particularly so in notorious cases. Closed-circuit viewing of these portions of the trial away from the courtroom alleviates the pressure of large numbers of people jamming into a single courtroom and makes it easier to control potentially emotional and explosive situations. Closed-circuit transmission is also an alternative for notorious trials that have been moved (e.g., change of venue), which generate substantial public interest in their original jurisdictions. This was the case in the Oklahoma City bombing trials, which were moved from Oklahoma City to Denver. In that case, the closed-circuit signal was encrypted to prevent any unauthorized tapping into the feed or rebroadcast of the trial.

Cable television broadcast. Another way of alleviating pressure on the courtroom and providing greater public access is to broadcast the proceedings over local cable television. One court did this with great success.

Judicial demeanor. One judge recommended that every trial judge should periodically watch how he or she comes across on television. This judge noted that during one in-court exchange, he came across much more harshly than he had intended. Watching oneself on television was recommended as a good means of monitoring one's own demeanor and appearance to avoid appearing unnecessarily angry, rude, or curt in court.

Judges who have tried notorious cases also stress the physical, psychological, and emotional exhaustion from the constant scrutiny of the television camera for days on end. They caution that trial judges should be aware of the temptations and insidious effects of intense media attention on themselves as well as on other participants in the trial. They suggest that judges in high-profile cases should expect a greater tendency toward theatrics and speechmaking from the trial lawyers who are on camera. In some cases, advocacy for a client merges with efforts to promote political or social agendas that are tangentially related to the case at trial. (Indeed, the reason for a trial's notoriety is often its relevance to controversial political or social issues.) For these reasons, a notorious trial can get out of control very quickly. It is important, particularly in a jury trial in a high-publicity case, that the trial judge keep a tight rein on the proceedings, always maintaining the jury's focus strictly on the issues at hand.

Other concerns regarding television coverage
Whether or not cameras are allowed in the courtroom, there are several other realities that arise when television reporters cover a notorious case.

Accommodation of broadcast equipment needs. To beam live transmissions back to their stations, television crews will need an area to set up microwave dishes and to park vans carrying remote broadcasting facilities. Court administrative staff should help the television crews place this equipment in appropriate locations. To the extent reasonably possible, the location of the television equipment should not add to the congestion of automobile traffic patterns around the courthouse or interfere with normal pedestrian traffic. The public should not have any perception that media vehicles are permitted to park illegally or given privileges or preferential treatment that ordinary citizens do not receive at the courthouse. Leasing an adjacent or nearby parking lot, at media expense, is one alternative.

The media may also need additional telephones, fax machines, PCs, or other equipment. Provided that the equipment, lines, and cables are installed in a safe and unobtrusive manner, court staff should attempt to accommodate reasonable requests whenever feasible. To the greatest extent possible, court staff should let the media handle their own logistics, subject to the review of the court and the court administrative staff. Given the proliferation of cellular telephones, laptop PCs, beepers, and other equipment, rules governing their use in the courtroom are advisable. Such rules should specify any prohibited use of technology (e.g., surreptitious broadcasting of court proceedings via cellular telephone or laptop PC). Rather than attempting to create an exhaustive list of permitted (or prohibited) equipment, it is generally sufficient to specify that equipment use is permitted provided that it does not disrupt the trial, violate existing court rules, or interfere with the ability of spectators to view the proceedings.

Interviews of participants. The question of where media interviews will be allowed is important and should be addressed early on by the trial judge. The court should also establish precisely what constitutes an interview. A talkative defendant can create a moving interview walking the length of a corridor. Our observations of the Marion Barry trial indicated that the mayor occasionally gave interviews while coming in and out of the courtroom, despite the court's policy that interviews were not allowed in the courthouse. If an interview is defined as any conversation or verbal exchange beyond standard pleasantries ("good morning" or "good afternoon"), a no-interview policy means that there must be no verbal interaction between the media and the parties until they are outside the courthouse. A security escort may be required to enforce this policy. Enforcing a no-interview policy is admittedly difficult, but might be a goal toward which the court strives.

Interviews, unless they are prohibited on court property, often are held in the hallway outside the courtroom door and can quickly degenerate into a chaotic, noisy shouting scene. Judges and courts have dealt with this problem in a number of ways:

- Prohibit all television (and radio/print) interviews on the same floor as the courtroom. Arrange for them to be held in other locations in the building, such as the pressroom, another less-congested floor, a room that can be reserved, a section of the lobby designated for that purpose, or outside the courthouse.
- Restrict such interviews to an area of the hallway away from the courtroom door, making certain that such interviews do not interfere with activity in other courtrooms. (Note: judges have found this difficult to enforce.)
- Allow interviews in the courtroom during recesses or after court has adjourned. Although many judges feel this should not be allowed, others have found it the easiest, least-disruptive way to handle the problem.

In one high-security case, a court required the media to schedule interviews with participants at other locations and had them transported there by law enforcement authorities. The Los Angeles Superior Court reports remarkable success with its requirement that prosecutors and defense attorneys arrange for interviews only in their respective offices within reasonable proximity of the courthouse.

Interviews by radio and print reporters should also be addressed. Because they are not as disruptive as television lights and cameras, some judges do not restrict them as tightly. This, however, inevitably draws an allegation of unfair or unequal treatment from television reporters. Those courts that have made a distinction have done it on the basis of the intrusiveness of television equipment as opposed to that of the radio or print media.

When cameras are not allowed in the courtroom, television organizations often employ sketch artists to render drawings for their reports. Sketch artists are usually seated as close to the front of the spectator section as possible so that they have an unimpeded view of the proceedings. In cases where a judge is concerned about protecting the privacy of a victim or witness, he or she may instruct the sketch artist to refrain from drawing too accurate a likeness of the individual or not to sketch the person at all. Generally, sketching jurors is prohibited.

Presence of still photographers

Even when television cameras are banned from the courtroom, still cameras may be allowed. The number of cameras permitted will usually be within the discretion of the trial judge. As with television cameras, pooling arrangements are often made among media organizations so that one or two still photographers provide photographs for the other members of the media. Restrictions are normally placed on the type of camera equipment used (it must operate silently) and on the freedom of movement of the photographer within the courtroom during court proceedings.

Jury-media coverage issues

Media coverage of a notorious jury trial raises a number of critical issues that should be weighed before the trial begins. (Chapter 3 discusses prescreening questionnaires and other approaches for dealing with the effect of pretrial publicity on the jury panel.)

Access to jury questionnaires. If jury-screening questionnaires are used in selecting a jury, the media may ask to see them. As a matter of law, the media have a right to inspect jurors' responses to voir dire questionnaires. If jurors have responded to questionnaires *in camera* and with assurances from the court that their answers will be kept confidential, this information should be withheld from the media. There is less explicit caselaw on the issue of whether the questionnaires of prospective jurors who are *not* selected to sit on the jury are public documents. Some judges make these materials available, while others do not. (See discussion of legal authority on this issue, Appendix 1.)

Names and addresses of jurors. Addresses of jurors in notorious cases should not be given to the media. The trial judge may elect to provide juror names after the jury is selected, but in some cases the names of jurors are not disclosed until after the verdict has been rendered. As a general rule, jurors' names are a matter of public record.[3] A decision to empanel an anonymous jury, discussed in greater detail in Chapter 3, should be supported by a specific finding that this measure is necessary to protect the rights of the defendant or the integrity of the judicial process. In such cases, the court should use a juror identification number to refer to the juror and to any materials provided by the juror (e.g., written questionnaires).

Coverage of voir dire. Although seating space may be further limited because of the presence of the jury panel in the courtroom, voir dire conducted in open court usually presents essentially the same issues of media access as the trial itself.

A more difficult problem may arise when individual voir dire is conducted away from the courtroom in chambers or in a separate room. Judges have dealt with this approach to voir dire by allowing a pool media representative to be present during these individual questioning sessions, subject to the same restrictions on what may be reported throughout the jury selection process. In this situation, a judge should ask prospective jurors whether the presence of the media in the questioning room or the courtroom would affect their attitudes toward the case or their service as jurors. In fact, prospective jurors should be asked whether the presence of the media would affect their ability to listen or to be fair and impartial during the trial.

It is not advisable to conduct jury screening and pretrial hearings at the same time because prospective jurors can be exposed to media coverage of the hearings.

Consecutive trials of codefendants or multiple defendants in the same case may raise special problems with regard to juror knowledge of the particular circumstances and outcomes of the prior proceedings. The publicity surrounding a prior trial will necessitate asking prospective jurors specific questions about the impact of that publicity on their ability to be fair and impartial. (But see discussion of *Mu'Min v. Virginia*, Appendix 1.)

In camera **and bench conferences.** At various stages of the case, bench and *in camera* proceedings may occur. Depending upon local custom or rule or statute these proceedings may or may not be reported. If they are not reported, it is usually very helpful if the trial judge makes a comment or

---

[3] *See, e.g.*, In re Globe Newspaper Co., 920 F.2d 88 (1st Cir. 1990); In re Baltimore Sun Co., 841 F.2d 74 (4th Cir. 1988).

"We found the defendant guilty as charged by the media."

statement that summarizes the purpose or subject matter of the unreported conference. Such a practice prevents the parties from misrepresenting the actual proceedings and avoids needless litigation of tangential issues. If the bench or *in camera* proceedings are reported, issues of media access are raised, especially where juror privacy, confidential information, or inadmissible and prejudicial evidence are at stake. (See Appendix 1.)

Shielding the jury from media coverage of proceedings and contact with the media. Intense media coverage of a notorious trial makes it necessary for the judge and the court to devise measures to ensure that such coverage does not affect jurors' consideration of the case. Equally important, the trial court must ensure an atmosphere that permits the jury to come and go from the courthouse unimpeded, safely, and insulated from extraneous influence to the greatest extent possible. Such measures should also ensure that jurors are protected from public demonstrations, including clothing (e.g., t-shirts) with messages intended to sway the jury, that might affect their consideration of the case. The Fully Informed Jury Association (FIJA), an organization that promotes informing jurors of their nullification powers, has been known to place pamphlets or brochures on jurors' automobiles.

Sequestration of the jury from the time of selection until the verdict is rendered is the most onerous means of insulating jurors from outside influences—both for jurors and for the court. Because it is expensive, ties up large numbers of personnel, and imposes burdens on jurors during a long trial, most judges are reluctant to sequester jurors. Sequestration should be used only in the most compelling circumstances, such as where there is a substantial risk of juror exposure to prejudicial media coverage, a risk of jury tampering, or a threat to the personal safety of the jurors. Absent such compelling reasons or other convincing rationale, the court should seek alternatives for dealing with the need for juror isolation and security.

Sequestration of the jury during deliberations, required by law in some states, may be ordered by the court to shield jurors during the most critical stage of their service.

Sequestration during the trial day (e.g., keeping jurors separated from trial participants, the media, and the public during recesses and the lunch hour) is sometimes used. Lunch may be ordered by the court and served to jurors in the jury room, courtroom, or elsewhere. Another approach is to reserve a section of the public cafeteria exclusively for jurors. Partial sequestration, however, does not solve the problem of juror access to television or print coverage of the trial once they leave the courthouse.

Jury admonition. The trial judge usually admonishes the jury daily not to watch television or read press accounts of the proceedings and not to discuss the case with anyone. This admonition should also prohibit jurors from reading about the case on the Internet. In cases receiving continuous media coverage, it is often necessary to question jurors each time a major news story appears.

An innovative approach taken by one judge was to tell the jury at the beginning of the trial that he would provide them with news clippings and video scrapbooks of the coverage at the conclusion of the trial. He arranged for clippings to be made from several local and national publications and obtained videotapes of the local television news stories from the sheriff's office, which routinely recorded news broadcasts each day. At the end of the trial, each juror received copies of these materials. This judge felt the technique was very successful in reducing jurors' temptations to read newspapers or watch television accounts of the trial.

Issuing gag orders. Another way judges have shielded jurors from media exposure is by restricting what counsel and the parties can say to the media. Such orders were often previously overturned on appeal as violative of the First Amendment freedom-of-speech guarantees. In recent years, however, appellate courts appear to have become more tolerant of these measures, provided that such orders are not overbroad and are narrowly tailored to protect the integrity of the judicial system and the defendant's right to a fair trial.

(See discussion of law regarding gag and protective orders in Chapter 1 and Appendix 1 discussions of the *Gentile* decision.)

Insulating the jury from media or other contacts. The court should try to ensure that jurors are insulated from inadvertent contact with the media within the courthouse. If possible, a separate entrance and exit to the courthouse and courtroom should be provided for the jury. Courts unable to provide this may reserve an elevator for jurors and have a bailiff or court attendant accompany them through the hallways and on and off the elevator. Jurors may be assembled at another location and transported to the courthouse, or special parking arrangements may be made for them. Jurors may also be sequestered during the lunch hour. The efforts made will depend upon the facilities and resources available, but some thought should be given to how best to accomplish this within the court's capabilities.

Media interviews with jurors. The media is strictly prohibited from talking to jurors during the proceedings. The vast majority of media professionals understand and willingly comply with this restriction. Unfortunately, not all reporters share such scruples. Therefore, the court may want to warn the media that attempts to interview sitting jurors or their immediate families are prohibited and that violations will be dealt with severely.

After the jury has returned its verdict and been dismissed, however, the media generally will request the chance to interview jurors. Judges have different attitudes toward this request. Some judges feel that jurors in a notorious case may need the catharsis of talking to the media once the decision is made and that the court should facilitate such interviews. Even jurors who prefer anonymity at the beginning of the trial often express interest in explaining the verdict after the trial. Judges may arrange for a televised press conference in the courthouse, as well as an off-camera interview for jurors. A press conference at the courthouse does offer one particular advantage for jurors over individual interviews with the press—namely, it decreases the likelihood that jurors will be hounded individually at their homes or places of employment following the trial. This is as true for those jurors who do not speak at the press conference as for those who do.

Other judges feel that the court should not facilitate media interviews but should simply advise the jury that they may talk to the media if they wish. Still others will advise the jury of the media's desire to interview them but discourage it by emphasizing that they have no obligation to do so and reminding them of the need to respect the privacy of their fellow jurors, who may not wish to have their deliberations disclosed. As part of its closing admonition, the court should advise jurors to contact the court if members of the media persist in questioning them, over their objections, about their jury service. (Sample media advisories are provided in Appendix 7. The advisories illustrate different approaches to media access to jurors.)

In all cases, jurors should be told that they may choose to talk to the media if they wish, but the decision is entirely theirs.

The issue of commercial transactions between jurors and the media, i.e., the sale of their stories to the press, is also of concern. In some states, such transactions are illegal while the jury is impaneled. (This issue is discussed in greater detail in Chapter 3.)

Pressures on courtroom staff

Handling a notorious case is likely to place significant burdens and pressures on the courtroom staff. In particular, high-profile cases dramatically increase the volume of mail, telephone calls, and in-person inquiries to the court, making it difficult for courtroom staff to finish routine work within reasonable business hours. The phone calls may continue for some time after the trial is over because of inquiries about the verdict; the names, addresses, and telephone numbers of counsel for the parties; and other aspects of the case. If left unrestricted, television and other media equipment may impede access to parts of the courtroom, making it more difficult for staff to perform some of their usual functions. Once the trial begins, staff may also feel increased concern about dealing with exhibits or other aspects of the proceedings because of the intense public interest and media focus on their work and the trial and the concern for error, which might jeopardize the trial.

Judges and courts should do whatever possible to mitigate the additional burdens on the trial court staff. Back-up clerks can be assigned to help with additional administrative duties or to perform work outside the courtroom during court hours.

Telephone calls can be routed, if possible, to a central location in the court administrative office or elsewhere by placing intercepts on the public lines to the courtroom and providing other private lines to the trial judge and his or her staff during the proceedings. If possible, a recorded message providing basic scheduling and seating information can be used to answer the bulk of the calls. These and other logistical concerns should be discussed with court staff in considerable detail before the trial.

If a media liaison is used, he or she should handle all media inquiries directed to the court. Neither the judge's staff nor the court's administrative staff should field any media telephone inquiries; they should all be directed to the media liaison to answer the questions or convey them to the judge. The liaison should relieve both the judge's staff and the court's staff from the burden of answering countless telephone inquiries from the media.

In a case attracting widespread media and public attention, the trial judge should emphasize how important it is that the courtroom staff project the best possible image in their treatment of both the press and the public. At the same time, court staff should be extremely circumspect in their conversations with media representatives and avoid appearing to favor one individual or organization over others. In fact, some orientation and training should be given to the court and trial staff in how to deal with the public and the media in an upcoming notorious case. Above all, staff members should understand the judge's ground rules and their particular authority, or lack thereof, with the media. The staff should be an extension of the trial judge for enforcing policies, procedures, and standard practices as they relate to the notorious case and dealings with the media.

Delivery of judge's decision in nonjury cases

The court may wish to provide for printing and disseminating the decision from a central location other than the courtroom. A contemporary solution is to release the opinion via the Internet, as was done by Judge Hiller Zobel in the *Massachusetts v. Woodward* case.

jury considerations

in a notorious trial

Lessons Learned

1. The trial judge must plan for the needs of jurors in a notorious trial. Early planning and clearly defined responsibilities are essential in determining the numbers of prospective jurors to be called, the prescreening methodology, sequestration logistics (if unfortunately required), and security needs.

2. Prescreening questionnaires should be well thought out in terms of what they ask and how they will be used and administered. The trial judge should take an active role in the drafting, review, and control of prescreening questionnaires to ensure that only relevant and meaningful information is elicited and the privacy rights of jurors are protected.

3. The possibility that jurors may have been or may be approached and offered payment in return for information concerning the notorious trial or for news stories and book, movie, or television rights should be explored with the jury before the start of evidence. If there is applicable law on the subject, that law should be explained to the jury.

4. Limited sequestration for jurors while they are in the courthouse is preferable to full sequestration—both for the jurors and for the court staff who are responsible for the jury's comfort and safety. In the rare cases that full sequestration is warranted, juror security, meal, entertainment, transportation, and personal needs should be arranged well in advance. Irrespective of sequestration orders, jurors should be kept apprised of trial schedules, including the anticipated length of various stages of the trial.

5. The trial judge should ensure that jurors feel comfortable enough to inform the judge about problems or concerns regarding improper exposure to media coverage or contact, improper comments by families or friends, or any sort of inadvertent taint.

6. The court should plan for possible demonstrations that may seek to influence jurors improperly, both inside and outside the courthouse.

7. Security plans should include specific provisions for safeguarding the jury's dismissal after delivering the verdict with regard to jurors' exit from the courthouse, press access to the jury, and community reaction to the verdict.

8. The trial judge should provide clear guidance to the jury regarding postverdict contact with the media and attorneys for the parties.

9. In the intense emotional setting of a notorious case, jurors may require postverdict emotional support or even psychological counseling. Judges should be sensitive to these needs and be prepared to respond to them.

CHAPTER THREE

Jury Considerations in a Notorious Trial

The notorious trial places different and magnified strains on the trial court's jury system. One of the foremost concerns of a judge who presides over a notorious case is the care, comfort, and safety of the prospective jurors, and of the jurors who are ultimately seated. While the care and feeding of jurors in a standard case can often become routine, the primary juror concern in a notorious case often is to maintain the needed isolation of the jurors from the parties, media, and the public. The well-being and safety of the jury should not be overlooked in this concern for isolation.

More than anything else, jurors want (and legitimately expect) to be kept well informed about a typical day's proceedings—the time of the start and conclusion of the trial each day and the time of the daily recesses in the morning and afternoon and for lunch. In addition, jurors appreciate periodic updates on the anticipated length of the various components of the trial: when the prosecutor's case will conclude; the length of the defense case (once it has commenced); how long the instruction conference may be; and when the jury can expect to be given the case. While these times will always be estimates, jurors are often reassured by having an idea of how long the next phase of the trial is expected to take and what their schedule will be in the coming days and weeks.

Because the case is of great public interest, the effect of pretrial publicity upon prospective jurors invariably becomes an issue that requires major attention during voir dire. The nature of the notorious criminal case, which may be gruesome, can be so offensive that few of the prospective jurors can honestly claim to be objective. The nature of the notorious civil case, such as the failure of a savings-and-loan association or a retirement investment program that touches many persons, can make it difficult to find a person unaffected by pretrial exposure. Although the U.S. Supreme Court in *Mu'Min v. Virginia*[1] relaxed the obligation on the court to investigate juror bias (see detailed discussion of this decision, Chapter One and Appendix 1), the need to ensure an appearance of fairness can result in many persons being unable to hear the case.

---

[1] Mu'Min v. Virginia, 111 S. Ct. 1899 (1991).

Each trial judge should be conversant with the specific legal criteria pertinent to change-of-venue determinations in his or her jurisdiction. The change-of-venue determination is not always clear. The *Mu'Min* decision reviews the legal history and standards of voir dire and exposure to pretrial publicity in a notorious case. The Court articulated the minimal permissible range of inquiry allowed during voir dire to meet Sixth Amendment requirements for selecting a fair and impartial jury. In doing so, the Court upheld severe limitations on the extent of voir dire permitted on the subject of exposure to pretrial publicity in a high-publicity case. The Court concluded that potential jurors do not have to be questioned about the specifics of what they know about the case, so long as they promise to be fair. Given the Supreme Court's pronouncements in *Mu'Min*, finding jurors who are totally ignorant of the facts and issues involved in a notorious case may be less necessary. Nevertheless, the trial judge must be satisfied that the jurors *can be believed* when they state that they have not formed an opinion about the case despite the widespread publicity surrounding it.

If the defendants in criminal cases are, or appear to be, threatening, then juror security and privacy are issues. However, in reality, the greater security and privacy problem for jurors may stem from the media's interest in them. Instances of jury tampering are very rare—almost nonexistent. Nevertheless, if jury members feel threatened—from whatever source—the court must take measures to protect them.

Constitutional challenges that the jury fails to represent a fair cross-section of the community can result from the alleged failure to comply with required local procedures. There may also be challenges stemming from the discriminatory use of peremptory challenges (*Batson*). In addition to all of the above considerations, and because of the added attention and scrutiny given notorious cases by the media and the public, the entire process becomes longer and more complex. This further burdens the jury system and those citizens called to serve as jurors. These jury considerations will be explored in this chapter.

Pretrial jury considerations

A notorious trial is likely to put additional pressure on jury staff because of the need to call a larger jury panel than usual and to use procedures not ordinarily used, such as administering prescreening questionnaires. Consequently, coordination among the judge, clerk, court administrator, and jury staff is crucial. Communication with the jury staff as early as possible and on a continuing basis is necessary when an especially large jury panel must be called because extra time and planning will likely be required to summon the jurors.

A pretrial-planning conference should be held with the parties to the trial as well as the security staff, building staff, press representatives, judge's staff, and the court reporter. Jury matters should be thoroughly explored. As basic policies become clearer, the judge and court staff should conduct additional planning conferences, again with all interested people in attendance, to fill in specific details related to the trial.

Jury topics at these pretrial-planning conferences should include the following:

- **Estimated length of trial**: What time frame can all parties agree on for planning purposes?
- **Trial schedule**: What holidays will be observed? What are the normal hours of trial for each day? Will there be evening sessions? Will there be weekend sessions?
- **Number of jurors needed**: Is a special venire required, or can the jurors be selected from the existing jury pool? How many names should be drawn from the source list? What is the expected yield of qualified jurors from the people summoned for jury service? Will the court need to print special jury summonses or notices? If so, who will be responsible for making those arrangements?
- **Jury management system**: Is the selection of names from the source list sufficiently random? Do the court's procedures for impaneling juries produce panels that reflect a representative cross-sample of the community? Would the court's jury management system survive a legal challenge?
- **Criteria for excusing prospective jurors from service**: Will court staff have the authority to excuse jurors for financial or medical hardship? Can prospective jurors be excused from service without appearing in court in person?
- **Juror instructions**: Should the jury panel be given instructions about appropriate juror conduct (e.g., reading or watching media accounts of the case) before reporting for voir dire? What instructions should be given to people who have been selected as jurors before the full jury has been selected and sworn? What should jurors be told about pretrial publicity, courthouse security, access to information about jurors, contacts with people involved in the case, or offers from media or publishers about jurors' stories?
- **Prescreening procedures**: Will juror questionnaires be used? Who will prepare the questionnaire? How much time can the judge give to supervising the preparation of the questionnaires? How will it be distributed? When and where will the jury panel complete it? Who will have access to the questionnaires?

- **Jury selection procedures**: How many members of the jury panel will be asked to report each day? How large will the panels be for voir dire? Where will voir dire take place? How will challenges for cause and peremptory challenges be made? Who may participate in sidebars concerning jury selection? How will *Batson* challenges be handled?
- **Alternates**: How many alternate jurors will be needed? How will they be selected? Will they be identified to other jurors? To the parties? Will they be identified before deliberations? Will they be permitted to sit in on deliberations? To participate in deliberations? When will they be dismissed? How will they be seated? At what point will the media be allowed to interview alternates?
- **Sequestration**: Is sequestration necessary? Have all alternatives to sequestration been fully explored? If sequestration is necessary, who will plan and make arrangements? How will hotels and restaurants be paid? For how long will jurors be sequestered? What rules will be established for jurors? What security precautions are necessary for sequestered jurors?
- **Courtroom facilities**: Are the jury facilities adequate given the anticipated length of the trial? Is the jury box large enough to accommodate all of the jurors? Are the chairs reasonably comfortable? Will jurors need a writing surface for taking notes? Will jurors have access to the courtroom, to restrooms, and to the courthouse that isolates them from the press and public? Will jurors who smoke have a separate smoking area? Are more seats needed for alternates?
- **Juror privacy**: Should the court use an anonymous jury for this case? If not, what information about the jurors will be made available to the press and public? When will this information be made available? Who will have access to confidential information about jurors? How will that information be kept secure? If cameras are permitted in the courtroom, may jurors be photographed or filmed?
- **Tools for jurors**: If jurors are promised a record of the proceedings, who will maintain this record? Will jurors be given notebooks? If so, what will they contain? Who will prepare and copy them? Where will notebooks be kept during breaks and recesses? What procedures need to be established for juror notetaking or submission of juror questions to witnesses? Will jurors be given preliminary instructions? If so, who will prepare them? What information will they contain? Who will prepare final instructions? Will jurors have a written copy of the final instructions?
- **Juror security**: Should prospective jurors be required to furnish positive identification when reporting for voir dire? Will jurors need special passes for parking or for access to the courthouse? What personal items (e.g., reading materials, lunch, clothing) will jurors be permitted to bring to the courthouse? How will those personal items be secured during trial? Who

among the court staff should jurors contact in case of an emergency? How will they reach that person? How can family members reach jurors in case of an emergency?

- **Verdict and dismissal**: What procedures need to be in place when the jury returns its verdict? Will the judge meet with the jurors after the verdict has been returned? If so, who else may participate in that meeting? What restrictions should the judge place on discussions with the jury? What instructions will jurors be given about postverdict conversations with the media? With the attorneys? What suggestions will the court give jurors about handling postverdict stress? How much protection will the court offer jurors from media harassment following the verdict?

Estimating numbers of prospective jurors needed[2]

In estimating the number of prospective jurors needed to be called for the trial, the court should consider reasons for which jurors will likely be eliminated. That is, will the nature of the case, the estimated length of the trial, or possible sequestration cause persons to ask to be excused? Jury personnel can provide the normal proportion of the jury pool that is qualified, able, and willing to serve on a given jury panel (called the *yield rate*).[3] That number must then be reduced because of factors specific to the notorious case (e.g., number of prospective jurors exposed to prejudicial pretrial publicity). A jurisdiction with experience in high-profile, notorious cases can provide yield rates for such cases.

One method of determining this yield rate is for the jury staff or court manager staff to survey the panels of prospective jurors reporting for non-notorious cases and determine from those the number who would be available under the notorious case's conditions. In one such exercise, reporting panels were asked how many persons could serve on an eighteen-month trial. Less than 10 percent of those summoned indicated that they could serve. (In that court, the normal yield was approximately 25 percent; therefore, the yield in a notorious case would be expected to be 2.5 percent.) The interesting result was that when the actual jury for the notorious case was selected, many times the 10 percent figure were available because of the "famous" nature of the case. That is, people were more willing to serve when it was known to be the "Pontiac Ten," rather then just an eighteen-month trial.

[2] In Brown v. Louisiana, 100 S. Ct. 2214, 2222 n. 9 (1980), the court noted that a small panel may affect the outcome of the trial. There is no case law on specific panel size requirements, however.

[3] The yield is the percentage of the names selected from the source list or lists that are qualified to serve as jurors and are available for voir dire. This rate reflects those excused because of financial or physical problems, statutory disqualifications, nonresponses, and undeliverable summonses. Typical yield rates are from 10 percent in major urban courts to 50 percent in suburban courts. G. THOMAS MUNSTERMAN, JURY SYSTEM MANAGEMENT 43-53 (National Center for State Courts, 1997).

Table 1
Large Jury Panels for Highly Publicized Cases
U.S. District Court for the District of Columbia

Jury Selection Dates	Case #	Title Of Case	Judge	Case Type (Subject Matter)	Panel Size	Number Selected	Challenged For Cause	Pre Challenged	Not Used	Actually Needed
9/2-3/80	80-289	U.S. v. Jenrette	Penn	Abscam	110	18	55	23	14	96
12/4-8/80	80-340	U.S. v. Kelly	Bryant	Abscam	162	18	45	15	84	78
5/5-5/08 5/11/81	78-367	U.S. v. Guillermo Sampol	Parker	Murder of Chilean Amb. Letelier	103	18	29	24	32	71
4/27-30/82	81-306	U.S. v. John W. Hinckley Jr.	Parker	Assasination Attempt of President	90	18	38	22	12	78
7/28-30/82	80-340	U.S. v. Ciuzio Weisz	Bryant	Abscam	74	16	17	17	24	50
10/19/87 10/26/87	87-96	U.S. v. Deaver	Jackson	Perjury	100	16	39	30	15	85
1/11/88 1/15/88	87-309	U.S. v. Nofziger, Et Al	Flannery	Ethics Violations	91	18	20	23	30	61
1/31/89 2/9/89	88-80-02	U.S. v. North	Gesell	Conspiracy	234	18	108	108	0	234
3/1/90 3/7/90	88-80-01	U.S. v. Poindexter	Greene	Conspiracy	206	18	30	20	138	68
6/16/90 6/18/90	90-68	U.S. v. Barry	Jackson	Narcotics	250	18	226	0	6	244
10/19/92 10/22/92	91-521	U.S. v. Clair George	Lamberth	Iran-Contra	93	16	16	10	45	48
11/22 11/29-30 12/1-2/94	94-167	U.S. v. Gatling, Jackson, Walker, Et Al	Sporkin	Illegal Bribes For DC Housing	179	18	104	31	26	153
3/13 3/16/95	94-447	U.S. v. Duran	Richey	Attempted Murder of President	104	18	26	27	33	71
10/26- 10/27/95	94-469	U.S. v. Billy Dale	Kessler	White House Travel Case	99	15	50	0	34	65
1/3/96	95-42	U.S. v. Fitzpatrick	Kessler	Defrauding The U.S. Govt	60	18	31	0	11	49
3/11-12/96	95-271	U.S. v. Gartman	Sullivan	Fraud	123	18	24	17	64	59
4/1 4/9-11 4/15-18 4/22/96	95-154	U.S. v. Alston	Sporkin	Death Penalty	251	18	231	0	2	249
4/11-12 5/1-2 5/6 5/20-21/96	95-88	U.S. v. Cunningham, Et Al	Kessler	Murder	212	20	162	26	4	208

The trial judge should consider, however, whether having persons seeking to be jurors is a good idea. This should be explored during voir dire.

District of Columbia court history

Another method of determining the required panel size is to research the experience of other judges who have presided over notorious cases. The U.S. District Court for the District of Columbia maintains records for all such cases heard in that court (see Table 1). A close correspondence between the size of

Table 1
Large Jury Panels for Highly Publicized Cases
U.S. District Court for the District of Columbia

Jury Selection Dates	Case #	Title Of Case	Judge	Case Type (Subject Matter)	Panel Size	Number Selected	Challenged For Cause	Pre Challenged	Not Used	Actually Needed
5/6/96	95-284	U.S. v. Brooks, Et Al	Lamberth	Kidnappping	75	14	23	21	17	58
5/21 5/23 5/28/96	91-1830	Amr Pharm Holland v. American Home Products	Hogan	Trademark Infringement	84	12	15	27	30	54
6/17 6/20-21/96	93-0284	U.S. v. Rezaq	Lamberth	Terrorist	103	18	84	0	1	102
7/17-18/96	39	U.S. v. Darron Gilliam, Et Al	Sullivan	Narcotics	85	14	10	26	35	50
9/9-10/96	96-193	U.S. v. Sun-Diamond Growers	Urbina	Bribery of Public Official	70	16	13	18	23	47
1/21 1/23-24 1/27/97	95-323	U.S. v. Neill	Joyce Green	Fraud	118	18	66	17	17	101
1/23/97	96-181	U.S. v. Hemmingson, Et Al	Kessler	Fraudulent Interstate Transaction	80	18	12	15	35	45
2/26 2/28/97	96-319	U.S. v. Wilson, Et Al	Johnson	Murder	93	16	49	28	0	93
5/1 5/8-9 5/12/97	96-105	U.S. v. Singh, Et Al	Lamberth	Fraud	100	18	60	19	3	97
5/20/97	96-374	U.S. v. Pupo	Joyce Green	Aircraft Regulation	75	16	18	16	25	50
9/25 9/29-30 10/1/97	96-070	U.S. v. Whitaker, Et Al	Sporkin	Embezzlement	139	18	113	0	8	111
10/22/97	91-0270	U.S. v. Shirosaki	Robertson	Murder	106	18	15	21	52	54
10/28/97	96-1692	Wiley v. GMC	Joyce Green	Product Liability	55	10	32	5	8	47
1/5-6/98	97-351	U.S. v. R. Stokes	Kollar-Kotelly	Bribery of Public Official	74	15	19	15	25	49
3/2-3/98	97-185	U.S. v. J. Robinson	Sullivan	Bank Fraud	100	16	9	1	74	26
3/9-10/98	97-072	U.S. v. A. Akers	Jackson	Narcotics	59	16	10	6	27	32

the initial panel brought in and the number of jurors actually needed to select a fair and impartial jury indicates an efficient and effective summoning and screening process. *Panel size* refers to the number of prospective jurors who are already qualified; that is, undelivered, nonresponses, or disqualified persons have already been eliminated.

What is impressive about the district court's results is the relatively small number of persons needed to select juries for these notorious cases. For example, the jury panel needed for jury selection for the trial of John Hinckley consisted of only seventy-eight people. Many courts routinely overestimate the number of prospective jurors needed for their jury panels, even in non–notorious cases. The result is large numbers of people who report for jury service and complete lengthy questionnaires but are not "reached"—that is, questioned—during voir dire.

Table 1 is included to illustrate the value of this type of historical data and to show the experience in one federal district court, albeit one of the most experienced in terms of notorious cases. The experience in other courts might include the use of larger panels. Courts may also look to the experience of other courts in their own states or other states for guidance on the size of jury panels needed for notorious cases. In addition, state administrative offices, clerks, or administrators in major urban courts may be able to identify experienced judges who possess data similar to that of the U.S. District Court for the District of Columbia.

Several methods can help the court bring in only the number needed and prescreen prospective jurors who obviously will be excused "for cause" without asking those persons to report. To prevent voir dire from becoming a matter of crowd control rather than due process, courts that normally summon a hundred persons, for example, should avoid sending out a thousand summonses, expecting hundreds to report.

If an unusually large call is necessary, judges have found innovative methods of crowd control. One judge solved a need for 500 prospective jurors by taking 80 people out of the regular jury pool every day for several days. Another judge called a manageable number each morning and afternoon for three or four days. Still another used the jury assembly room as a courtroom and conducted initial qualifying screenings there. Each of these judges felt that these methods were effective and resulted in fewer unhappy jurors due to a more expeditious process.

Prescreening prospective jurors

Some prescreening of prospective jurors is done in all cases, such as simply asking on a qualification questionnaire whether the person fulfills the basic statutory qualifications of citizenship, residency, age, ability to communicate in English, and whether the prospective juror is a convicted felon whose rights have not been restored. In notorious cases, this screening must be far more extensive.

Pretrial screening encompasses the entire process of jury selection, from drawing names of prospective jurors from the source list to examining prospective jurors. It includes administrative matters such as the elimination of persons disqualified or not found from the list of prospective jurors, voir dire examination of prospective jurors (including the exercise of peremptory and for-cause challenges), and the swearing of the jury. In notorious cases, this entire process requires judicial oversight, coordination, and planning. Monitoring this process could include establishing guidelines for administrative staff and voir dire procedures for the attorneys, including the timing, location, and scope of questions asked of prospective jurors. There are various types of possible screening of prospective jurors:

- **Screening for statutory qualifications**: This is done in all cases and is usually repeated in orientation and possibly at the beginning of voir dire.
- **Screening for case type**: Some courts handle so many cases of a similar nature (e.g., drugs) that prescreening jurors for experience with those types of cases can save a tremendous amount of time and energy—both for court staff and for the prospective jurors. A questionnaire asking prospective jurors if they had been a victim of a drug-related crime, or if they or members of their family had used drugs, is useful for identifying people who would obviously be excused for cause. The judge, attorneys, and parties then screen these questionnaires. Jury staff may also be permitted —by stipulation of the parties, by court order, or by statute—to eliminate from the panel those persons giving particular responses, although this delegation of authority is often examined closely when jury systems are challenged.
- **Screening for trial length**: Courts may prescreen prospective jurors in the jury assembly room or at their homes via a questionnaire as to whether they could sit as a juror in a case that is expected to continue for a specified length of time. Persons who indicate that it would cause a hardship are eliminated from consideration, again by the proper authority. The U.S. District Court, Northern District of California, reported a savings of over $30,000 in seven cases using this form of pretrial screening.[4] In a study of this technique, the court found that 64 percent of persons called for a three-month trial asked to be excused. For a six-month trial, 75 percent asked to be excused. Most of those requesting to be excused were excused. A remarkable finding of this study was that those persons who could serve on longer trials were very similar demographically to those who were not able to serve. Notwithstanding that study, the impact of a long trial on the composition of the jury pool can vary widely from one jurisdiction to another. In addition, the changing nature of the economy over time and the changing demographics of jury pools can also have an effect on who serves in long cases.

The number of companies willing to pay for extended jury duty has declined in some areas, causing a corresponding increase in the number of private-sector workers who, for financial reasons, are unable to serve on a

[4] Dennis Bilecki, *A More Efficient Method of Jury Selection for Lengthy Trials*, 73 JUDICATURE 43 (June-July 1989).

long trial. There may, in fact, be demographic differences among the jurors able to serve in longer trials. Jurors in lower-status occupations may be prevented from serving because they lack the economic independence (or the financial support of employers) that allows more well-to-do jurors to serve for a long trial. Prospective jurors with higher paying managerial and professional jobs also often seek to be excused, claiming preexisting professional commitments.

• **Case-specific screening**: Screening potential jurors according to factors specific to the case is often an effective and orderly way of obtaining an adequate panel of prospective jurors for a notorious case. It tends to save in-court time and inconvenience to prospective jurors.[5] In addition, case-specific screening helps identify and weed out persons who "volunteer" to serve as jurors in a notorious trial for personal reasons (e.g., political or financial interest). As a noted defense attorney once quipped, voir dire in notorious cases is often better characterized as jury audition, not jury selection.

Case-specific questionnaires usually encompass the basic statutory qualifications as well as screening for case type and trial length. Carefully drafted and properly administered questionnaires can be very useful for screening jurors before they appear in court. These questionnaires are much less time-consuming and costly than questioning hundreds of jurors individually, or even en masse if many of the panel require individual follow-up questioning. The questionnaires must be thoughtfully prepared and used in such a way that jurors are not asked the same questions during oral/in-court voir dire.

Preparation and use of prescreening questionnaires

In some state courts, where court administrative support is limited, attorneys usually submit suggested prescreening questions, which are then reviewed by the trial judge. Often, the lawyers are responsible for the final preparation of the questionnaire. In the federal courts, it is more common for the judge to prepare the questionnaire and submit it to the parties for comment; the court then takes responsibility for preparing and distributing the final questionnaire. In major cases, however, the court may ask both sides to submit drafts or work together on one draft. Regardless of who actually drafts the questionnaires, the court should always authorize their preparation and directly supervise their distribution to prospective jurors.[6]

---

[5] Robert M. Takasugi, *Jury Selection in a High Profile Case—United States v. Delorean*, 40 AM. U.L. REV. 837 (1991).
[6] Louisiana v. Bates, 508 So.2d 1346 (1987)(holding that a prosecutor's practice of preparing and distributing questionnaires to prospective jurors without the knowledge or authorization of the trial court or defense counsel was reversible error).

Practicality and efficiency suggest that court supervision of the questionnaire is important. Lengthy questionnaires for large jury panels present a logistical nightmare as well as a daunting copying problem. The questionnaire in the O.J. Simpson criminal trial consisted of 225 questions and was over eighty pages long. **The trial judge must assert control over the questionnaire to ensure that only strictly relevant matters are explored and to avoid excessive burdens on jurors. Each prospective question should be tested by answering the following: "What is this question designed to do or elicit?"**

Once the questionnaires have been prepared, they must be distributed to the jurors for completion. Some courts will send the questionnaires to the prospective jurors with a letter explaining the need for them to complete the questionnaires without assistance, the oath that must be sworn, and a statement as to the serious and important nature of jury duty. The questionnaires are returned in envelopes provided by the court.

An alternative is to ask all of the prospective jurors to complete the questionnaires in the courtroom or assembly room after an orientation by the judge. Some courts have several groups report on the same day if the facilities are inadequate for the total number completing the questionnaire. In very high profile cases, courts often require jurors to complete the form in the courtroom. Bringing in the entire panel, many of whom will be excused, is expensive for the court and for prospective jurors and their employers. There have been no serious irregularities reported when questionnaires are completed at home. If the case is not yet notorious, or if the questionnaire does not indicate the names of the parties, completion at home should be feasible. For example, the prescreening questionnaire used in the selection of the jury to try former federal judge Harry Claiborne was only eleven pages long and had no references to the defendant, lawyers, or witnesses.

Typically, the responses to juror questionnaires are no longer needed after the jury has been selected and sworn. None of the panel questionnaires for notorious cases should be discarded, even for those persons who were not selected for the jury. Appellate review of jury matters, including *Batson* challenges or responses in oral voir dire, may encompass review of the jurors' responses to questionnaires. The trial judge must ensure that they are properly identified and preserved. Proper procedure may include marking pertinent questionnaires as exhibits.

Questionnaire design

In designing the questionnaire, the court should determine the degree to which the questionnaire seeks to highlight areas for further exploration during in-court voir dire or to resolve "for-cause" considerations and permit the court to excuse persons without calling them to the court. Closed-ended questions—that is, those that can be answered with a single, determinative answer (e.g., yes/no, multiple-choice answers, dates, locations)—are useful for identifying topics that require additional inquiry during voir dire. For instance, some questionnaires will list the potential witnesses or persons who are expected to be mentioned in testimony and ask the potential jurors, "If you know or have any connection (personal, social, or business) with any of the individuals listed below, please circle the name of that person." Obviously, no judgment about the prospective juror's objectivity or impartiality could be made based on that response alone. Other questionnaires will add "Please explain," which could provide information for excusing the juror from reporting.

The questionnaire used in *Oakland Raiders, Ltd. v. National Football League*, for example, listed 251 persons and organizations and gave prospective jurors the following five, not necessarily mutually exclusive, categories to consider for each name:

1. I am aware who this person, company, or public body is.
2. I believe I have a financial interest in this person, company, or public body.
3. I have no opinion about this person, company, or public body.
4. I have an opinion about this person, company, or public body.
5. I have a strong opinion about this person, company, or public body.

The primary advantage of multiple-choice questions is that they are easily coded and analyzed. In this case, however, it is not clear that multiple-choice responses, as opposed to a single response, are particularly helpful in seating qualified jurors or in directing follow-up inquires. Note that the five choices do not include two of the most important things judges and attorneys want to know about prospective jurors. Does the prospective juror personally know any of the people listed (as friends, acquaintances, or relatives)? And does the prospective juror have any business relationships with any of the people, companies, or public bodies?

Open-ended questions—that is, those that cannot be answered with a single, determinative answer—are more difficult to manage logistically. They require more time and effort to read and categorize and to prioritize for future inquiry. However, they also permit jurors to put their opinions, knowledge, or experiences in their own words, rather than being forced into the categories the attorneys and judge think are appropriate.

A good questionnaire balances multiple-choice questions and open-ended questions, with the open-ended section reserved for the most important attitude and awareness questions, such as "What have you heard about this case?" "What are your impressions of the defendant?" and "What opinions do you have about the guilt or innocence of the defendant?" It is sometimes confusing to jurors to mix affiliation questions, such as knowing someone or doing business with them or their employer, and attitude questions. A way to avoid this confusion is to create a list of questions about various kinds of affiliations and to ask opinion questions in another section.

All questionnaires should include an introduction that informs the jury panel about the purpose of the questionnaires. The introduction should not make false assurances about the confidentiality of jury panel responses, which are subject to limitations concerning public access to juror information revealed during voir dire. If the questionnaire seeks potentially embarrassing or particularly sensitive information, the introduction should inform jurors about alternatives for providing that information (e.g., *in camera* voir dire). Appendix 8 contains a sample introduction to a questionnaire that addresses the fact that the information is not necessarily confidential.

Any questionnaire should be tested before it is given to prospective jurors, if only by asking a few court staff members to complete it. Attorneys or trial consultants might themselves be asked to complete a questionnaire as part of this test. Testing the questionnaire helps identify questions that are ambiguous, intrusive, or excessively long.

Juror questionnaires typically ask jury panel members to answer questions about five basic areas:

- Biographical and demographic information
- Knowledge of the parties in the case, including the attorneys representing the parties and witnesses testifying for the parties
- Awareness of the case, including firsthand knowledge or knowledge gained from pretrial publicity
- Opinions about the case, including preexisting attitudes and beliefs about relevant case information
- Preexisting attitudes, beliefs, values, and experiences, including prior jury service or prior experience with the justice system as a victim, party, or witness

In addition to these basic areas of inquiry, prescreening questionnaires from several notorious cases included questions about

- Jurors' health and the health of their immediate family members
- Jurors' ability to serve in lengthy or sequestered trials
- Jurors' ability to follow instructions concerning publicity, and contact with others[7]

---

[7] Questionnaires were from trials of Marion Barry, Jr., Bess Meyerson, Oliver L. North, John Poindexter, John Delorean, Michael Deaver, John Gotti, Rayful Edmond, Oakland Raiders v. NFL, and Evan Mecham.

Some questionnaires appear to go a bit far afield and do not elicit particularly relevant information relating to the qualifications of the prospective juror. Screening questionnaires should not be used for pop psychology explorations. One questionnaire contained three pictures of the three defendants being somewhat harassed by the press as they entered what appeared to be a courthouse. The first question asked for each picture was, "Have you seen this picture?" followed by the open-ended question, "What do you think is happening in this picture?" The Agent Orange questionnaire asked if the juror, juror's spouse, live-in companion, close friend, or close relative suffered from any of a long list of problems from acne, to birth defects, to loss of sexual drive. The questionnaire in *United States v. John Delorean* asked about the prospective juror's attendance at religious services, television-viewing habits, reading habits, use of cocaine or marijuana, and beliefs about the severity of the criminal law and the impact of wealth on criminal justice. Another questionnaire asked prospective jurors to explain bumper stickers on their cars.

There is little case law on the permissible scope of questions. A Florida intermediate appellate court held in one case "that the questionnaires submitted to prospective jurors went beyond questions that properly might be asked during voir dire" and was therefore improper and should not have been used.[8] Some lawyers believe that submitting excessive and irrelevant questions for the prescreening questionnaire is the path of least resistance to securing information about jurors for voir dire. They recognize that many judges lack the time, resources, or inclination to conduct a careful review of the questionnaire or to edit the submitted questions heavily. **Nevertheless, courts should regard prescreening questionnaires merely as a surrogate for in-court voir dire. They should not be used for time-consuming, irrelevant, and meaningless inquiries.** If the trial judge is unable to dedicate sufficient time to supervising the preparation of the questionnaire, he or she should consider asking a judicial colleague to assist in this task. If a tandem judge approach is used for managing the notorious trial (see "Trial judge selection," Chapter 1), the second judge may assume responsibility for this task.

Yet one must remember that the great strength of questionnaires is precision in eliciting information about bias, including both attitudes about the specific case as well as underlying attitudes about subjects such as race. Numerous studies have documented that people feel more at liberty to state their honest opinions on paper than in a crowded courtroom with the media present.[9] People are also more likely to reveal sensitive personal information, such as experience with sexual assault and family violence, on questionnaires

[8] State v. Thayer, 528 So. 2d 67 (Fla. Dist. Ct. App. 1988).

[9] *See generally* David Suggs & Bruce D. Sales, *Juror Self-Disclosure in the Voir Dire: A Social Science Analysis*, 56 IND. L. J. 245 (1981) (examining the social science literature relevant to group conformity and its significance during voir dire).

than in open court.[10] Questions that pertain to attitudes about the case are thus particularly appropriate for questionnaires.

Some find the idea of replacing voir dire with questionnaires disturbing, arguing that questionnaires should be used *only* to highlight areas requiring follow-up with individual jurors. For example, the Michigan Supreme Court, in criticizing the use of a questionnaire as a substitute for voir dire, noted that questionnaires do not permit the court and counsel to observe the demeanors of prospective jurors to assess credibility.[11] It recommended that such devices be used as a starting point to identify potential jurors who are severely tainted by extensive or prejudicial publicity about a high-profile case.

The general consensus among the judges and attorneys is that case-specific prescreening questionnaires were very helpful in notorious cases but that the scope of the questions can easily get out of hand. The following guidelines are suggested when considering screening questions:

- Will the question elicit a more honest and more complete response than the person might give in open court?
- Will the question lead more directly and quickly to follow-up questions?
- Can the question provide adequate information for a challenge for cause without further inquiry?
- Is the question respectful of the person's privacy and within bounds of a reasonable expectation of privacy?
- Would the question be permitted or proper in open court?
- Will the prospective juror be more comfortable providing the information on a questionnaire than in a crowded courtroom?
- Is there an appropriate alternative to providing the requested information on the questionnaire (e.g., *in camera* discussion with the trial judge and attorneys)? Have the jurors been advised of this alternative?

Scheduling oral voir dire after completion of the juror questionnaire

Completed questionnaires are copied at the court and screened by the judge. Persons not qualified, excused by the court, or challenged for cause based on the responses to the questionnaires are not asked to report. Those qualified are then scheduled to appear. This can be done in several ways depending on the method of voir dire. After completing the questionnaire, the jurors are usually given a time and date to report. Each juror can be given a different time based on the expected individual voir dire time or asked to report in small groups if there is to be more group voir dire. A slip of paper with the time,

[10] *Id.*
[11] Michigan v. Tyburski, 445 Mich. 606, 623 (1994).

date, and phone number of the court will help remind them of their scheduled reporting time. If the jurors' questionnaires are numbered and the numbers are used to identify the jurors, the numbers should also be on this
reminder slip. Based on the review of the questionnaires, some persons may
be phoned and told not to report.

When planning for voir dire in a notorious case, the court should always
use a call-in system with a telephone-answering machine or voice-mail system to inform jurors of scheduling delays. Even if jurors are given a specific
time and date to report, a change in the court's schedule, particularly in a
notorious case, is always possible. Individuals or groups can not only be
rescheduled via the call-in telephone message, but also excused if the in-court
screening of several groups has resulted in enough prospective jurors.

Juror privacy

The Supreme Court has held that the jury selection process is presumptively
open and that there is a public right of access to voir dire.[12] A trial court may
find that a juror's privacy interest may rise to the level of a compelling interest when questions concern deeply personal matters. This can be the basis for
closure in certain exceptional situations. Before conducting closed proceedings, however, the court must explore alternatives (such as securing the juror's
consent to *in camera* disclosure) and determine whether the juror has a compelling privacy interest that outweighs the presumption favoring public access
to judicial proceedings. A trial judge who finds that closure or partial closure
is appropriate should spell out the reasons in detail on the record so that a
reviewing court can determine the propriety of the closure order. A court
must balance juror privacy against the value of openness; only the absence of
any realistic alternatives justifies closure.

The California Court of Appeal has considered in-depth the confidentiality of jurors' qualifications questionnaires in two decisions. (See discussions
of *Pantos v. City and County of San Francisco* and *Copley Press, Inc. v. San Diego
County Superior Court*, Appendix 1, "Protection of Juror Privacy.") The *Copley
Press* decision, in its discussion of several types of questions found on juror
questionnaires, articulated different standards concerning the level of public
or media access to juror questionnaires.[13] The *Copley* court held that questions
concerning juror qualification information (e.g., address, telephone number,
Social Security number, driver's license number) were included for the purpose of jury management and administration rather than for voir dire.[14] Thus,
there was no First Amendment right to that information.

[12] Press-Enterprises v. Superior Court, 104 S. Ct. 819 (1984).
[13] Copley Press v. San Diego County Superior Court, 278 Cal.Rptr. 443 (1991).
[14] *Id.* at 445.

The court also recognized that juror questionnaires often solicit information about which the prospective juror might have a legitimate privacy interest. The court held that questionnaires are public documents, and prospective jurors should be informed that their responses are not confidential. It provided, however, that trial courts must inform prospective jurors of their right to request an *in camera* hearing to answer specific sensitive questions rather than filling out those answers on the questionnaire form. It also limited the amount of time that the press would have access to the questionnaires to the period that the prospective juror is subject to oral voir dire. The questionnaires of prospective jurors not called for oral voir are not available for public scrutiny at any time.[15]

Jurors as authors

The idea that a notorious trial might make for interesting reading is hardly new. Many judges, lawyers, and laypersons have written first-person accounts of jury trials.[16] A few former jurors have written books describing their experiences. Only recently, however, has this form of free enterprise become profitable enough to cause concern during trials. The trials of General Westmoreland, Pennzoil, and Bernard Goetz all produced publicized books. The O.J. Simpson criminal trial holds the record for producing the most books by jurors, including one by a juror who was excused from the jury during the trial.

Because of the concern that juror authors may not always give priority to the best interests of justice and from fear about improper approaches or jury tampering by literary agents, legislatures have responded with legislation concerning jurors who might sell their stories. In New Jersey, persons impaneled as petit or grand jurors cannot "solicit, negotiate, accept or agree to accept a contract for a movie, book, magazine article, other literary expression, recording, radio, or television production or live entertainment of any kind which would depict his service as a juror" before the termination of service.[17] It is likewise a crime to offer or solicit such a contract.

In New York, the statute defining the pretrial admonitions to be given to the jury states "that prior to discharge they (jurors) may not request, accept, agree to accept or discuss with any person receiving or accepting any payment or benefit in consideration for supplying any information concerning the trial."[18] Note that both the New Jersey and New York statutes apply only to

[15] *Id.* at 450.
[16] *See, e.g.*, Shirley Abrahamson, *A View from the Other Side of the Bench*, 69 MARQ. L. REV. 463 (1986). *See also* Carole L. Hinchcliff, *Portrait of a Juror: A Selected Bibliography*, 69 MARQ. L. REV. 495 (1986) (containing references to 188 articles by or about jurors).
[17] N.J. Stat. Ann. 29-8.1 (1989)
[18] N.Y. Crim. Proc. Law 270.40 (1990).

sitting jurors. Attempts to prohibit postverdict compensation for information about jury deliberations will generally not survive appellate scrutiny on constitutional grounds.[19]

Some judges interviewed felt that raising the publication issue could provide the idea to jurors where none existed and thereby generate a problem. The New York statute reduces this concern by including admonitions against contacts with media or publishers with the admonitions given to the jury not to discuss the case with anyone and not to visit the premises of the occurrence. If anyone approaches a sitting juror to talk about the case, the juror is instructed to inform the judge. Thus, a special anti-publication admonition is generally unnecessary.

If a notorious case can be expected to attract extensive national publicity or lead to sensationalism (O.J. Simpson, Timothy McVeigh and Terry Nichols, Theodore Kaczynski), judges should inquire whether any of the impaneled jurors have been approached concerning payment for posttrial interviews or book, television, or movie rights concerning the case. Depending on the jurisdiction, this may disqualify the prospective juror automatically. It may even be illegal. But the matter is serious and ought to be explored in terms of the juror's ability to maintain fairness and impartiality throughout the trial in light of having agreed to supply information concerning the trial once the trial is concluded.

Multiple juries[20]

The technique of "severing" cases involving multiple defendants into separate trials for each defendant is a tried-and-true method of caseload management in criminal trials.[21] The cases are then tried consecutively with separate juries. This technique reduces the level of trial complexity significantly. It prevents jurors from confusing the charges brought against the defendants or the evidence presented against them at trial. Nevertheless, severance can have several disadvantages. Jurors selected for the second trial may be exposed to media reports of the first trial. Trying the same case to two or more juries also requires the duplicative presentation of evidence in all of the trials.

An alternative to severance is the use of "dual juries" or "multiple juries." Dual juries permit the presentation of otherwise duplicative testimony and evidence and reduce the complexity of questions to be asked of any one jury. In cases raising *Bruton* problems (out-of-court statements by a nontestifying defen-

[19] *See, e.g.*, Dove Audio, Inc. v. Lungren, No. 95-2570 (C.D. Cal. May 22, 1995) (enjoining enforcement of a California statute making it a misdemeanor to pay a juror for information relating to trials).
[20] G. THOMAS MUNSTERMAN, PAULA L. HANNAFORD & G. MARC WHITEHEAD, JURY TRIAL INNOVATIONS 135-37 (National Center for State Courts, 1997).
[21] *See generally* discussion of severance in United States v. Andrews, 754 F.Supp. 1161, 1168-75 (N.D. Ill 1990).

dant implicating a codefendant) or where other types of evidence may be admissible against one defendant but not another, dual juries allow the court to try two or more defendants simultaneously.[22] This technique poses the risk of inconsistent verdicts, although this risk is no greater in dual jury trials than in completely separate trials.

In practice, dual juries are impaneled separately. Opening and closing statements are generally presented to the juries separately. If presented jointly, the attorneys, particularly the prosecutor, must take great care not to make reference to evidence admissible against one defendant but inadmissible against the other. The jury for one defendant can be removed from the courtroom when evidence inadmissible against that defendant will be presented against the other defendant. This procedure has been widely upheld, although the appellate courts have not given blanket endorsement to the process.[23] The technique has been used frequently; e.g., in the "Big Dan" rape trial in Massachusetts, in the first trial of the Bensonhurst defendants in Brooklyn, in the Malice Green murder trial in Detroit, and in the first Menendez brothers trial in Los Angeles.

Problems certainly arise as to facilities, personnel coordination, and additional security concerns involving both the defendants and the juries. Can two full juries fit in the jury box? Will the jury for one defendant be sequestered while evidence against other defendants is presented? Will the verdicts be announced as each jury completes its deliberations? Or will both verdicts be announced simultaneously? Trial logistics become much more complicated, and the trial judge must be alert to shifting juries, counsel, and evidence. Nevertheless, judicial economy and the ability to avoid a greater potential for juror bias in subsequent trials argue in favor of this technique.

Anonymous juries

Notorious cases, by definition, generate a great deal of public and media interest. For criminal defendants, or parties in civil cases, the trial is a very high stakes affair. Because of the potential for outside inference or intimidation of the jury, many courts keep the identities of the jurors confidential until at least after the verdict has been announced and the jury dismissed. The level of anonymity may vary from case to case depending on the circumstances. For example, the identity of the jurors may be withheld from the parties, and even their lawyers, if there is a substantial risk of jury tampering by these individuals. In other cases, the court may only restrict media and public access to the jurors' names. The use of anonymous juries is permitted in both state and fed-

---

[22] Bruton v. United States, 391 U.S. 123 (1968).
[23] Annotation, Propriety of Use of Multiple Juries at Joint Trial of Multiple Defendants in Federal Criminal Cases, 72 A.L.R. Fed. 875 (1985). Annotation, Propriety of Use of Multiple Juries at Joint Trial of Multiple Defendants in State Criminal Prosecutions, 41 A.L.R. 4th 1189 (1985 & Supp. 1991).

eral courts. Guidelines to determine the advisability and permissibility of an anonymous jury include

- the defendant's participation in "dangerous and unscrupulous conduct"
- evidence of any past attempt by the defendant to interfere with the judicial process
- the extent of pretrial publicity
- the possibility that public knowledge of jurors' identities will subject them to intimidation[24]

As a practical matter, the media will eventually discover the identities of the jurors. Unless the court has significant concerns that members of the media will publicize the jurors' names or attempt to contact jurors or their friends and families during the trial, there are very few measures for preventing the media from investigating jurors' backgrounds. However, in cases where the court has a significant concern about jury tampering or intimidation by the parties, anonymity should be employed with other jury protection measures, such as sequestration.

Total anonymity may not be appropriate in all cases. But it can be used where the seriousness of the charges, the extensive pretrial publicity, or the defendant's willingness to interfere with the judicial process places the safety and privacy of the jurors in jeopardy.[25] Critics contend that anonymous jury procedures interfere with meaningful voir dire and thus undermine a defendant's right to an impartial jury. They also argue that telling jurors to guard their identities effectively violates a defendant's right to be presumed innocent until proven guilty. If an anonymous jury is used, the trial judge should explain why these procedures have been implemented. The following is an example of such a jury instruction:

> This case could receive considerable publicity, in the newspapers, on the radio, and on television. The media and members of the public may be curious about the identity of the participants, the witnesses, the lawyers, and the jurors. As a result the jury might be exposed to opinions, comments, and inquiries which could impair its ability to be impartial. The court does not wish to allow such outside influences to divert the jury's attention from the evidence or to cause people to pry into the personal affairs of the jurors.
>
> Thus the court has decided that your name, address, and place of employment will remain anonymous. That is why you have received numbers. Anonymity will ward off curiosity that might infringe on a juror's privacy

[24] United States v. Persico, 832 F. 2d 705 (2d Cir. 1982).
[25] United States v. Barnes, 604 F.2d 121 (2d Cir. 1979), and United States v. Thomas, 757 F-2d 1359 (2d Cir. 1985).

and will insulate the jury from improper influence that might interfere with its sworn duty to judge the evidence fairly.[26]

The number of lists providing the cross-references between the jurors' numbers and the jurors' names and addresses should be kept to a minimum, and the location and persons having access to these lists should be recorded by the trial judge. In the U.S. District Court for the Southern District of New York, which employed the first anonymous jury, not even the judge knew the jurors' names.[27] Data on the jurors should be well guarded. It may be kept on either a standalone or a host computer; in either case, data should be secured, and only two or three people should have access to it. In the Timothy McVeigh trial, jurors' identification numbers were randomly reassigned daily to prevent identification of jurors should an earlier list be leaked. Jurors should be told about security of their names.

Regardless of the method that the court and attorneys use to refer to jurors, the trial judge must ensure consistency so that an appellate court can easily identify particular jurors, if necessary. For example, if numbers are used, the court must ensure that all court reporters, the court clerks, and the attorneys are using the same numerical system as the court.

As a practical matter, only the payroll clerk really needs to know the identities of the jurors. Computer-generated checks for jurors should bear the jurors' identification numbers, and the payroll clerk should manually type in the jurors' names. Eventually, the jurors' names should be entered in the prior jury service records of the court, unless the records could be used to determine the case, trial, and, eventually, the jurors' identities. This permits verification of each juror's service (e.g., for employers or for subsequent jury service).

In using anonymous juries, the court provides transportation to and from either the jurors' homes or a meeting point away from the court.

Juror identification problems

During a trial of a major drug dealer in Washington, D.C., the court learned of a promise in certain sections of the community that anyone identifying a juror by name, address, or other means would receive a reward. The court was using an anonymous jury in this trial in anticipation of threats against jurors or tampering. The jurors were told that if they recognized any of the courtroom spectators or felt that anyone was watching them "too carefully," they

---

[26] United States v. Thomas, 757 F.2d 1359 (2d Cir. 1985).
[27] PAUL RILEY, HANDBOOK ON MANAGEMENT OF LARGE JURY TRIALS 14 (S.D.N.Y. undated local monograph).

should report this to the court. The trial was stopped at least once to discuss with a juror the possibility he had been identified.

The trial judge proposed several options for protecting the jurors' identities, including closing the courtroom to the public and designing a closed-circuit television arrangement from which the public could watch the trial but not see the jury. Another proposed solution was the erection of large vertical "venetian blinds," which would be angled such that the public could see the bench and witness stand but not the jury box. Although an appellate court ultimately overruled all of the trial judge's proposals on First Amendment grounds, the options he considered represent the sort of imaginative planning and innovative measures that may be required during a notorious case.[28]

Interference by the media may also be an issue. In the *U.S. v. McVeigh* trial, the court used a partition that prevented spectators in the court gallery (including the media) from seeing the jury. In the O.J. Simpson criminal trial, a reporter offered court personnel $5,000 to identify and provide the address of one of the jurors who was a court employee.

Jury issues during trial

Assistance to jurors

A notorious case requires special considerations and skills. The case will receive special attention by the parties from the selection of attorneys to the hiring of trial consultants. Yet once the jury is sworn, it may seem like business as usual. It should not be treated that way. If the trial is complex as well as notorious, the jury is faced with a difficult and, some would say, impossible task. In fact, asking a citizen to give a long period of time away from his or her employment is seen by many as clearly improper, if not cruel and unusual. Some aspects of jury service such as separation from family, interruption of employment, and disruption of daily routine are unavoidable. Judges should acknowledge these hardships—over which they have little control—and soften the hard edges of jury service whenever possible, particularly in a long and difficult notorious case. Helping jurors to comprehend the evidence and correctly apply the law is a very effective way to increase jurors' satisfaction with their appointed role as fact finder in the trial. Courts around the country use several techniques to help jurors in this regard. These include permitting jurors to take notes and to submit questions to the judge during trial, providing juror notebooks, preinstructing the jurors about the law, providing jurors with written instructions, and using special verdict forms and written interrogatories to help guide jurors' deliberations.

---

[28] None of these options were implemented, and the trial progressed to a conviction with no further jury problems.

Permitting jurors to take notes is becoming more widespread. Notes serve as a useful memory aid for the evidence presented during trial and make it easier for jurors to follow and comprehend the issues and arguments in complex litigation. The court should furnish notepads and writing utensils and should instruct the jury about court policy as to juror retention of notes when the court is in recess. Jury instructions about notetaking may include the following:

- juror notetaking is permitted, but not required
- jurors should not try to take verbatim or all-inclusive notes
- notetaking should not distract the jury's attention from the trial proceedings
- jurors' notes are confidential
- notes are for the private use of jurors and will not become an official document or part of the trial record
- jurors should use their notes to refresh their memory of evidence presented at trial, but notes should not be relied upon as definitive fact
- notes have no greater weight than memory
- in deliberations, note-aided and non-aided memory are of equal significance
- jurors should not permit themselves to be influenced by another juror's notes

Many courts also permit jurors to submit questions to witnesses. At the beginning of the trial, the judge explains to the jurors that if a witness's testimony is confusing or complicated, they may submit clarifying questions in writing through the judge. The judge reviews the questions with the attorneys on the record, but out of the presence of the jury. After the judge has ruled on any objections to the questions, the trial commences with either the judge reading the question to the witness or instructing the appropriate attorney to address the issue during the direct or cross-examination. Judges and attorneys who have used this technique report that the vast majority of juror questions are serious, concise, and relevant to the trial proceedings.

Some judges have gone beyond letting the jurors take notes to giving them a notebook in which to take notes and including materials that would be helpful to the jury.[29] This notebook would include lists and pictures of witnesses, copies of instructions and important documents or exhibits, and definitions of terms likely to be used. Anything that would assist the jury without causing bias may be included. The materials are provided by the parties or the court. The court supervises the preparation of the notebooks and may give the jurors additional pages as the trial progresses.

---

[29] John V. Singleton & Miriam Kass, *Helping the Jury Understand Complex Cases*, 12 LITIGATION 11 (Spring 1986).

"Preinstructions" about the basic principles of law that govern the trial provide a conceptual framework that enhances jurors' ability to remember information presented at trial and to link the evidence to relevant issues. Preinstructions introduce jurors to the parties and their claims, present matters not in dispute, and provide guidance on the contested issues and governing legal principles. They are particularly helpful in cases involving multiple defendants or charges and complex legal issues, such as RICO cases. Preinstructions may also address such basic issues as the burden of proof, the use of direct and circumstantial evidence, and the jury's role to assess witness credibility and to make reasonable inferences based on the evidence.

Numerous studies support the practice of providing written instructions to juries before they begin deliberations. Written instructions provide a necessary reference for jurors during deliberations that reduces the number of questions by the jury about the instructions and prevents jurors from failing to consider critical elements of the legal claims or offenses. The Dupont murder trial, in which the jury requested the court to repeat the intent element of first-degree murder from its verbal instructions *five times*, is perhaps the most poignant example of how written instructions can help the jury with its deliberations. The jury's last request in that trial was that the instructions be repeated "slowly, please."

Special verdicts and written interrogatories are particularly useful for cases in which the governing law is particularly complicated, counterintuitive, or otherwise difficult to apply. They tend to focus the jury's attention on the pivotal issues in the case. In addition, they minimize the necessity of elaborate instructions to the jury on legal doctrine, as well as the reliance on lay persons to understand and follow such instructions. In multiparty cases, special verdicts can also prevent prejudicial spillover from one defendant to another by requiring the jury to delineate the acts of each defendant.

Outside contact with jurors

It is common each day to admonish the jury to avoid outside contacts concerning the case, conversations about the case, media reports of the case, and any contact with the parties. One technique to enhance this admonition was used during the trial of Bernard Goetz in New York. The judge spent a few minutes individually with each juror every Monday morning before the start of the trial proceedings. During these more relaxed bench discussions, the jurors could discuss problems, concerns, or apprehensions about possible outside exposure regarding the case. They were specifically asked about media exposure inside and outside of the courthouse and any attempts to influence them. The jurors felt they could be honest and open with the trial judge during these interviews as opposed to the usual head nodding or group silence during the standard court admonition or inquiry. This procedure also put the jurors on notice that next week they would once again be personally asked, "Is there anything you would like to discuss about any contacts you have had pertaining to the case, or anything that concerns you?" The judge reported that this mechanism helped avert problems and ease concerns. Moreover, an atmosphere of rapport and trust was established between the trial judge and the jurors. The parties were present during these sessions, and a record was made of the discussions. Any matters raising concern were discussed on the record with the parties outside the presence of the jury.

Juror access to courthouse

Once the jury is sworn, and particularly during deliberations, the press will give jurors extensive coverage because there may be little else to show of the trial. Providing jurors with parking spaces and badges for easier access to the courthouse, allowing them to use special entrances, or assembling jurors away from the courtroom can shield jurors from the press and keep them away from areas where witnesses, defendants, or the press may be gathering.

If the jury is subject to a "limited sequestration" order (see "Limited sequestration," *infra*), the judge should consider meeting the jurors at pre-arranged locations away from the court, driving them to the court, and entering through a secured parking area. Similar planning for juror egress is important. For example, if a juror must be picked up for a ride home, a secure place to wait should be provided that is not in front of the courthouse. It is useful to develop lists of "cleared" restaurants and caterers to provide meals to jurors. Jury administrators should use a staging area and work closely with security to move jurors from that site to the courtroom. In lengthy trials, it is advisable for security reasons to select several routes that can be varied on a random basis. Jurors should use judicial corridors as much as possible. Emergency exits, lighting, and cameras to monitor juror ingress and egress should be used when warranted. These techniques are also useful for anonymous juries and juries under full sequestration orders.

Juror pay during trial

The juror's daily fee, while rarely generous, should be paid at regular intervals. These fees actually reimburse jurors for costs personally advanced, e.g., parking, meals, and snacks. Because many courts pay jurors only at the completion of their duty, special provisions to pay at regular intervals during extended trials should be established and made known to the jurors at the start of the trial. In addition, if employers need verification of service to pay the salaries of the jurors, these details should be worked out before the trial begins. A payment schedule of the jurors' fees should be provided.

Sequestration[30]

Sequestration, whether done from the opening of the trial, midtrial, or only during deliberations, should not come as a surprise to the jury. Prospective jurors should be told of this possibility during voir dire at the earliest opportunity, and sequestration should be a standard area of inquiry on prescreening questionnaires.

"When they said they were going to sequester us, they weren't kidding!"

Copyright 1998. Reprinted courtesy of Bunny Hoest and Parade Magazine.

Sequestration is rarely fun for jurors.[31] Radios and televisions in hotel rooms are usually disconnected because monitoring is difficult. Telephone conversations often are monitored. Court staff is kept busy trying to provide for security, personal needs, and group entertainment. In a nutshell, sequestration is not desirable. It should be used only in the most serious cases, and even then for the shortest possible period of time. Jurors in the O.J. Simpson criminal trial, who were sequestered for the entire nine-month trial, revolted over the conditions of sequestration.

It is helpful in sequestration cases to have a list of "cleared" hotels—that is, hotels with a reputation for adequate safety and amenities. As a general rule of thumb, if judges or court staff would be reluctant to stay in a particular hotel, jurors should not be required to stay there under sequestration orders.

[30] James P. Levine, *The Impact of Sequestration on Juries*, 79 JUDICATURE 266 (1996).
[31] Greenberg, *Twelve Tough Muthuhs*, PLAYBOY 164 (December 1978).

A number of issues should be considered in planning for sequestration:

Security
- outside interference
- television, radio, mail, e-mail, Internet access, and phones, including cellular digital phones (both at the hotel and in court)
- background checks for hotel staff, caterers, etc.

Emergencies
- medical emergencies
- family emergencies, escorts for jurors during visits away from the sequestered area
- court and hotel evacuation

Conjugal Visits
- married, unmarried (enough said)

Room Searches
- before, after hotel staff, upon departure

Transportation
- who provides?
- are jurors' cars secure?

Chain of Command
- means for reporting irregularities
- reporting grievances directly to the judge

Juror Personal Needs
- laundry: how often, who pays?
- are jurors permitted to drink alcoholic beverages, and if so, at whose expense?
- permissible use of room service
- group or individual dining
- presence of court staff or security while not in court
- availability of snacks, soft drinks

Entertainment/Other
- television monitoring
- newspaper screening
- group events (are all jurors required to attend?)
- book and magazine screening
- exercise, jogging/walking escorts
- religious services and escorts

Medical Needs
- obtaining prescription medicines
- doctor's appointments
- names/addresses/phone numbers of family physicians and specialists
- eyeglass repair
- obtaining cold/flu remedies
- allergy medications
- personal hygiene supplies

Financial
- how hotel and meal bills are paid
- jurors' incidental expenses

Juror ombudsman

For cases in which the jury is placed under substantial restrictions (e.g., prolonged full sequestration), the judge should consider appointing a member of the court staff as the "juror ombudsman" for the duration of the trial. The ombudsman functions as a sounding board for jurors to express their concerns or vent frustration about the conditions of jury service. This individual also serves as a conduit to the trial judge, relaying any specific grievances or suggestions from the jury for improving the conditions of sequestration. To perform this role effectively, the ombudsman should be subject to the same restrictions as the jury (e.g., living arrangements, dining arrangements) and be available to the jurors at all times when the jury is not seated in the jury box listening to trial evidence.

In routine cases, the bailiff or sheriff often serves in this capacity. In notorious cases, however, these individuals are responsible for enforcing the court's sequestration orders—in effect, becoming the jury's jailers. Their relationship with the jurors is generally formal and professional, rather than open and friendly. As a result, the jurors may resent their presence in the jury room or be less willing to inform them of grievances (particularly if those grievances concern security restrictions imposed on the jury).

Limited sequestration

Even when not sequestered overnight, jurors on notorious cases are often sequestered while in the courthouse and even escorted to and from the courthouse. In addition to a meeting place other than the jury assembly room, the court must provide a special dining area and meals. In this way, jurors do not mix with the public, press, or parties to the case. (See discussion in Chapter 2, "Shielding the jury from media coverage of proceedings and contact with the media.") This, however, does not mean that the jurors should be held captive. Jurors should have time to stretch, relax, and make personal telephone calls.

Public demonstrations during trial

The court should try to ascertain when a demonstration is to be held. This might be learned through police intelligence, or by monitoring news reports or seeing to it that the press office or media liaison knows that the court needs to be made aware of such a situation. A liaison with local and federal law enforcement may also be helpful. A demonstration could cause the judge to sequester the jury, plan for extra security to maintain order, or even close the courthouse. The judge may need to prepare an evacuation plan for the jurors in case of emergencies (e.g., bomb threats).

Keep in mind that a public demonstration may be conducted through very subtle means. Messages printed on t-shirts or buttons on clothing can convey messages to the jury just as effectively as large placards and bullhorns. A demonstration by mothers of children born with birth defects was organized during the Bendectin trial in Columbus, Ohio. The defects were blamed on the mothers' use of Bendectin during pregnancy. The children were to be brought into the courtroom and seated with their mothers so that the jury could see the deformities of the children. When the judge heard of the plans, he closed the courtroom to all persons under a certain age and installed closed-circuit television so that anyone, including those excluded, could watch the courtroom proceedings. A nurse was also on hand to provide medical assistance for the children. The ability to anticipate and detect the unusual, to plan, and to react to potential disruptions is essential during a notorious trial.

Medical assistance for jurors

The court should be aware of the jurors' medical needs. Jurors should also be told that if situations arise that could require medical attention, the trial court should be informed so that medical staff can be placed on alert.

Planning for and receiving the verdict

As with all other matters in notorious trials, the delivery of the verdict and the dismissal of the jury requires planning. The following topics should be considered:

- Security: Will security or police require time to prepare for the receipt of the verdict? In the first Bensonhurst trial the police asked for a one-hour lead time before receiving the verdict.

- Juror dismissal: Jury staff and security should develop evacuation procedures for jurors. This may include multiple site planning, evacuation courses, or security coverage teams.
- Jurors and the press: Will jurors meet the press? In notorious trials in Los Angeles, the court sometimes offers the jurors the option of holding a press conference immediately after the verdict is delivered. This permits the jury to present a unified front to the media, thus making it easier for jurors to refuse individual media interviews after their release from jury service. It also tends to lessen media incentives to pursue jurors individually after the trial. Before making such arrangements, the trial judge should appoint an appropriate individual to preside over the press conference, such as the media liaison (if a member of the court staff) or a judicial colleague. Is an alternative to meeting the press available? Will jurors be escorted to autos or parking lots?
- Press deadlines: Many of the press will want to rush to broadcast the verdict and interview the jurors. Timing will also be crucial to meeting deadlines for afternoon and evening editions. If there are prohibitions on the use of cellular telephones in the courtroom, the judge should consider whether a reminder about surreptitious broadcasting from inside the courtroom is necessary.
- Community reaction: The 1980 Miami riots, which followed the acquittal of the police officers accused of beating Arthur McDuffie, were blamed, to a degree, on the fact that the verdict was received at midafternoon on a hot Saturday.

Postverdict considerations

Dismissal procedures

Following the reading of the verdict and juror polling, the judge will usually give the jurors some word of thanks, without commenting on the verdict, and some statement as to possible discussions of the verdict.[32] The following instruction might be considered:

> Ladies and gentlemen:
> Now that the case has been concluded, some of you may have questions about the confidentiality of the proceedings. Many times jurors ask if they are now at liberty to discuss the case with anyone. Now that the case is over, you are of course free to discuss it with any person you choose. By the same

[32] AMERICAN BAR ASSOCIATION, JUDICIAL ADMINISTRATION DIVISION, STANDARDS RELATING TO JUROR USE AND MANAGEMENT Standard 16 (1993).

token, however, I would advise you that you are under *no obligation whatso-ever* to discuss this case with any person. If you *do* decide to discuss the case with anyone, I would suggest you treat it with a degree of solemnity in that whatever you do decide to say, you would be willing to say in the presence of your fellow jurors or under oath here in open court in the presence of all the parties. Also always keep in mind if you do decide to discuss this case, that your fellow jurors fully and freely stated their opinions with the understanding they were being expressed in confidence. Please respect the privacy of the views of your fellow jurors.[33]

In addition to any final instructions concerning jurors' postverdict discussions with media, the court should advise jurors to contact the court if members of the public or media persist in questioning them over their objections.[34] The court should be prepared to offer ongoing protection for jurors—through contempt orders, if necessary.

After the verdict has been delivered, the judge or bailiff should instruct the jurors on where to report before leaving and whether they are free to leave. It is incongruous that the jury is watched, escorted, and protected during the duration of the trial, only to be simply set free in the middle of the courtroom at the conclusion of the trial. The trial judge may ask to speak with the jury privately (see "Interviews by the judge," p. 96). The press will surely want to speak with them, the attorneys may want to speak with them, and one party may want to thank them. If the verdict has resulted in emotional reactions from a criminal defendant, spectators, or witnesses, these persons may want to confront the jurors. A dismissal plan providing for the safety and comfort of the jury should be formulated and made known to the parties, court personnel, and the jury at the appropriate time.

One technique to help the jurors escape the courthouse without contact from the parties and the press is for the judge to give any final statement to the jurors and let them return to the deliberation room for any personal belongings. The court officer then escorts them from the courthouse *before* the persons in the courtroom are dismissed. Jurors can leave the courthouse via side exits, to parking lots, or even to court vehicles before the verdict is known outside the courtroom and before the parties and courtroom press are allowed to leave. However, hordes of media may hover outside and may be posted at every entrance to the parking lot and at jurors' homes—even when the jury is anonymous.

---

[33] JURY MANAGEMENT AND UTILIZATION COMMITTEE OF THE UNITED STATES NINTH CIRCUIT COURT OF APPEALS, A MANUAL ON JURY TRIAL PROCEDURES (1990).

[34] U.S. v. Cleveland, No. 97-30756 (5th Cir. Oct. 29, 1997) (upholding the trial judge's postverdict instruction to jurors that they could not discuss the case) is a clear departure from the recent trend to respect jurors as citizen participants in the justice system.

Contacts by attorneys

For a number of reasons, the attorneys may wish to contact the jurors after the verdict has been returned. The most common purpose of postverdict interviews is to investigate whether juror misconduct has occurred that would provide grounds for appeal. The federal courts, and several state courts, use evidentiary law to discourage contact with jurors for pursuing frivolous appeals by limiting the areas of the deliberations upon which a juror may testify.

Counsel frequently ask trial consultants to do posttrial interviews, so they can tell the jurors that they are "neutral" interviewers, even though they are being paid by one side. Jurors often feel more comfortable talking to trial consultants than to the lawyer they have voted against. Many federal courts, however, prohibit contact by the attorneys with jurors without the permission of the court.[35] (See Chapter 2, "Media interviews with jurors.")

Interviews by the judge

There is a strong difference of opinion as to the advisability of the judge interviewing or speaking with jurors after the trial. Trial judges who have used this technique report that they learn a great deal from jurors during these meetings, and they almost never find themselves in detailed discussions about the jury's deliberative process or in situations that might permit a new trial. Jurors generally appreciate the chance for a personal meeting with the judge.

These posttrial interviews, which can be held informally in the jury deliberation room, provide a personal conclusion or closure to the jury experience, not merely an administrative checkout or the more formal procedure in the courtroom. Some judges may invite the attorneys to participate as a courtesy or as a matter of policy. Other judges look upon this as an informal gathering at which attorneys, though not formally excluded, are not usually invited. Jurors seem to appreciate a personal thank-you from the judge. If questions are solicited, judges usually preface the questions with some ground rules or explanation about the proper areas of discussion. The first question from the jury is usually, "Did we do the right thing?"—to which the judge demurs. One judge routinely answers "I'm glad you, rather than I, decided this case." Judges report that questions usually split equally between administrative and legal matters. Judges favoring these postverdict interviews do not report the kinds of problems predicted by those opposed to the practice, who believe that at the end of a long and difficult trial, judges should want to preserve the verdict and not look for trouble.

Following the appreciation expressed from the bench, judges should have some comments in mind to begin the postverdict sessions. Judges should reinforce their statements concerning postverdict conduct by attorneys and

---

[35] ELISSA KRAUSS & BETH BONORA (eds.), 2 JURYWORK: SYSTEMATIC TECHNIQUES, ch. 16, pp. 1-24.

the media and reemphasize the need for consideration of other jurors' privacy as a means of limiting detailed discussions of the deliberations.

Postverdict trauma

If the jury has undergone considerable emotional stress such that the judge is concerned for the future mental well-being of some jurors, the judge might offer suggestions for relieving stress or, in more extreme cases, recommend professional counseling for the jurors. Concern for postverdict trauma is relatively new, although postverdict trauma itself has probably always existed. At least one state offers postverdict counseling for jurors. And other states are beginning to consider this option for notorious trials. (See Appendix 11 for a sample brochure on "Tips for Coping after Jury Duty.")

Serving as a juror is an intensely personal experience. Years after persons serve on jury duty, they can recall details of the testimony and of the overall experience with amazing accuracy. Even if the trial is modest by notorious-trial standards, the one or two days spent in the jury box leave an indelible impression on many jurors' memories. It is a point of reference for their view of the justice system—both civil and criminal. This intensity stems from the uniqueness of the experience—of being an intimate participant with the other parties in the jury trial and in the justice system, as well as having the unique role as the finder of facts in the case before them. Articulate lawyers, in their opening and closing statements, stress the importance and forcefully define the role of the juror.

The trial also forces jurors into behavior that, for them, may be abnormal. In many courts, jurors cannot take notes; they must sit placidly and listen to often mind-numbing testimony. Jurors receive admonitions not to discuss the case until after all the evidence is heard and they have been instructed. For persons who rely on external contacts for comfort and as a means of accepting and processing knowledge, this silence is an excruciating punishment.

Given the additional attention that the juror receives in a notorious trial, these problems will be intensified. If the notoriety is based on the heinous nature of the crime, the intensity is even greater. Viewing photographs of mutilation, listening to a coroner's testimony of abuse, examining articles of a deceased's clothing, or handling a murder weapon are never pleasant. If jurors are asked to make a life/death decision in a capital case, the experience will be extremely difficult, as jurors may look ahead to the execution and know that it will be the result of their verdict.

Just as with postverdict interviews of jurors, judges in cases with disturbing evidence or difficult deliberations sometimes fear causing more problems by intervening than may actually exist. Some jurors may easily handle these intense psychological pressures. Others may not, however. Most courts are somewhat hesitant to raise issues—in effect, saying, "It's best to let the juror get back to a normal life, away from the courthouse, the parties, and the public, as soon as possible." Other courts are more proactive. The Maricopa County (Phoenix) Superior Court provides a brochure to jurors that describes common symptoms of stress and recommends techniques for reducing stress. In particularly difficult cases, court staff from the L.A. Superior Court will contact jurors for months—or even up to a year or more, depending on the circumstances—to ask about their welfare and to offer referrals to community mental health resources, if necessary.

Over the past decade, trial judges and court staff have become more sensitive to the psychological impact that notorious cases can have on jurors—in part because judges and court staff have experienced this impact themselves. Juror stress has also become a topic of great interest to researchers.[36] One study found that jurors who served in the Pamela Basu murder trials in Columbia and Baltimore, Maryland, experienced significant levels of stress, even three months after the completion of the trial.[37]

The balance between additional intrusion into the lives of the jurors and the possibility of exacerbating existing problems, and the help that the court can provide in these cases, requires an ongoing sensitivity by the trial judge to the psychological trauma of jurors during the a notorious case. This sensitivity should be exercised from voir dire through the dismissal of the jury.[38]

---

[36] *See, e.g.,* T. B. Feldmann and R. A. Bell, *Crisis Debriefing of a Jury After a Murder Trial*, HOSPITAL AND COMMUNITY PSYCHIATRY 79 (1991); Thomas L. Hafemeister & W. Larry Ventis, *Juror Stress: Sources and Implications*, TRIAL 68 (October 1994).

[37] Hafemeister & Ventis, *supra* at note 36.

[38] The National Center for State Courts (NCSC) recently completed a project entitled "Responding to Juror Stress," which produced a monograph (THROUGH THE EYES OF THE JUROR: A MANUAL FOR ADDRESSING JUROR STRESS, 1998) that discusses various issues associated with juror stress.

planning for security

in a notorious trial

Planning for Security

Lessons Learned

1. The judge, security personnel, and court administrator should assess and determine the level of security risk posed by the trial. Security personnel should plan for and take proper measures to ensure that sufficient personnel and equipment are in place to deal with realistic threats to court security.

2. The trial judge and security personnel should review the adequacy of current security measures and procedures in and around the courthouse.

3. The need for separate security measures for jurors, judges, and the parties should be determined.

4. The location and size of the courtroom should be evaluated in terms of security considerations.

5. Public and media access to the courtroom should be reviewed, particularly with regard to reserved seating arrangements, courtroom entry screening, when the media and public may enter and leave the courtroom, and whether there will be any differentiation between the media and the public in terms of courtroom access.

6. Absent compelling security concerns, preferential parking and special entrances into the courthouse for the media, the parties, lawyers, and witnesses are not recommended.

7. The security plan should be sufficiently flexible to adjust as necessary to unexpected circumstances.

8. Security in notorious trials often extends beyond the physical confines of the courthouse. Collaborate with law enforcement agencies, private security in adjacent buildings, and any other security personnel with overlapping or neighboring jurisdiction who are needed to implement the security plan for this trial.

9. Security personnel, court staff, and the media liaison should be introduced to one another and apprised of their respective roles. Court staff and the media liaison should be informed of all security arrangements to avoid inadvertent interference with legitimate security plans.

10. Think ahead. Be prepared. Once the contours of the security plan have been determined, security personnel should not be micromanaged and should, with supervision, be allowed to do their job—a job they know best.

Planning for Security in a Notorious Trial

Planning for security in a notorious case is essential. The level and degree of security is a function of the type of case being tried. The criminal trials of notorious underworld defendants or of white supremacist organizers raise different sorts of security concerns than the trials of celebrities like O.J. Simpson. A defining characteristic of notorious trials is intense public interest—including that of persons who are often mentally and emotionally disturbed. A common element of security in most notorious trials is preventing interference from such individuals. Each notorious trial is unique, however, and security plans should reflect the actual needs of each trial. The trial involving a major drug trafficker, where there is a threat of witness intimidation and violence, requires a different security response than the trial of someone like former Arizona governor J. Fife Symington. What follows are considerations for overall security plans, which should be examined in planning for the trial of a notorious case.

Notorious trials raise a variety of security issues. The trial judge should meet well in advance of the trial with representatives of the court, law enforcement (or other agencies responsible for security in and around the courthouse), and the parties to the trial to discuss security needs and concerns. A security plan should be prepared that takes into account the contingencies that may arise during the trial. If different agencies are responsible for security inside and outside the courthouse, they should establish good communication and develop an interagency plan of cooperation. Everyone involved should know exactly who is in charge of each aspect of the security plan.

Level of risk involved

Before developing security the court must ascertain the level of risk involved. The following checklist of items should be covered in making security preparations:

- Will security be required simply to control crowds?
- Are problems with spectators and disruptions in the courtroom likely?

- In a criminal trial, how many defendants will be tried? Are they considered dangerous or potentially disruptive in the courtroom?
- Have threats of any kind been made to the court, judge, or participants in the trial?
- Are there likely to be demonstrations or protests inside or outside the courthouse?

Some trials will require attention only to what occurs in the courtroom, while others will also require awareness and attention to what may happen beyond the confines of the courtroom and the courthouse.

Permanent security measures and features

Court security should review the permanent, routine security measures and features that are already established or in place in the courthouse. The questions below may be used as a checklist for specific measures and features that should be implemented. The review should be presented to the trial judge with any recommendations for modification.

- Is there a high-security courtroom available that might be suitable for the trial?
- Are there alarms in each courtroom? Where are they located? How are they activated? Who responds to them? Do the courtrooms have telephones, radio transmitters? Are bailiffs or court attendants equipped with portable transceivers?
- Are courtrooms equipped with bulletproof glass to protect the judge, witnesses, the jury? Is the bench reinforced to make it bullet resistant?
- Are backup security officers available, either to augment normal courtroom staff or to respond quickly to an emergency? How is their assistance obtained?
- Is there a policy for firearms carried into the courtroom by bailiffs or court attendants, law enforcement officers, witnesses, spectators, or other security personnel?
- Are people entering the courthouse routinely screened by magnetometers?
- Are surveillance cameras used in the lobby, hallways, and parking areas?
- Is there a screening procedure at the courtroom door for people entering the courtrooms?
- Can entrances to the courthouse and courtroom, including elevators, be secured from public and media access?
- How are in-custody defendants transported to and within the courthouse? Where are they held in the courthouse?

- Are waiting rooms available for witnesses? Are attorney-client conference rooms provided? Are they secure?
- What procedures are in place for evacuating defendants, the judge, and jurors from the courtroom?
- What are the routine evacuation procedures for bomb threats, fire, and other emergency situations? Are these procedures known and understood by all courthouse personnel?

Court administrative staff should ensure that all employees understand routine evacuation procedures, and they may find it helpful to hold a meeting with key staff to review procedures shortly before the trial starts.

Number and posting of security personnel

Based upon the level of risk foreseen, the court should determine how many security officers will be needed, whether additional personnel will be required and available, and where they will be posted. The senior security officer should make this determination in consultation with the judge and the court administrator.

The number of security personnel needed inside the courtroom will depend on the extent to which it is anticipated that defendants or spectators may cause disruptions or the level of concern about the potential for violence. In a very high security trial, a number of security personnel may be assigned to protect certain parties, witnesses, counsel, the judge, and the jury. Plainclothes officers may be stationed randomly throughout the spectators' gallery. In such a case, sufficient seating in key locations in the courtroom must be reserved for the extra officers.

Security officers may also escort parties or witnesses to and from the courthouse. In some instances, twenty-four-hour protective services may be required for some trial participants. In the trial of Texas separatist Richard McLaren, for example, there was a sufficient risk of kidnapping or violence against the judge so bodyguards were assigned to protect him and his family for the duration of the trial. Additional security officers may be needed outside the courtroom and in the hallway to control crowds, maintain order, and screen members of the public, media, and others seeking to enter the courtroom.

Depending on the level of security required, security officers may be assigned to additional screening posts on the floor where the courtroom is located or at other key points in the building, such as entrances, elevators, and stairwells. Backup officers may be stationed in rooms adjacent to the courtroom or elsewhere throughout the courthouse. Additional personnel may be required in the holding area for in-custody defendants or witnesses. Officers may patrol the building on a regular basis. Assigning the same officers to the same screening post every day enables them to become familiar with people entering and leaving their areas of responsibility.

For a very high security trial, or one in which demonstrations outside the courthouse are anticipated, security officers may be stationed outside the courthouse, at entrances and exits, on the roof, and at other key locations. In extraordinary circumstances, security may even be required to form a virtual cordon around the perimeter of the courthouse. In most localities, security outside the courthouse will require extensive coordination with other state and local law enforcement agencies. Federal law enforcement personnel may also be available to assist in high-risk security situations.

Location and size of courtroom

Although many older courthouses do not allow for very much flexibility, the size of the courtroom should be considered: Is it too small for the number of participants and required security personnel? Or is it so large that it might be conducive to disruptive activity by spectators?

If the trial judge's regular courtroom will not be large enough or sufficiently secure, an alternate courtroom should be selected that meets the necessary requirements. Access to the courthouse, whether from inside the courthouse or outside, should be easy to keep secure from the public and the media. Attention should be given to whether offices, courtrooms, or other rooms located on the floors directly above, below, and adjacent to the proposed courtroom present a security hazard. In a very high security trial, it may also be important to consider whether buildings or other structures with windows facing the courtroom might pose a potential security threat.

Pay attention to the extent of adjacent courtroom activity on the floor. Is it possible to seal off the corridor leading to the courtroom without unduly interfering with other courtrooms in the same area? In a very high security trial, is it possible to close off the entire floor without causing major problems in the courthouse? Can stairways leading to the courtroom or the corridor be locked or guarded? Is there another courtroom or room nearby that can be secured as a possible holding area for backup security personnel or as a private area for the use of defendants, plaintiffs, or other participants?

Access to the courtroom

Plans should be made for how the public, media, and other spectators will be granted access to the courtroom.

- Will it be necessary or desirable to set up barricades or barriers in the hallway? One court found that rented 4' x 8' partitions were the least expensive and most effective barricades. In conjunction with, or in lieu of, barricades, ropes and stanchions can be used for crowd control and to prevent people waiting in line from interfering with other activity in the hallway.
- Will there be separate lines for the media and the public and other spectators (e.g. defendant's family, victims)?
- Will picture identification, press passes, or press credentials be required?
- If press credentials are required, what level of access do these credentials guarantee? For the Oklahoma City bombing cases, the court issued three levels of press credentials, only one of which secured access to the courtroom. The other two limited access to the pressroom and the courthouse, respectively.
- What seating arrangements will be made? Will seats or blocks of seats be assigned, or will all seats be allocated on a first-come/first-served basis?
- Will all spectators be allowed to exit and reenter at will? Will exit and reentry be restricted to breaks in court proceedings?
- Will seats be assigned to the next person in line whenever vacated?
- Will the media be treated the same as the public, or will media representatives be allowed more leeway in coming and going from the courtroom? Note that granting preferential treatment to the press with respect to basic rules of access to the courtroom can cause tremendous resentment in the public spectators.
- What kind of entry screening will be done?
- Will spectators, including the media, be subjected to handheld detectors? Will they be required to pass through a stationary magnetometer?
- Will hand searches of briefcases, purses, and other items be conducted?

As discussed in Chapter 2, security personnel should be extensively involved in planning for the presence of the media and for their activities in and around the courthouse. At minimum, security personnel should be fully apprised of all arrangements made with the media. Security personnel also should work with media representatives to ensure that courthouse and courtroom access are not impaired by media equipment and that the presence of TV equipment, cables, and the like does not pose a threat to the safety of participants in the trial or the public in general.

Court staff information
Court staff, including the media liaison, should be fully briefed about all security arrangements. They should know what to do and who to contact in the event of an emergency. **Make certain that *all* court staff likely to be**

involved in the trial (e.g., clerks, court reporters, interpreters, janitorial staff, secretaries) are informed about such arrangements. One court described an embarrassing incident in which one of the janitors picked up a piece of loose paper left on the defense table during a court recess and gave it to a reporter. If court staff are to be restricted from certain areas of the courthouse or courtroom during the trial, this information should be communicated by the trial judge directly. This will prevent needless antagonism between court staff and security personnel.

Access to the courthouse

Consideration should also be given to the need for security outside the courthouse:

- Is there a need for roadblocks or other barriers around the courthouse?
- Should parking around and near the courthouse be curtailed or prohibited?
- Should plans be made to cordon off an access route to and from the courthouse entrance for participants?
- Should the media be restricted from certain areas of the courthouse (e.g., separate entrances for jurors, judges' parking areas)?
- Should separate access be provided for parties or witnesses?
- How many entrances will be kept open for the entry of court staff or the public? If some ordinarily open entrances are closed, notices indicating where the public may enter should be prepared and posted. If possible, court staff and the public should not use the same entrances.
- How many security personnel will be needed to guard entrances and other key locations throughout the day and night?
- Will a magnetometer or other screening device be used for everyone entering the courthouse, including staff, at all times? In buildings that house many other government agencies, it may be too burdensome to screen all entrants during regular business hours, but a magnetometer or other screening procedure may be used at the entrance to the courtroom for all entrants.
- Who will be permitted access to the building after hours? Will they be required to show identification? Will they be screened? If other agencies usually conduct business in the courthouse after hours, they may need to be persuaded to meet elsewhere for the duration of the trial.
- Will staff be required to show or wear identification during working hours?
- Will the media have access to the courthouse (e.g., on-site media center) after regular working hours? If so, the media should pay for any additional security personnel needed to accommodate media access.

- Is it possible to lock doors to offices in the building and allow entry by buzzer or other means? If so, is this necessary in this case?
- Will access by elevator be restricted to certain floors of the courthouse? Will staff be allowed unrestricted access to the basement or storage areas?

Security precautions for jurors, judge, and participants

In any jury trial that attracts significant public attention, it is important to limit juror contact with media representatives and the public. Depending on the level of risk involved, more-stringent efforts may be required to protect jurors, the judge, and participants in a notorious trial. In making juror security decisions, courts should keep in mind that even the apprehension of danger is sufficient to cause extreme distress to jurors.

In a high-security trial, it may be necessary to screen prospective jurors as they arrive. For example, security officers may ask jurors to show their subpoenas or summonses and some form of positive identification before allowing them to enter the jury assembly area. The procedure for assembly and reporting should be spelled out clearly so that as they arrive, members of the jury panel are directed immediately to the proper location. Security personnel should be well briefed on the plans for how, when, and where prospective jurors will initially gather and how and where they will assemble during jury selection.

The court and judge should be aware of the possibility that the presence of visible, elaborate security precautions at this stage may have a negative impact on prospective jurors' interest in serving on the jury. For that reason, the level of risk during this phase, as throughout the proceedings, should be carefully assessed and the least obtrusive means deemed acceptable used.

As with the influence of the media on the jury panel, it may be necessary to ask prospective jurors during voir dire about the effect of security measures on them. Because of the possible influence such measures may have on the attitudes of jurors toward a criminal defendant, for example, in cases where a device such as a magnetometer is used, an instruction in the following language, if requested by the defendant, may be appropriate:

> You may have noticed a screening device on this floor of the courthouse. The sheriff from time to time monitors or screens all persons within the court environs. It is a normal course of court procedure to utilize such devices in various parts of the courthouse facility. You should not attach any importance or significance to its random use on various floors of the courthouse. It certainly has nothing to do with the merits of this case now on trial.

How and where jurors, the judge, and other participants will enter and leave the courtroom and courthouse are also important questions:

- Will there be special parking arrangements made for jurors, the parties and their counsel, and witnesses? Will jurors assemble at a separate location and be transported to the courthouse by security personnel?
- Will security personnel transport the judge or other participants to the courthouse each day? Is there a rear or restricted entrance with a controlled passageway to the courtroom that can be used?
- Will everyone except the judge be required to pass through a magnetometer or other screening process before entering the courtroom each day?
- Will jurors, parties, or other participants be escorted throughout the courthouse? If so, when and by whom?

The trial judge should give security personnel notice of the impending verdict in sufficient time to permit security to deploy additional officers and to arrange for special precautions for handling the defendants and dealing with any possible outbursts or demonstrations.

Special treatment of parties and witnesses

As a general rule, most judges advise against providing special or preferential treatment for parties or witnesses involved in the lawsuit (e.g., preferential parking or special entry and exit arrangements). Special treatment can give rise to allegations of favoritism or partiality on the part of the court or the trial judge. In notorious cases, however, genuine security concerns may give rise to special arrangements for defendants and their attorneys. Separate access to the courthouse, protected from media inquiries, may also provide a means to facilitate the parties' compliance with attorney gag orders. (See discussion on this issue in Chapter 1, "Attorney gag orders.")

Jury sequestration

The security plan for the trial should also address the possibility of full or partial sequestration of the jury. Full sequestration will require security personnel on a twenty-four-hour basis and daily transportation for jurors. (See discussion of sequestration in Chapter 3.) Sequestration of jurors (and perhaps parties at their request) during lunch or breaks in the proceedings may require additional personnel to escort them to reserved areas in the lunchroom or elsewhere in the courthouse. Security personnel may also be required to provide them with lunch in the courtroom or other secured area.

If the jury is transported to a local restaurant, efforts should be made to provide meals in a private dining area, removed from public contact.

Other measures to provide security for jurors, the judge, parties, and other participants may also be considered, such as putting their telephone numbers into the 911 system so that they will be assured of an instant response to any emergency. Security precautions will necessarily be intensified if an anonymous jury is used.

As a general rule, jurors should be kept informed of routine security arrangements made on their behalf. Knowledge about extraordinary measures, however, may inadvertently influence the jurors' ability to remain fair and impartial. The murder convictions of two Detroit police officers were overturned, in part, because jurors found out about National Guard plans to respond to potential riots, which were believed to be highly likely in the event of an acquittal.[1]

Additional security precautions and considerations

- Is it necessary to do a bomb sweep of the courtroom and courthouse every day?
- Is it possible to trace incoming telephone calls to the courthouse in the event of bomb threats?
- Is a special security plan needed for the return of the verdict by the jury because of the high emotions connected with the verdict or the expectation of demonstrations?
- Are special seating arrangements likely to be required to accommodate overflow and reduce the likelihood of disruption in the courtroom?
- Can the proceedings be telecast by closed-circuit television to another room in the courthouse or adjoining building?
- Is it necessary and feasible to set up a special command center in the courthouse for coordination and communication among security personnel and to enable security personnel to view the trial on closed-circuit television?
- Should all mail sent to the courthouse be screened at a central location before distribution?
- Should telephone calls to the judge and the court during and after hours be monitored by security personnel?
- Are the windows in the jury deliberation room, the courtroom, and in other parts of the secured area equipped with drapes, blinds, shades, or other means of blocking the view from the outside? If not, can some means be devised to accomplish this if necessary?

[1] Michigan v. Budzyn, 566 N.W.2d 229 (1997); Nevers v. Killinger, 1997 WL 816107 (E.D. Mich.).

• Should the airspace above the courthouse be secured from helicopter or other aircraft traffic?

The planning and thought that must go into developing a comprehensive security plan is considerable and important. (The trial security plan used in the White Aryan Resistance trial, which required extraordinarily high security, is provided in Appendix 10.)

Planning for the unthinkable

In the best of all possible worlds, the security plan for a notorious trial will adequately control crowds and deter violence with sufficient flexibility to adjust to unexpected circumstances as they arise. A part of this plan should include a contingency plan for catastrophes—the witness or spectator that manages to smuggle a weapon into the courtroom and threatens the lives of the trial participants or innocent spectators. Judges typically resist giving up control of their courtrooms. They often view themselves as the captain of their ship, prepared to go down with her in the event of a disaster. Such false bravado during an eruption of violence in the courtroom needlessly risks the lives and safety of the judge, jurors, trial participants, and innocent bystanders.

Security personnel are specially trained to handle incidents involving violence. In notorious trials, their first consideration is to secure the safety of the judge, the jurors, the parties and their attorneys, witnesses, and media and spectators—in that order. **In the event of a violent incident, the trial judge should be prepared to accede command of the situation to security personnel and follow their instructions.** After the immediate security situation is back under control, the judge can reassert his or her authority in the courtroom and make any trial modifications—including a mistrial, if necessary—that are warranted in response to the breach in security.

Appendices

Legal Materials

Appendix 1 provides judges and court managers with a primer on the legal issues that arise during a notorious trial. Neither the range of subject areas treated nor the collection of case law is meant to be exhaustive. The legal materials included provide an overview and a context for most legal research on common topics that arise during a notorious trial.

In preparing this appendix, the authors have relied in great measure on the work of Mr. Donald I. Pollock, director of the legal division in the Administrative Office of the Courts of the Eleventh Judicial Circuit, Dade County (Miami), Florida. Mr. Pollock's publication *Issues in Sensational or Widely Publicized Cases* (April 1990) is the basis for the organization of this appendix, and its text has been freely incorporated into this material. We found his work to be the only formal source on legal issues specific to notorious trials, and we have not attempted to improve many portions of it. It is for this reason that the reader will note that there are numerous references to Florida case law in this appendix.

APPENDIX ONE

Background Legal Materials

I. RIGHT OF ACCESS

A. *First Amendment right of access to judicial proceedings*

The United States Supreme Court's 1980 decision in *Richmond Newspapers, Inc. v. Virginia*[1] revolutionized the law of access to criminal trials by announcing a First Amendment right of public access to such trials to guarantee a self-informed citizenry. In so ruling, the Court concluded that the press and public cannot be excluded from criminal trials absent findings of a compelling or overriding interest sufficient to overcome the presumption of open trials.[2] The press and public may attend the trial, and the media may report on what they have observed.[3] The media and public, however, may be limited to these observations and may not be allowed access to certain records[4] or to copy evidence.[5] This qualified right of access applies not only to the criminal trial as such but to the voir dire proceedings in which the jury is selected,[6] and to preliminary hearings as well.[7] The right of access has also been extended to pretrial suppression hearings. *Waller v. Georgia*[8] held under the Sixth Amendment that any closure of a suppression hearing over the objection of the accused must meet the *Press-Enterprise* test applicable to the closure of trial proceedings.[9]

Although the Supreme Court has expressly applied such a right of access only to criminal proceedings, lower courts have recognized the right in civil cases, as well as a variety of other circumstances.[10] As the Sixth Circuit noted in *Brown & Williamson Tobacco Corp. v. Federal Trade Commission:* "The

[1] 100 S. Ct. 2814 (1980).
[2] *See also* Waller v. Georgia, 104 S. Ct. 2210, 2215 (1984); Fenner and Koley, *Access to Judicial Proceedings*, 16 HARV. C.R.-C.L. L. REV. 415, 440 (1981).
[3] *See* Nixon v. Warner Communications Inc., 98 S. Ct. 1306(1978); United States v. Edwards, 785 F.2d 1293 (5th Cir. 1986).
[4] *See* Calder v. I.R.S., 890 F.2d 781 (1989) (holding no right of access to IRS records of Al Capone).
[5] Group W. Television v. Maryland, 626 A.2d 1032 (1993) (holding no First Amendment right of the media or public to copy trial evidence).
[6] Press-Enterprise Co. v. Superior Court (I), 104 S. Ct. 819 (1984).
[7] Press-Enterprise Co. v. Superior Court (II), 106 S. Ct. 2735 (1986).
[8] 104 S. Ct. 2210.
[9] *But see* Gannett Co. v. De Pasquale, 99 S. Ct. 2898 (1979), in which the Court held that the Sixth Amendment guarantee of a public trial does not preclude the closure of a pretrial suppression hearing upon motion of the defense in order to curb the disclosure of prejudicial information and to protect the defendant's right to a fair trial. *See also* United States v. Charga, 701 F.2d 354 (5th Cir. 1983); In re Globe Newspaper Co., 729 F.2d 47 (lst Cir. 1984), regarding the right of the public and press to attend pretrial bail hearings.
[10] *See* Brown & Williamson Tobacco Corp. v. Federal Trade Commission, 710 F. 2d 1165, 179 (1983).

Supreme Court's analysis of the justifications for access to the criminal courtroom apply as well to the civil trial. . . . In either the civil or the criminal
courtroom, secrecy insulates the participants, masking impropriety, obscuring
incompetence, and concealing corruption."[11]

In deciding whether a First Amendment right of access attaches to a judicial proceeding, the court must determine (1) whether the place and the
process has historically been open to the press and general public and (2)
whether public access plays a significant role in the functioning of the particular process in question.[12]

In a criminal case, the initial presumption is always that the proceeding
should be open. The Supreme Court insisted in *Richmond Newspapers, Inc. v.
Virginia* that "absent an overriding interest articulated in findings, the trial of
a criminal case must be open to the public." 100 S. Ct. at 2839.

In the *Press-Enterprise (II)* decision, however, the Supreme Court ruled
that when a right of access attaches to a proceeding, closure may be ordered
only if it serves a compelling interest; there is a "substantial probability" that,
in the absence of closure, this compelling interest would be harmed; and there
are no alternatives to closure that would adequately protect the compelling
interest. As both *Press-Enterprise* rulings emphasize, a closure order must be
narrow and based on specific findings on the record that enable a reviewing
court to determine whether the closure order was properly entered. A number of courts have adopted very strict tests for closure: *United States v. Brooklier*,
685 F.2d 1162 (9th Cir. 1982); *In re Washington Post Co.*, 807 F.2d 383 (4th
Cir. 1986); *Associated Press v. Bell*, 510 N.E.2d 313 (N.Y. 1987).

In the third edition of the *ABA Standards for Criminal Justice, Fair Trial and
Free Press*, published in 1991 (ABA Standards), the ABA recommends a similar three-part test for closure. (See Standard 8-3.2.) Under Standard 8-3.2,
before a court may issue a closure order with reference to judicial proceedings
or records, reasonable notice and an opportunity to be heard must be afford-
ed. To close a proceeding under the ABA standards, a court must find that:

> (1) unrestricted access would pose a substantial probability of harm to the
> fairness of the trial or other overriding interest which substantially outweighs
> the defendant's right to a public trial;

> (2) the proposed order will effectively prevent the aforesaid harm, and

> (3) there is no less restrictive alternative reasonably available to prevent the
> aforesaid harm.

---

[11] *Id.*
[12] Globe Newspaper Co. v. Superior Ct. for County of Norfolk, 102 S. Ct. 2613.2615 (1982).

B. *Permissible restrictions on right of access*

1. *Constitutional concerns.* A judge's failure to insulate the judicial proceedings from massive, pervasive prejudicial publicity and disruptive influences is a clear violation of the Fourteenth Amendment.[13] The admonition in the *Sheppard* case concerning the need to protect the trial process from prejudicial outside influence is as valid today as it was in 1966.

> Given the persuasiveness of modern communications and the difficulty of effacing prejudicial publicity from the minds of the jurors, the trial courts must take strong measures to insure that the balance is never weighed against the accused. The court must take such steps by rule and regulation that will protect their process from prejudicial outside interferences. 86 S. Ct. at 1522.

Although many of the concerns that underlie the *Sheppard* decision have been allayed by the development of less obtrusive methods of television coverage in the courtroom, the Supreme Court has reaffirmed its support for many of the measures recommended by that decision designed to maintain order and decorum during notorious trials.[14] Those measures include:

- Adoption of strict rules governing the use of the courtroom by the media such as limiting the number of newsmen allowed in the courtroom and prohibiting the placement of reporters inside the bar.[15]
- Restriction on conduct of newsmen in the courtroom such as prohibiting the handling or photographing of trial exhibits.
- Insulation of witnesses from publicity during the trial.
- Controlling the release of leads, information, and gossip to the press by police officers, witnesses, and counsel for both sides. More specifically, a judge can proscribe extrajudicial statements by any lawyer, party, witness, or court official which divulge prejudicial matters.[16]

With reference to the last measure, see the discussion of ABA Standards 8-1.1 (extrajudicial statements by attorney), 8-2.1 (disclosure by court personnel), and 8-3.6 (conduct of the trial), *infra*. See also the discussion of *Gentile v. State Bar of Nevada* on extrajudicial statements by attorneys, *infra*.

---

[13] Sheppard v. Maxwell, 86 S. Ct. 1507, 1521 (1966).

[14] *See* Nebraska Press Association v. Stuart, 96 S. Ct. 2791 (1976).

[15] The provision of a press table inside the bar was deemed unprecedented in *Sheppard*. The bar of the court is designed to protect the witnesses and jury from any distractions, intrusions, or influences and to permit bench discussion of the judge's rulings away from the hearing of the public and the jury. *Sheppard*, 86 S. Ct. at 1518.

[16] As an outgrowth of Sheppard, the Judicial Conference Committee on the Operation of the Jury System on the "Free Press-Fair Trial" issued strongly recommended limitations on control by the court of the release of prejudicial information by attorneys and courthouse personnel in criminal cases. 87 F.R.D. 525 (1980).

2. *Restrictions on electronic media.* The Supreme Court in *Chandler v. Florida*, 101 S. Ct. 802 (1981) removed the constitutional obstacles to television cameras in the courtroom. However, the Court has not addressed directly the question of whether the First Amendment right of access extends specifically to the electronic media. Lower courts that have confronted the issue have held that it does not. See *Westmoreland v. CBS*, 752 F.2d 16 (2d Cir. 1984.); *United States v. Hastings*, 695 F.2d 1278 (11th Cir. 1983); *United States v. Edwards*, 785 F.2d 1293 (5th Cir. 1986). These decisions have been questioned in light of the *Chandler* ruling. See, e.g., Ares, *Chandler v. Florida: Television, Criminal Trials and Due Process*, 81 Sup. Ct. Rev. 157,189 (1982); Frank, *Cameras in the Courtroom: A First Amendment Right of Access*, 9 Comm/Ent. L.J. 749 (1987).

Standards for camera coverage vary widely among the states. Only the state of Florida has created a presumptive right of access for television cameras in the courtroom. See *State v. Palm Beach Newspapers*, 395 So. 2d 544 (Fla. 1981); *State v. Green*, 395 So. 2d 532 (Fla. 1981). ABA Standard 8-3.8 adopts an essentially neutral position based on the *Chandler* decision. It provides for camera and electronic access to the courtroom and adjacent areas only "under rules prescribed by a supervising appellate court or other appropriate authority."

3. *Time, place, and manner restrictions.* It is axiomatic that courts have the inherent power to preserve order and decorum in the courtroom, to protect the rights of the parties and witnesses, and generally to further the administration of justice. In so doing, a trial judge may impose reasonable time, place, and manner restrictions on access to a trial.[17] The courts' implied power to maintain decorum has traditionally been liberally construed.[18] ABA Standard 8-3.2(c), concerning prohibition of direct restraints on media, cautions, however, that "such limitations should not operate as the functional equivalent of a closure order."

To ensure that proceedings are conducted with a measure of dignity and decorum, as well as for security reasons, a court may require restrictions on both admission to the courtroom and behavior of the audience once admitted. Persons can be screened upon entry into the courtroom. Admittance to the courthouse can be conditioned upon passing through a magnetometer or x-ray machine.

The following cases are representative of those holding that the government, consistent with the Fourth Amendment's prohibition against unrea-

[17] *See* Globe Newspaper Co. v. Superior Court, 102 S. Ct. 2613 (1982); Richmond Newspaper, Inc. v. Virginia, 100 S. Ct, at 2829 n.18.
[18] *E.g.*, Dorfman v. Meiszner, 430 F.2d 558 (7th Cir. 1970); Seymour v. U.S., 373 F.2d 629 (5th Cir. 1967). *But see* United States v. CBS, Inc., 497 F.2d 102 (5th Cir. 1974).

sonable searches and seizures, may condition entry into a public courthouse upon the requirement that each citizen submit to the least offensive screening procedure that will detect the presence of weapons, explosives, or other destructive devices: *Downing v. Kunzig*, 454 F.2d 1230 (6th Cir. 1972) (denial of entry to federal courthouse unless packages are submitted for examination); *McMorris v. Alioto*, 567 F.2d 897 (9th Cir. 1978) (inspection of briefcases and parcels as condition to enter courthouse); *Rhode Island Defense Attorneys Ass'n v. Dodd*, 463 A.2d 1370 (R.I. 1983) (parcels, objects, or briefcases brought into courthouse inspected for firearms or explosives); *Commonwealth v. Harris*, 421 N.E.2d 447 (Mass. 1981) (packages, briefcases, or other items carried by a person must be offered for an inspection); *Barrett v. Kunzig*, 331 F. Supp. 266 (M.D. Tenn. 1971) (casual eye inspection of briefcases, packages, etc.); *Justice v. Elrod*, 649 F. Supp. 30 (N.D. 111. 1986) (local rule requiring all persons to submit to a search upheld).

In the trial of William Lozano (a Miami police officer charged with the fatal shooting of a black man, which touched off three days of rioting), persons seeking entry were required to walk past armed guards in the hall, submit to a pat-down search, and pass through a metal detector. Even this sort of conspicuous deployment of uniformed security personnel in a courthouse is recognized as reflective of "a normal, official concern for the safety and order of courtroom proceedings."[19]

In widely publicized notorious cases, the trial judge or designated court manager should issue directives relating to the seating and conduct in the courtroom of spectators and news media representatives as necessary to preserve order and decorum. Such directives, for example, might relate to clearing entrances and hallways in the courthouse and insulating witnesses from news interviews during the trial. A judge may restrict talking among members of the audience to ensure that testimony is heard. Reasonable restrictions may be placed upon access to exhibits.[20] Because courtrooms have limited seating capacities, there will often be occasions in notorious cases when not everyone who wishes to attend can reasonably be accommodated. In such situations, reasonable restrictions on general access may be imposed, including allowing for preferential seating for media representatives.[21]

4. *Partial closure and news timing.* Partial closure has been advocated in circumstances where the court could otherwise have ordered closure.[22] In such instances, the judge could have limited the person's attendance upon agree-

19 Holbrook v. Flynn, 106 S. Ct. 1340 (1986).
20 *See* Fenner and Koley, ACCESS TO JUDICIAL PROCEEDINGS, supra note 2, at 444.
21 Richmond Newspapers v. Virginia, 100 S. Ct. 2814.
22 *See* Mayer v. State, 523 So. 2d 1171 (Fla. Dist. Ct. App. 1988). *See also ABA Standard for Criminal Justice, Free Trial, and Free Press,* Rule 8-3.6(a), "Conduct of the Trial" (1991).

ment to the court's order restricting the time at which persons in attendance
may disclose to others those matters occurring at the proceeding. In some circumstances, a court might either deny access or seek to delay the dissemination of the information obtained. For example, there have been occasions
where the government has withheld publishing a kidnapping or extortion
threat until the incident was resolved. In such kidnapping cases, the media
agrees to postpone coverage, but usually with an understanding that the
media's blackout is voluntary and that they will be kept well informed of
important developments.[23] Unlike total closure of cases, limited closure of
trial court proceedings does not violate the Constitution.[24]

   5.   *Protection of minors or sexual assault victims.* In *Globe Newspaper Co. v.
Superior Court*,[25] the Supreme Court recognized that safeguarding the psychological and physical well-being of minors is a compelling interest, which may
justify the closure of criminal trials in certain circumstances. The Court
noted, however, that a case-by-case review should be used because "circumstances of the particular case may affect the significance of the interest."[26]
   Historically, exclusion orders have been used to minimize the embarrassment of witnesses in rape and sexual assault trials.[27] The Supreme Court has
acknowledged that the trial court does have an obligation "to take special
pains" to protect certain witnesses (e.g., children, victims of sex crimes, some
informants, and even the very timid witness or party) from the glare of publicity and the tensions of being "on camera."[28]

   6.   *Bench conferences or conferences in chambers.* The press and public may be
excluded from bench conferences or conferences in chambers without the
necessity of notice or hearing. This exclusion was specifically addressed by
Justice Brennan in his concurrence in *Richmond Newspapers*:

> When engaging in interchanges at the bench, the trial judge is not required
> to allow public or press intrusion upon the huddle. Nor (are judges) restrict-
> ed in their ability to conduct conferences in chambers, inasmuch as such
> conferences are distinct from the proceeding. 100 S. Ct. at 2839.

   Within the scope of a judge's *inherent* authority to adopt rules governing
"the use of the courtroom by newsmen," a judge can prohibit the press from
being "placed inside the bar."[29]

---

[23] *See* Moffitt, *Regulating the Media's Coverage*, 8 COMPUTER L.J. 227 253 (1988).
[24] People v. Benson, 621 N.E.2d 981, 984 (1993).
[25] Globe Newspaper Co., 102 S. Ct. 2613 (1982).
[26] *Id.* at 2621.
[27] *See* Gannett Co., 99 S. Ct. at 2910.
[28] Chandler v. Florida, 101 S. Ct. 802 (1981).

Nevertheless, the *ABA Standards for Criminal Justice*, Commentary to Standard 8-3.2(c), suggests that a "limitation on access [to side-bar or *in camera* proceedings] is reasonable only if alternative means of providing the underlying information, such as a written transcript, are provided."

"The Fair Trial and Free Press Standards" (Chapter Eight) of the *ABA Standards for Criminal Justice* (1991) are a valuable source of guidance and information on a wide variety of topics that arise during a notorious trial: public access to judicial proceedings, change of venue or continuance, severance, jury selection, conduct of the trial, setting aside of the verdict, televising and photographing of the proceedings. Judges should become familiar with the contents of these standards but understand that the standards are aspirational in nature and do not always conform to the realities of many of the situations judges must confront.

II. ACCESS TO JUDICIAL RECORDS

Historically and presumptively, judicial records are open to the public, subject to the court's supervisory powers. Many lower courts have applied the right of access articulated in *Richmond Newspapers* to judicial records as well as proceedings. See *United States v. Peters*, 754 F.2d 753 (7th Cir. 1985) (trial exhibits); *Seattle Times Co. v. District Court*, 845 F. 2d 1513 (9th Cir. 1988) (pretrial motion papers); *In re Washington Post Co.*, 807 F. 2d 383 (4th Cir. 1986) (plea hearings and related documents); *In re Baltimore Sun*, 841 F.2d 74 (4th Cir. 1988) ("venire list" of prospective jurors); *Valley Broadcasting v. District Court*, 798 F.2d 1289 (9th Cir. 1986) (copying of tape exhibits); *Sarasota Herald Tribune v. Holtzendorf*, 507 So. 2d 667 (Fla. Dist. Ct. App. 1987) (psychiatric report of defendant). See generally note, *Access to Pretrial Documents Under the First Amendment*, 84 Colum. L.Rev. 1813 (1984).

Based on *Richmond*, some courts have invalidated traditional designations of confidentiality of records. E.g., *Globe Newspaper. v. Polaski*, 868 F.2d 497 (1st Cir. 1989) (voids state statute requiring sealing of records of acquittal); *United States v. Haller*, 837 F.2d 84 (2d Cir. 1988) (sealed plea agreement); *Matter of Chase*, 446 N.Y.S.2d 1000 (Fam. Ct. 1982) (juvenile proceedings).

Access cannot be denied except for compelling countervailing reasons.[30] Among the competing interests that must be considered are: (a) whether the

---

[29] Sheppard v. Maxwell, 86 S. Ct. at 1521; *Revised Free-Fair Trial Guidelines of the Judicial Conference of the United States - 1980*, 87 F.R.D. 525 (recommendation that no member of the press or public be at anytime permitted within the bar railing).

[30] *See* Pantos v. City and County of San Francisco, 198 Cal. Rptr. 489 (Cal. Ct. App. 1984). *See also* Nixon v. Warner Communications, Inc., 98 S. Ct. 1306 (1978), which holds that the press could be denied physical access to certain tape recordings for copying where reporters were permitted to listen to the tapes and report on what was heard and were furnished transcripts of the tapes, which they were free to comment upon and publish. However, it was held that the videotaped deposition of Jodi Foster in the John Hinkley prosecution need not be made available to the media for recordation or rebroadcast. In re ABC, 537 F. Supp. 1168, 1172 (D.D.C. 1982); *see also* United States v. Edwards, 672 F.2d 1289 (7th Cir. 1982).

records are sought for improper purposes such as promoting public scandal or gaining unfair commercial advantage; (b) whether access is likely to promote understanding of historically significant events; (c) whether the press already has been permitted substantial access to the contents of the records; and (d) whether the rights of third parties will be affected.[31]

The right to inspect and copy records may be curtailed if it interferes with the administration of justice.[32] In *United States v. Beckham*,[33] the Sixth Circuit Court of Appeals indicated that a judge can consider "the community turmoil and tense atmosphere which could permeate the courtroom" in deciding whether to grant the media the immediate right to copy and broadcast certain tape recordings, noting the "detrimental effects of the tapes on a fragile community climate." In denying the copying and broadcast request, the court suggested that because of the "furor in the community," the courtroom might have "become less orderly" if the subject tapes had been copied and broadcast.

In its commentary to Standard 8-3.2(a), the ABA takes issue with the *Beckham* decision, noting that "[a]ccess should not depend on the manner in which a court maintains records of various proceedings, documents or exhibits." It cites the decision in *Ohio v. Bender*, 494 N.E.2d 1135 (Ohio 1986), as standing for the proposition that a "court record by any other name is still subject to public access. Also cited is Hanson et al., *Special Topic: Telecommunications in the Courtroom*, 38 U. Miami L. Rev. 611 (1984).

III. RESTRAINTS ON DISSEMINATION OF INFORMATION AND EXTRAJUDICIAL COMMUNICATIONS

A. Prior restraints on publishing

The term *prior restraint* is customarily applied to orders prohibiting publication or broadcast of information already in the possession of the press.[34] In *Nebraska Press Ass'n v. Stuart*,[35] a state court entered a "gag order" in a criminal case restraining the news media from publishing information "strongly implicative" of the accused until the jury had been selected and impaneled. The Supreme Court held that the order violated the First Amendment, observing that:

> Prior restraints on speech and publication are the most serious and the least
> tolerable infringement on First Amendment rights [because prior restraint

---

[31] *See* Barron v. Florida Freedom Newspapers, Inc., 531 So. 2d 113, 118 (Fla. 1989).
[32] *See, e.g.*, United States v. Rosenthal, 763 F.2d 1291, 1294 (11th Cir. 1985); United States v. Baez Alcaino, 718 F. Supp. 1503 (M.D. Fla. 1989) *(in camera* filing of plea agreement).
[33] 789 F.2d 401, 410, 415 (6th Cir. 1986).
[34] *See* Nebraska Press Ass'n v. Stuart, 96 S. Ct. 2791 (1976); Sheppard v. Maxwell, 86 S. Ct. 1521 (1966); Near v. Minnesota, 51 S. Ct. 625 (193 1); Comment, *Indirect Gag Orders*, 44 U. MIAMI L. REV. 165 (1989).
[35] 96 S. Ct. at 2791.

has an] immediate and irreversible sanction. . . . If it can be said that a threat of criminal or civil sanctions after publication "chills" speech, prior restraint "freezes" it at least for the time.[36]

The *Nebraska Press* decision set out an all-but-absolute ban on prior restraints on publishing.

The courts have extended the prohibitions of *Nebraska Press* to a variety of indirect restraints: One judicial measure held to be an unconstitutional prior restraint was a trial court's order requiring a newspaper to have counsel attend pretrial proceedings "in order to advise his client . . . so that the publication of the proceedings in these hearings shall not require change of venue . . . or alternative actions by the Court." *Keene Publishing Corp. v. Cheshire County Superior Court.*, 406 A. 2d 137 (1979) (citing ABA Standard 8-3.1 with approval). In *Shermon Publishing Co. v. Goldberg*, 443 A.2d 1252 (R.I. 1982), the trial court provided "conditional access" to the press. Because the press had previously published the names of juveniles in family court proceedings to which the press had been admitted, the court barred the press from future juvenile proceedings unless they agreed not to publish the juveniles' names. This was held to be an unconstitutional prior restraint. In *KUTV-V, Inc. v. Conder*, 668 P.2d 513 (Utah 1983), the trial court employed a "limited" gag order to bar the press from referring to the rape defendant as the "Sugarhouse rapist," a reference to a notorious ten-year-old set of rape convictions of the defendant. This, too, was held to be an unconstitutional prior restraint. And in *News American Div. Hearst Corp. v. State*, 447 A.2d 1264 (Md. 1982), the trial court issued an "indirect" gag order that applied directly only to court personnel and trial participants. The Maryland Court of Appeals held that the press had sufficient standing to challenge the gag order. But see *KUTV, Inc. v. Wilkinson*, 686 P.2d 456 (Utah 1984), which upheld a prior restraint on any publication of the defendant's alleged connections with organized crime.

A number of Supreme Court cases[37] suggest that a court cannot constitutionally restrain dissemination of information obtained from public records.[38]

---

[36] *Id.*

[37] *See* Cox Broadcasting Corp. v. Cohn, 95 S. Ct. 1029 (1975) (civil damages award entered against a television station for broadcasting the name of a rape-murder victim, which the station had obtained from courthouse records, held unconstitutional); Oklahoma Publishing Co. v. District Court, 97 S. Ct. 1045 (1977) (state court's pretrial order enjoining the media from publishing the name or photograph of an eleven-year-old boy in connection with a juvenile proceeding involving that child, which reporters had attended, held unconstitutional); Smith v. Daily Mail Publishing Co., 99 S. Ct. 2667 (1979) (publishing of information obtained from police band radio not violative of state statute forbidding newspapers to publish, without written approval of the juvenile court, the name of any youth charged as a juvenile offender); The Florida Star v. B.J.F., 109 S. Ct. 2603(1989)(imposition of damages upon a newspaper for publishing the name of a rape victim in violation of Fla. Stat. §794-03, where the press learned of the victim's name from a publicly disseminated police report, held unconstitutional).

[38] The court has *declined* to hold that truthful publication is automatically constitutionally protected, or that there is no zone of personal privacy within which the state may protect the individual from intrusion by the press, or even that a state may never punish publication of the name of a victim of a sexual offense.

But the more-narrow principle to be extrapolated from the cases is that where a newspaper publishes truthful information that it has lawfully obtained, punishment may lawfully be imposed, if at all, only when it is narrowly tailored to a state interest of the highest order. Hence, the media may still be sanctioned for disseminating the name, age, or address of a juvenile if the information was gained from *privileged, confidential, or nonpublic sources*.[39]

Under the *Nebraska Press* decision, to determine whether the heavy presumption against prior restraint is overcome, a court must examine (1) "the nature and extent of pretrial news coverage"; (2) whether there are less-restrictive alternatives that would "mitigate the effects of unrestrained pretrial publicity"; and (3) "how effectively a restraining order would operate to prevent the threatened danger."

Under ABA Standard 8-3.1, "Prohibition of Direct Restraints on Media," prior restraints are prohibited "[a]bsent a clear and present danger to the fairness of a trial or other compelling interest."

B. Prohibition of extrajudicial comments by other participants in court proceedings

1. *Attorneys*. The difficulty of dealing with constraints on attorney speech was illustrated by the Supreme Court in the June 1991 decision of *Gentile v. State Bar of Nevada*, 111 S. Ct. 2720 (1991). The Court was asked to evaluate a Nevada rule patterned after the American Bar Association Model Rule of Professional Conduct 3.6, "Trial Publicity" (1989, hereafter Rule 3.6), as it applied to a defense attorney's comments made at a scheduled press conference. At the press conference held the day after his client's indictment, six months before the trial, the defense attorney asserted the innocence of his client, implicated a police detective in the theft with which his client was charged, accused the police of a coverup, and accused other witnesses of being drug dealers and money launderers. The defense attorney admitted in the disciplinary hearing that he had sought to stop a wave of publicity he perceived as poisoning the prospective juror pool, prejudicing potential jurors against his client, and injuring his client's reputation.

Although the discipline imposed on the defense attorney was vacated upon a finding of vagueness in the Nevada rule arising from a grammatical interpretation of the rule and the state's failure to clarify its meaning (which was at variance with the ABA wording of the rule), a majority of the Court found that the "substantial likelihood of material prejudice" standard, applied to attorney speech by the Nevada rule and by most states, satisfies the First Amendment.

---

[39] *See* Cape Publications Inc. v. Hitchner, 549 So. 2d 1374 (Fla. 1989); White v. City of Coral Springs, 49 Fla. Supp. 136, 140 (Brevard County Ct. 1979); Mayer v. State, 523 So. 2d 1171 (Fla. Dist. Ct. App. 1988).

The Court pointed to the statement of Justice Holmes in *Patterson v. Colorado*, 27 S. Ct. 556, 558 (1907), that "when a case is finished, courts are subject to the same criticism as other people, but the propriety and necessity of preventing interference with the course of justice by premature statement, argument, or intimidation hardly can be denied." The Court went on to note that "the outcome of a criminal trial is to be decided by impartial jurors, who know as little as possible of the case. . . . Extrajudicial comments on, or discussion of evidence which might never be admitted at trial and exparte statements by counsel giving their version of the facts obviously threaten to undermine this basic tenet." *Gentile* at 111 S. Ct. at 2742.

The Court asserted that its decision in *Sheppard* contemplated that "the speech of those participating before courts could be limited"; that lawyers are not "protected by the First Amendment to the same extent as those engaged in business"; and that "the speech of lawyers representing clients in pending cases may be regulated under a less demanding standard than that established for regulation of the press in *Nebraska Press Ass'n v. Stuart*, 96 S. Ct. 539 (1976), and the cases which preceded it." *Id.* at 2743, 2744.

The Court concluded that the " 'substantial likelihood of material prejudice' standard constitutes a constitutionally permissible balance between the First Amendment rights of attorneys in pending cases and the state's interest in fair trials." *Gentile*, 111 S. Ct. at 2745. The rationale for this conclusion was summarized as follows:

> Even if a fair trial can ultimately be ensured through voir dire, change of venue, or some other device, these measures entail serious costs to the system. Extensive voir dire may not be able to filter out all of the aspects of pretrial publicity, and with increasingly widespread media coverage of criminal trials, a change of venue may not suffice to undo the effects of statements such as those made by petitioner. The State has a substantial interest in preventing officers of the court, such as lawyers, from imposing such costs on the judicial system and on the litigants. *Gentile*, 111 S. Ct. at 2745.

The *Gentile* decision has been criticized for the split nature of the ruling and for the fact that it does not explicitly state what lawyers may now say about their cases. In adopting the "substantial likelihood of material prejudice" standard, rather than the standard suggested by *Gentile* requiring that the speech present a "clear and present danger" of actual prejudice, the majority of the court on this issue rejected the position of the other four members of the court. Justice Kennedy, joined by three other justices, wrote that an attorney "may take reasonable steps to defend a client's reputation and reduce the adverse consequences of an indictment" and pursue "lawful strategies to obtain dismissal of an indictment . . . including attempting to demonstrate in the court of public opinion that the client does not deserve to be tried." *Gentile*, 111 S. Ct. at 2728, 2729.

While the *Gentile* decision focused on the ABA Model Rule 3.6, Standard 8-1.1 of the American Bar Association *Standards for Criminal Justice*, "Chapter Eight: Fair Trial and Free Press" (1991), addresses precisely the same sorts of concerns regarding extrajudicial statements by attorneys. Although the "Fair Trial and Free Press" Standards predate the *Gentile* decision, Standard 8-1.1 employs the "substantial likelihood" test of Model Rule 3.6 and offers some guidance regarding the specific types of statements made by attorneys that are permissible, and those that are impermissible, regarding pending criminal cases. As such, Standard 8-1.1 answers some of the questions left unanswered by the *Gentile* decision in terms of what sorts of statements by attorneys are permitted and what types of statements are impermissible concerning a pending criminal case.

Standard 8-1.1 sets out two contrasting lists of statements: those that "are ordinarily likely to have a substantial likelihood of prejudicing a criminal proceeding" and those that are "deemed least likely to promote prejudice" and are therefore per se permissible. The descriptive list of statements that are considered most likely to prejudice a proceeding include comments on such matters as

- the prior criminal record (including arrests, indictments, or other charges of crime) of a suspect or defendant
- the character or reputation of a suspect or defendant
- the opinion of the lawyer on the guilt of the defendant, the merits of the case, or the merits of the evidence in the case
- the existence or contents of any confession, admission, or statement given by the accused, or the refusal or failure of the accused to make a statement
- the performance of any examinations or tests, or the accused's refusal or failure to submit to an examination or test
- the identity, testimony, or credibility of prospective witnesses
- the possibility of a plea of guilty to the offense charged, or other disposition
- information which the lawyer knows or has reason to know should be inadmissible as evidence in a trial

By contrast, permissible statements, according to Standard 8-1.1, include

- the general nature of the charges against the accused
- the general nature of the defense to the charges or to other public accusations against the accused, including that the accused has no prior criminal record

- the name, age, residence, occupation, and family status of the accused
- information necessary to aid in the apprehension of the accused or to warn the public of any dangers that may exist
- a request for assistance in obtaining evidence
- the existence of an investigation in progress, including the general length and scope of the investigation, the charge, or defense involved, and the identity of the investigating officer or agency
- the facts and circumstances of an arrest, including the time and place and the identity of the arresting officer or agency
- the identity of the victim, where the release of that information is not otherwise prohibited by the law or would not be harmful to the victim
- at the time of seizure, a description of any physical evidence seized, not including any admission, confession, or statement by the accused
- information contained within a public record, without further comment
- the scheduling or result of any stage in the judicial process

Trial judges should not hesitate to bring the above standards to the attention of attorneys appearing before them in a notorious case. They can form the basis for a voluntary agreement to limit statements to the media without the unpleasant aspects of a gag order. The *Gentile* decision and these standards should guide trial judges in their efforts to ensure that counsel do not try the case on the courthouse steps. (See Chapter 1, "Trying the case in the media.")[40]

2. *Law enforcement and court personnel.* The speech of law enforcement personnel and court employees is also subject to restriction to prevent prejudice to a fair trial. ABA Standard 8-2.1 specifies that law enforcement personnel are subject to the same standard as attorneys. It should be noted, however, that appellate courts have not specifically decided the extent of a court's authority to regulate extrajudicial speech by executive branch employees. In *Rizzo v. Goode*, 96 S. Ct. 598, 604 (1976), the Supreme Court suggested that the courts are without power to issue regulatory orders against the police absent an actual case or controversy. In view of the lack of certainty on this issue, a trial judge should probably seek voluntary cooperation from law enforcement officials, based on Standard 8-2.1, before resorting to more coercive means to enforce it.

On the other hand, there is little question of the authority of the courts to impose speech restrictions on court personnel. See *Landmark Communications, Inc. v. Virginia*, 98 S. Ct. 1535, 1545 (1978). Consequently, ABA Standard 8-2.2 proscribes disclosures by court employees whenever they "may be" prejudicial to a fair trial.

---

[40] Note that Gentile has been distinguished from attorney statements unrelated to matters not pending before the court. *See* Standing Comm. v. Yagman, 55 F 3d 1430, 1443 (1995). Such statements may only be sanctioned if they pose "a clear and present danger to the administration of justice." *Id.*

3. *Parties and witnesses*. Regarding parties and witnesses who are not agents of the state, a recent Supreme Court decision indicates that a court may only caution them about the dangers of extrajudicial publicity. See *Butterworth v. Smith*, 110 S. Ct. 1376 (1990). This approach is adopted by the ABA in Standard 8-3.6(c). In this regard, however, a U.S. District Court decision concerning extrajudicial speech by a defendant deserves note. In *United States v. Northrop Corp.* 58 U.S.L.W. 2513 (Cal. Ct. App. Feb. 15, 1990) (No. CR 89-303 PAR), a corporate defendant facing trial on charges that it cut corners in fulfilling government contracts was restrained from airing, on the eve of jury selection, a series of television commercials that portrayed it in a favorable light. The court declared that postponing this "targeted advertising campaign," and thus limiting the defendant's right of free speech, was justified to prevent improper influencing of potential jurors. Under the circumstances, the court said the defendant's First Amendment right to commercial speech was outweighed by the court's obligation to ensure the integrity of the judicial process.

Judges should also be familiar with the Supreme Court decisions in *Nebraska Press* and *Sheppard v. Maxwell*, which outlined acceptable means of restraining speech jeopardizing defendants' trial rights.[41]

C. Use of court liaison officer to communicate with media
The United States Supreme Court in dicta approved a procedure whereby a trial judge in a notorious case instructed court personnel, counsel, witnesses, and jurors not to speak directly to the press, but instead appointed a court employee as "liaison" with the media to provide a "unified and singular source to the media concerning these proceedings."[42] Similarly, in Dade County, Florida, the chief judge has appointed a "communications director" to provide information to the public and the news media about events affecting the operations of the courts and the court clerk's office. During trials, the director relays information to reporters from the trial judge and from the prosecutor and defense lawyers.

See detailed discussions of media liaison position alternatives, Chapter 2.

D. Adoption of bench–bar–press voluntary guidelines
There have been efforts to develop voluntary guidelines for courts, lawyers, the press, and broadcasters. Voluntary bench-bar-press guidelines adopted in several states outline factual matters that may appropriately be reported and list those items that are generally not appropriate for reporting.[43] Typically, the

---

[41] *See* discussion *supra* this appendix, permissible restrictions on right of access.
[42] KPNX Broadcasting Co. v. Arizona Superior Court, 103 S. Ct. 584 (1982).
[43] *See* Sheldon, *The Effect of Voluntary Bench-Bar-Press Guidelines*, 72 JUDICATURE 114 (Aug.-Sept. 1988).

guidelines provide that the press should avoid publication in the following areas: confessions, opinions on guilt or innocence, the results of tests or examinations, comments on the credibility of witnesses, and the prior criminal record or discreditable acts of the accused.[44] The guidelines often set out standards for the taking and publishing of photographs and can set up a mechanism to resolve in advance problems concerning press coverage.

IV. SELECTION OF AN IMPARTIAL JURY IN A NOTORIOUS CASE

A. Sixth Amendment guarantee of trial by impartial jury
The Sixth Amendment assures a criminal defendant a trial by an impartial jury. This guarantee requires that those called for jury duty will come to the trial free of knowledge of the events related to the cause and that their actions as jurors will be based solely on evidence and argument in open court and the applicable law.[45]

1. *Voir dire inquiry with regard to pretrial publicity.* Once a prospective juror's exposure to pretrial publicity has been established, ABA Fair Trial and Fair Press Standard 8-3.5, "Selecting the Jury," recommends that jurors be individually examined outside the presence of other jurors regarding "not only the jurors' subjective self-evaluation of their ability to remain impartial but also the objective nature of the material and degree of exposure." The individual approach, which has been adopted by many courts,[46] has been thrown into some question by the Supreme Court decision, *Mu'Min v. Virginia,* 111 S. Ct. 1899 (1991). That decision reviews the legal history and standards in the area of voir dire and pretrial publicity and articulates the minimal permissible range of interrogation on the issue of pretrial publicity exposure necessary to meet Sixth Amendment requirements when impaneling a jury. The Court upheld severe limitations on the extent of voir dire permitted on the subject of exposure to pretrial publicity in a notorious case and concluded that potential jurors do not have to be questioned about what they know about the case so long as they promise to be fair.

In *Mu'Min,* the Court held that where potential jurors indicated that they had acquired some information about the alleged offense or the accused from the media, if the court found that they had not formed an opinion about the case and could remain fair and impartial, no further content inquiry by

---

[44] *See, e.g.,* Nebraska Press Ass'n, 96 S. Ct. 2791 (1976).

[45] Singer v. State, 109 So. 2d 7, 16 (Fla. 1959).

[46] *See* Press-Enterprise (I), 104 S. Ct. 819 (1984); United States v. Blanion, 719 F.2d 815, 822 (6th Cir. 1983); United States v. Booher, 641 F.2d 218 (5th Cir. 1981).

defense counsel need be permitted. The defense attorney in *Mu'Min* was not allowed individual voir dire, and his questions concerning the content of news items that potential jurors might have read or seen were not allowed. Although eight of the twelve jurors had indicated that they had read or heard something about the case, the Court affirmed the lower court's ruling that "while a criminal defendant may properly ask on voir dire whether a juror has previously acquired any information about the case, the defendant does not have a constitutional right to explore the content of the acquired information. Rather, an accused is only entitled to know whether the juror can remain impartial in light of the previously obtained information." *Mu'Min*, 111 S. Ct. at 1903.

The Supreme Court concluded "under the constitutional standard, . . . 'the relevant question is not whether the community remembered the case, but whether the jurors . . . had such fixed opinions that they could not judge impartially the guilt of the defendant.'" (quoting *Patton v. Yount*, 104 S. Ct. 2885 at 2891 (1984)). Under this constitutional standard, answers to questions about content alone, which reveal that a juror remembered the facts about this case, would not be sufficient to disqualify a juror. "'It is not required . . . that the jurors be totally ignorant of the facts and issues involved'" (111 S. Ct. at 1908, quoting *Irvin v. Dowd*, 81 S. Ct. 1639 at 1642 (1961)).

From a defendant's point of view, this decision delineates the most restrictive boundaries of permissible voir dire in terms of assessing the extent to which pretrial publicity has tainted a jury panel. It concludes that the Constitution does not require "content" questions and that the failure of the trial court to ask or permit "content" questions did not render the defendant's trial fundamentally unfair.

State constitutions may require more detailed content voir dire examination than the Sixth Amendment currently requires. Because a notorious case requires the expenditure of so much time, effort, and energy, the trial judge must exercise extraordinary caution to avoid appellate error of even the most innocuous sort. Therefore, out of an abundance of caution and in an effort to ensure fundamental fairness in the relatively unique notorious case setting, judges should refer to and be guided by the ABA Standards for Criminal Justice in this area. The ABA Standard of Criminal Justice 8-3.5, "Selecting the Jury," states:

> If there is a substantial possibility that individual jurors will be ineligible to serve because of exposure to potentially prejudicial material, the examination of each juror with respect to exposure shall take place outside the presence of other chosen and prospective jurors. . . . The questioning shall be conducted for the purpose of determining what the prospective juror has read and

heard about the case and how any exposure has affected that person's attitude toward the trial.

In reviewing this ABA standard in *Mu'Min*, the Supreme Court concluded that the standard "is a stricter standard of juror eligibility than that which we have held the Constitution to require." 111 S. Ct. at 1908. Nevertheless, this manual recommends that in the demanding setting of a notorious case, judges may be better served by allowing a wide latitude during voir dire when examining potential jurors concerning direct exposure to pretrial publicity.

While the Supreme Court ruling in *Mu'Min* permitting a more restrictive voir dire examination is at some variance with this recommendation, our recommendation is based on the recognition of the sensitive nature of notorious cases and of the tremendous time, resources, and energy invested in bringing those cases to trial. That investment in these sorts of cases should not be jeopardized by the precarious sensibilities of jurors unsure of their unexamined and unexplored ability to be fair and impartial. By the same token, trial judges should be aware that the Supreme Court has stated explicitly that in a notorious case "[i]t is not required that the jurors be totally ignorant of the facts and issues involved." *Mu'Min* at 1908. The critical question to be decided is "whether the jurors [have] such fixed opinions that they cannot judge impartially the guilt of the defendant." *Id.*

In summary, the Supreme Court has sanctioned a limited voir dire. Other courts, and the ABA, advocate a more thorough and searching voir dire. This manual prefers to err on the side of caution and suggests a thorough and detailed voir dire examination.

2.   *Voir dire inquiry with regard to racial prejudice.* While the scope of voir dire on the question of media exposure has been limited by the Supreme Court, examination of jurors on the topic of race may still be conducted.

Decisions regarding permissible voir dire inquiry with regard to racial prejudice are:

Aldridge v. United States, 51 S. Ct. 470 (1931)
Reversible error for a court to refuse to put to a jury a question of whether any of them might be prejudiced against the defendant because of his race.

Ham v. South Carolina, 93 S. Ct. 848 (1973)
Due process clause requires the jury be asked questions with respect to racial prejudice.

Rosales-Lopez v. United States, 101 S. Ct. 1629 (1981)

An inquiry into racial or ethnic prejudice need not be made in every case, but where the defendant was accused of a violent crime and the defendant and the victim were of different racial or ethnic groups, such an inquiry was required.

Turner v. Murray, 106 S. Ct. 1683 (1986)

In capital cases involving the alleged murder of a white person by a black defendant, the court must permit questions regarding racial prejudice.

3. *Error for failing to grant change of venue.* The William Lozano case involved a police shooting over the Super Bowl weekend that resulted in extensive rioting and civil disturbances in Miami. A motion for change of venue was denied, although there was a history or rioting in Miami in similar cases following other acquittals. Following the defendant's conviction, the appeals court concluded that it could not "approve the result of a trial conducted, as was this one, in an atmosphere in which the entire community—including the jury—was so obviously, and, it must be said, so justifiably concerned with the dangers which would follow an acquittal, but which would be and were obviated if, as actually occurred, the defendant was convicted."[47] The district court of appeal went on to say that "the fear that one's own county would respond to a not guilty verdict by erupting into violence is a highly impermissible factor,"[48] which came into play to deny the defendant a trial free of prejudice.

This case illustrates the difficult decision that must be made in deciding a motion for change of venue. The unstated presumption is that a court would prefer to try any case in the venue of origin. However, in those instances where it is actually impossible to impanel a jury free of bias and prejudice, the court must, if reluctantly, conclude that a change of venue is warranted.

B. Claims of potential prejudice arising after trial commences

When a claim of potentially prejudicial publicity arises after a jury has been selected, the trial court should determine whether the published material has the potential for prejudice and, if it does, then inquire whether any jurors actually read or saw the material in question. If so, the jurors should be questioned to determine the effect of the publicity.[49] ABA Fair Trial and Free Press Standard 8-3.5(a), "Selecting the Jury," recommends that jurors be questioned individually and that the standard for retaining a juror be the same as

---

[47] Lozano v. State of Florida, 584 So.2d 19 (1991).
[48] *Id.*
[49] *See* Salas v. State, 544 So. 2d 1040 (Fla. Dist. Ct. App. 1989).

the standard for initial acceptance found in ABA Fair Trial and Free Press Standard 8-3.5(b). In deciding whether to voir dire the jury about its members' exposure to potentially prejudicial publicity, a trial court may consider matters such as the prominence of the newspaper article or television story, the likelihood of the jury's contact with the article or story, the likelihood of the article or story's actual influence over the jury's decision making, and the content of instruction that had been given to prevent the jury from coming into contact with media coverage of the trial. Periodic monitoring of jurors during notorious cases as to media contact is advisable.

C. Cautionary instruction to jury

In cases involving extensive media coverage, a cautionary instruction should be given to jurors regarding contact with any news media coverage. ABA Fair Trial and Free Press Standard 8-3.6(d), "Conduct of the Trial," sets out a recommended admonition:

> During the time you serve on this jury, there may appear in the newspaper or on radio or television reports concerning this case, and you may be tempted to read, listen to, or watch them. Please do not do so. Due process of law requires that the evidence to be considered by you in reaching your verdict meet certain standards; for example, a witness may testify about events personally seen or heard but not about matters told to the witness by others. Also, witnesses must be sworn to tell the truth and must be subject to cross-examination. News reports about the case are not subject to these standards, and if you read, listen to, or watch these reports, you may be exposed to information which unduly favors one side and to which the other side is unable to respond. In fairness to both sides, therefore, it is essential that you comply with this instruction.

Standard 3.6(d) further suggests that at the end of each day of trial, and at other recess periods, if the court deems necessary, an instruction such as the following be given:

> For the reasons stated earlier in the trial, I must remind you not to read, listen to, or watch any news reports concerning this case while you are serving on this jury.

V. PROTECTION OF JUROR PRIVACY

A. *In camera voir dire*

The United States Supreme Court in *Press-Enterprise Co. (I)* recognized a juror's privacy interest as a valid concern that must be safeguarded and commented that the jury selection process may give rise to a compelling interest of a prospective juror when interrogation touches on personal matters that a person has legitimate reason for keeping out of the public domain. Hence, to preserve fairness and at the same time protect legitimate privacy interests, a trial judge should maintain control of the process of jury selection and should inform prospective jurors that once the nature of a sensitive question is made known to them, those individuals believing public questioning will prove damaging because of embarrassment may properly request an opportunity to present the problem to the judge *in camera* but with counsel present and on the record. The Supreme Court described the process as follows:

> By requiring the prospective juror to make an affirmative request, the trial judge can ensure that there is in fact a valid basis for a belief that disclosure infringes a significant interest in privacy. This process will minimize the risk of unnecessary closure. The exercise of sound discretion by the court may lead to excusing such a person from jury service. When limited closure is ordered, the constitutional values sought to be protected by holding open proceedings may be satisfied later by making a transcript of the closed proceedings available within a reasonable time, if the judge determines that disclosure can be accomplished while safeguarding the juror's valid privacy interests. Even then a valid privacy right may rise to a level that part of the transcript should be sealed, or the name of a juror withheld, to protect the person from embarrassment.[50]

The question of access to and the confidentiality of juror qualification questionnaires is often a source of contention between the media and the courts. The California Court of Appeals has considered in-depth the confidentiality of juror qualifications questionnaires in three decisions. In *Pantos v. City and County of San Francisco*,[51] the California Court of Appeals held that the disclosure of the identities of potential jurors without disclosure of other personal information is not a violation of jurors' right to privacy. The qualification questionnaires were not to be made available to the public because it was stated that these were confidential and that these forms were not judicial records open to the public, but are informative sources gathered to determine the qualifications of prospective jurors.

[50] 104 S. Ct. at 820.
[51] 198 Cal. Rptr. 489 (1984).

Another case of interest is *Copley Press, Inc. v. San Diego County Superior Court*.[52] Voir dire prescreening questionnaires containing 219 questions were used in a death penalty case in San Diego for 300 prospective jurors. Copley Press filed a motion requesting release of the questionnaires. The request was denied. The superior court responded that it recognized the right of access to the voir dire examination of the jury in a criminal trial. The questionnaires were used to equalize access for the parties' discovery of juror backgrounds; however, jurors had given open and complete information relying on the assurances in the instructions that they would be kept confidential. In this case the appellate court found that a blanket denial of access to the questionnaires was unconstitutional. However, because of the assurance given to the prospective jurors of the confidentiality of the questionnaires, the questionnaires were not to be released. The appeals court asserted nonetheless that in all future cases in which jury questionnaires are used, the trial court should: "(1) segregate juror qualification information from other questions, (2) plainly instruct the venirepersons in the body of the questionnaire that (a) the written responses are not confidential . . . , and (b) the venirepersons have a right to request an *in camera* hearing to discuss their responses to any questions they do not wish to answer in writing, and (3) provide access to the questionnaires." Furthermore, the court in *Lesher Communications v. Superior Court* has held that only those questionnaires of prospective jurors who made it into the jury box would be made available in the future.[53] All questionnaires from the prospective jurors who did not make it to the jury box could be withheld from the court record.[54] This decision places further demands upon the trial court to assure that unnecessary questions of a personal nature are avoided in the jury selection process, unless they are absolutely necessary to the determination of whether an individual can serve as a fair and impartial juror.

B. *Confidentiality of jurors' names and addresses*

To protect juror privacy, some lower courts have recognized a judge's right to withhold jurors' names and addresses from the media.[55] A more drastic approach is to ensure the anonymity of the jury not only from the media, but from all parties and their counsel. Courts have established cautious guidelines for this, but the practice has been upheld. See *United States v. Thomas*, 757 F.2d 1359 (2d Cir. 1985); *United States v. Persico*, 832 F.2d 7O5 (2d Cir. 1987); *United States v. Scarfo*, 850 F.2d 1015 (3d Cir. 1988); *United States v. Tutino*, 883 F.2d 1125 (2d Cir. 1989). Other courts however, have taken a different

---

[52] Id 278 Cal. Rptr. 443, 452 (1991).
[53] 224 Cal. App. 3d 774, 779 (1990).
[54] *Id.*
[55] *See, e.g.*, United States v. Gurney, 558 F.2d 1202, 1210 (5th Cir. 1977); United States v. Barnes, 604 F.2d 121, 140 (2d. Cir. 1979) (jurors need not publicly disclose their identities); Gannett v. Delaware, 567 A.2d 420 (Del. Super. Ct. 1990). *See also* United States v. Edmond, 886 F.2d 442 (D.C. Cir. 1990).

approach. The court in *In Re Baltimore Sun Co.*, for example, has disagreed, claiming the names and addresses of seated jurors should be made part of public record.[56]

C. Photographing jurors

Many commentators recommend against the photographing of jurors where cameras are allowed in the courtrooms.[57] There is language in *Chandler v. Florida*[58] disapproving the photographing of jurors. At the very least, a juror who expresses prior objection should not be photographed.[59]

D. Posttrial juror privacy

Jurors, even after completing their duty, are entitled to privacy and to protection against harassment. Jurors have no obligation to speak to the news media or anyone else about their service. The juror's freedom of speech is also the freedom not to speak.[60] Thus, it should be permissible for a court to instruct jurors not to discuss the specific votes and opinions of other jurors in order to encourage free deliberation in the jury room. Likewise, a court may instruct jurors that they may refuse interviews and seek the aid of the court if interviewers persist after they express a reluctance to speak. Recently the Supreme Court stated that "full and frank discussion in the jury room, jurors' willingness to return an unpopular verdict, and the community's trust in a system that relies on the decisions of laypeople would all be undermined by a barrage of post-verdict scrutiny of juror conduct."[61]

Courts disfavor lawyer contact with jurors after the conclusion of litigation except when there is a showing of illegal or prejudicial intrusion into the jury process.[62] Most jurisdictions have rules that not only prohibit attorneys from interviewing jurors after a trial without the court's permission, but also strictly limit the scope of any allowed inquiry.

At the conclusion of trial, the judge should refrain from commenting upon or discussing the substance of any aspect or feature of the trial and should cautiously respond to juror's questions.[63]

---

[56] 841 F.2d 74, 75 (4th Cir. 1988).

[57] *See, e.g.*, Note, *Cameras in the Courtroom*, 84 MICH. L. REV. 475, 497-99, 511 (1985) (filming the jury during voir dire poses such serious danger it should be banned); Frank, *Cameras in the Courtroom: A First Amendment Right of Access*, 9 COMM. ENT. L.J. 749, 802 (1989) (many states do not allow coverage of the jury in a manner by which any juror may be identified); *Report of the Committee on the Operation of the Jury System* on the "Free Press-Fair Trial" Issue, 45 F.R.D. 391, 411 (no photograph can be taken of any juror within environs of the court).

[58] 101 S. Ct. 802, 805 (1981).

[59] *See, e.g.*, *Bench-Bar-Press Committee of Washington Statement of Principles*, 72 JUDICATURE 120-21 (Aug-Sept. 1985).

[60] In re Express News Corporation, 695 F. 2d 807, 811 (5th Cir. 1982).

[61] Tanner v. United States, 107 S. Ct. 2739 at 2748 (1987) (citing Note, *Public Disclosures of jury Deliberations*, 96 HARV. L. REV. 886 at 888-92 (1983)).

[62] United States v. Garcia, 732 F.2d 1221 (5th Cir. 1984) (quoting *United States v. Riley*, 544 F.2d 237 (5th Cir. 1976)).

[63] *See* Canon 3A(4).

California Change of Venue Guidelines

CALIFORNIA RULES OF COURT, APPENDIX, DIVISION I STANDARDS OF JUDICIAL ADMINISTRATION

Section 4. Policies to be considered before ordering and transferring a criminal case on change of venue

(a) [Attempt to impanel jury] Before ordering a change of venue in a criminal case, the court should consider attempting to impanel a jury that would give the defendant a fair and impartial trial.

(b) [Moving the jury] After a change of venue has been ordered, the court should determine, pursuant to Penal Code section 1036.7, whether it would be in the interests of the administration of justice to move the jury rather than to move the pending action. In so doing, the court should give particular consideration to the convenience of the jurors.
Adopted, eff. July 1, 1989.

Advisory Committee Comment – *Section 4(a) is not intended to imply that the court should attempt to impanel a jury in every case before granting a change of venue. If there is clear evidence of a reasonable likelihood that a fair and impartial trial cannot be had in the county, a change of venue should be ordered.*

Section 4.1 Change of venue case to be tried by judge from county in which the case originated—criminal cases

A criminal case in which a change in venue has been ordered should be tried in the court receiving the case by a judge from the court in which the case originated, unless the originating and receiving courts agree otherwise.
Adopted, eff. July 1, 1989.

Section 4.2 Guidelines for reimbursement of costs in change of venue cases – criminal cases

(a) [General] Consistent with Penal Code section 1037(c), the county in which an action originated should reimburse the county receiving a case after an order for change of venue for any ordinary expenditure and any extraordinary but reasonable-and-necessary expenditure which would not have been incurred by the receiving county but for the change of venue.

(b) [Reimbursable ordinary expenditures — court related] Court-related reimbursable ordinary expenses include:

(1) For prospective jurors on the panel from which the jury is selected and for the trial jurors and alternates seated:
(i)   Normal juror per diem and mileage at the rates of the receiving county. The cost of the juror should only be charged to a change of venue case if the juror was not used in any other case on the day the juror was excused from the change of venue case.
(ii)   If jurors are sequestered, actual lodging, meals, mileage, and parking expenses up to state Board of Control limits.
(iii) If jurors are transported to a different courthouse or county, actual mileage and parking expenses.

(2) For court reporters:
(i)   The cost of pro tem reporters, even if not used in the change of venue trial, but not the salaries of regular official reporters who would have been paid in any event. The rate of compensation for pro tem reporters should be that of the receiving county.
(ii)   The cost of transcripts requested during trial and for any new trial or appeal, using the folio rate of the receiving county.
(iii) The cost of additional reporters necessary to allow production of a daily or expedited transcript.

(3) For assigned judges: The assigned judge's per diem, travel, and other expenses, up to state Board of Control limits, if the judge is assigned to the receiving court because of the change of venue case, regardless of whether the assigned judge is hearing the change of venue case.

(4) For interpreters and translators:
(i)   The cost of the services of interpreters and translators, not on the court staff, if those services are required under Evidence Code sections 750 through 754. Using the receiving county's fee schedule, this cost should be paid whether the services are used in a change of venue trial or to cover staff interpreters and translators assigned to the change of venue trial.
(ii)   Interpreter's and translator's actual mileage, per diem and lodging expenses, if any, which were incurred in connection with the trial, up to state Board of Control limits.

(5) For maintenance of evidence: The cost of handling, storing, or maintaining evidence beyond the expenses normally incurred by the receiving county.

(6) For services and supplies: The cost of services and supplies incurred only because of the change of venue trial, for example, copying and printing charges (e.g., juror questionnaires), long-distance telephone calls, and postage. A pro rata share of the costs of routine services and supplies should not be reimbursable.

(7) For court or county employees:
(i) Overtime expenditures and compensatory time for staff incurred because of the change of venue case.
(ii) Salaries and benefit costs of extra help or temporary help incurred either because of the change of venue case or to replace staff assigned to the change of venue case.

(c) [Reimbursable ordinary expenses—defendant related] Defendant-related reimbursable ordinary expenses include the actual costs incurred for guarding, keeping, and transporting the defendant, including:

(1) Expenses related to health care: Costs incurred by or on behalf of the defendant such as doctors, hospital expenses, medicines, therapists, and counseling for diagnosis, evaluation, and treatment.

(2) Cost of food and special clothing for an in-custody defendant.

(3) Transportation: Nonroutine expenses, such as transporting an in-custody defendant from the originating county to the receiving county. Routine transportation expenses if defendant is transported by usual means used for other receiving county prisoners should not be reimbursable.

(d) [Reimbursable ordinary expenditures—defense expenses] Reimbursable ordinary expenses related to providing defense for the defendant include:

(1) Matters covered by Penal Code section 987.9 as determined by the court in which the action originated or by a judge designated under that section.

(2) Payment of other defense costs in accordance with policies of the county in which the action originated, unless good cause to the contrary is shown to the trial court.

(3) Unless Penal Code section 987.9 applies, the trial court in the receiving county may, in its sound discretion, approve all trial-related expenses including:
(i)   Attorney fees for defense Counsel and, if any, co-counsel, and actual travel-related expenses, up to state Board of Control limits, for staying in the receiving county during trial and hearings.
(ii) Paralegal and extraordinary secretarial or office expenditures of defense counsel.
(iii) Expert witness costs and expenses.
(iv) The cost of experts assisting in preparation before trial or during trial, for example, persons preparing demonstrative evidence.
(v)   Investigator expenses.
(vi) Defense witness expenses, including reasonable-and-necessary witness fees and travel expenses.

(e) [Extraordinary but reasonable-and-necessary expenses] Except in emergencies or unless it is impracticable to do so, a receiving county should give notice before incurring any extraordinary expenditures to the county in which the action originated, in accordance with Penal Code section 1037(d). Extraordinary but reasonable-and-necessary expenditures include:

(1) Security-related expenditures: The cost of extra security precautions taken because of the risk of escape or suicide or threats of, or the potential for, violence during the trial. These precautions might include, for example, extra bailiffs or correctional officers, special transportation to the courthouse for trial, television monitoring, and security checks of those entering the courtroom.

(2) Facility remodeling or modification: Alterations to buildings or courtrooms to accommodate the change of venue case.

(3) Renting or leasing of space or equipment: Renting or leasing of space for courtrooms, offices, and other facilities, or equipment to accommodate the change of venue case.

(f) [Nonreimbursable expenses] Nonreimbursable expenses include:

(1) Normal operating expenses including the overhead of the receiving county, for example:

(i) Salary and benefits of existing county or court staff which would have been paid even if there were no change of venue case.

(ii) The cost of operating the jail, for example, detention staff costs, normal inmate clothing, utility costs, overhead costs, and jail construction costs.

These expenditures would have been incurred whether or not the case was transferred to the receiving county. It is, therefore, inappropriate to seek reimbursement from the county in which the action originated.

(2) Equipment which is purchased and then kept by the receiving county and which can be used for other purposes or cases.

(g) [Miscellaneous]

(1) Documentation of costs: No expense should be submitted for reimbursement without supporting documentation, such as a claim, invoice, bill, statement, or time sheet. In unusual circumstances, a declaration under penalty of perjury may be necessary. The declaration should describe the cost and state it was incurred because of the change of venue case. Any required court order or approval of costs also should be sent to the originating court.

(2) Timing of reimbursement: Unless both counties agree to other terms, reimbursement of all expenses which are not questioned by the originating county should be made within 60 days of receipt of the claim for reimbursement. Payment of disputed amounts should be made within 60 days of the resolution of the dispute.

Adopted, eff. July 1, 1989; as amended Jan. 1, 1998.

Decorum Orders

UNITED STATES DISTRICT COURT
FOR THE DISTRICT OF COLUMBIA

UNITED STATES OF AMERICA

v.

MARION S. BARRY, JR.

Criminal Case No. 90-0068 (TPJ)

ORDER

In the exercise of its inherent power to provide for the orderly disposition of this case, it is, by the Court sua sponte, this _____ day of June, 1990,

ORDERED, as follows:

1. Only members of the prospective juror panel will be admitted to the spectator section of the courtroom until the Prospective Juror Questionnaires have been completed.

2. During individual *voir dire* and the trial a portion of the spectator section of the courtroom will be reserved for the press in accordance with a predetermined seating plan. The public will be admitted to the press portion of the courtroom only if seating remains available after all journalists have been seated. Journalists may be admitted to the public portion of the courtroom only if seating remains available after all members of the public have been seated.

3. The press and the public are reminded that any attempt by anyone, without leave of court, to communicate with a member of the jury panel respecting the case prior to selection of a jury, other than in the course of *voir dire*, and any attempt by anyone, without leave of court, to communicate with a member of the jury once selected respecting the case, other than in the course of trial, until the conclusion of the case, may be punished as a criminal contempt of court.

4.   No media interviews whatsoever will be permitted in the courtroom at any time.

5.   No member of the press or public will be admitted within the well of the courtroom at any time.

6.   All spectators, whether press or public, must be seated before the court is in session, and must remain in the courtroom (except for emergencies) until the next recess is called. No spectators will routinely be admitted to or allowed to depart the courtroom while court is in session.

7.   The courtroom will be cleared of press and public until 9:45 a.m., for the duration of the noontime recess, and at adjournment. The parties, counsel, and their staffs may be present in the courtroom at any time from 9:00 a.m. until 6:00 p.m.

8.   Any violation of the foregoing, and any conduct the Court finds disruptive of the proceedings, may result in an order of temporary or permanent exclusion of the offender(s) from the trial.

Thomas Penfield Jackson
U.S. District Judge

Decorum Orders

ORDER

PEOPLE V. RAYMOND BUCKEY

IT IS HEREBY ORDERED that no attorney, party or witness in this matter shall participate in any televised, filmed or electronically recorded interview on any portion of the 11th floor of the Criminal Courts Building.

IT IS FURTHER ORDERED that any television camera, radio, or recording equipment that is permitted in the courtroom shall only be turned on and operating when court is in session.

IT IS FURTHER ORDERED that all those participating in film or electronic media coverage comply with Rule 980 of the California Rules of Court.

IT IS SO ORDERED.

DATED: May 7, 1990

/S/

Stanley M. Weisberg
Judge of the Superior Court

Decorum Orders

NOTICE TO THE VISUAL MEDIA

The privacy of the alleged victims, their parents, and the jurors being of paramount importance to this Court, any visual media agency which broadcasts or otherwise disseminates the image or names of such persons will be precluded from further visual coverage of the McMartin trial.

PRESENCE OF JURORS AT TELEPHONE BANK

Media representatives who make telephonic reports to their agencies should not use the public telephones on this floor to avoid being overheard by jurors in this case.

Handling News Media Arrangements During High Visibility Trials

Judge Gerhard A. Gesell (D.D.C) presided over a criminal trial that attracted wide-spread local and national news media coverage. Judge Gesell was asked to describe some of the techniques he used to permit media access but avoid disruption. His description follows:

A recent case that fell my way[1] was obviously going to be one of those occasional very high visibility criminal trials preceded by extensive pretrial proceedings that would attract the full weight of daily coverage by local and all major national news organizations. The case also involved a large volume of classified material, raising other problems of access. Drawing on lessons learned during the Watergate and other nationally publicized cases, we developed procedures to assure maximum press access and avoid expected disruption of the proceedings by a "full court press." The following arrangements worked fairly well.

First, we set up the usual code-a-phone system, immediately recording on the assigned number each pretrial and trial development and all announcements of future scheduling as dates were set. The press and members of the public were encouraged to telephone the code-a-phone for information.

But, of course, this arrangement met only some of the problems. Following my normal practice, I declined all picture taking, television panels, and interview requests. Yet there were bound to be some press matters that required contact with the court, as, indeed, there were. Seating for the courtroom immediately became an acute problem of vital interest to the press as well as the court's administrative staff.

I had refused to go to the larger ceremonial courtroom because of the circus atmosphere it might create and other difficulties. My regular courtroom seats 100 behind the rail. Approximately 75 different print and TV news organizations, foreign and domestic, would be covering every development, day to day, through what promised to be extensive pretrial proceedings and trial. Other members of the press anticipated dropping in from time to time. Some news organizations worked in relays, some needed room for sketch artists. Apart from the media, there was an enormous demand for seats from all quar-

[1] United States v. Poindexter, North, Secord and Hakem, Criminal No. 88-80

ters competing for space with the press. We needed space for the public, for the defendant's family, for families of the lawyers on both sides, for counsel advising witnesses, for court personnel interested in the proceedings, for security and classification specialists, for VIPs, and others. When push came to shove, only 45 seats at most could be set aside for the press. The court was ill-equipped to allocate these seats, given the large press interest, and, of course, access to the courtroom was vital, considering the lack of any electronic coverage which could be viewed or heard elsewhere.

While courthouse personnel could and did handle other demands for space, allocating press seats involved an expertise no one at the courthouse had. I designated a senior, well-respected member of the press to act as liaison between the court and all branches of the media. He had covered other high visibility criminal cases for a major TV network and understood the needs of the press. A notice was put out on the city wire service notifying news agencies that they could apply for seats by writing to a designated court official. The name and office telephone number of the liaison representative was made available so that he—not the court—would receive questions and complaints.

I made it clear that the press could not sit beyond the bar of the courtroom or attempt to interview anyone in the courtroom during recess or otherwise. Passes for the trial, entitling the holder to sit in one of the press rows, were assigned by the liaison representative without involvement of the court. Applicants other than the major newspapers, networks, and news services were put in pools sharing a single pass. Once this was arranged, courthouse administrative personnel made certain the press passes were being used and that each pooled seat was rotated property.

Several passes were cancelled after the news organizations to which they were issued failed to use them at least half of the time. Forfeited passes went to the news organizations next in line on a waiting list compiled by date of application. Reporters without permanent passes were permitted to form a special line and were given any press seats not occupied within 20 minutes of the start of the morning or afternoon session. Most of the reporters were accommodated. The first row was reserved for sketch artists. Wire service reporters, who frequently must leave to file, were given aisle seats near the rear to minimize distraction.

The liaison representative also assisted in another significant way. Through him I learned of press needs and problems anticipated or unexpected and was able to satisfy many concerns. He was designated to pick up copies of exhibits from the courtroom clerk and to arrange for their duplication on a photocopy machine rented by the pressroom regulars. The liaison representative also arranged a rotating pool of the television stations to make videotape copies of photographic exhibits. If the arrangements made for assuring availability of copies of exhibits, orders and memoranda, or names of jurors chosen, etc. happened to break down in some respect, the difficulties were brought to the court's attention by the liaison representative and were ironed out where possible, or explained. The reporters regularly assigned to the courthouse had no special privileges as far as the coverage of the case was concerned.

Because of the large volume of classified material involved in the case and the consequent need for closing the courtroom at various times during pretrial and for nonjury matters during trial, many novel problems of media access developed. Techniques for promptly supplying as much material from closed sessions as possible to the press were put in place in consultation with the liaison representative and court personnel.

In a case of this character, the press needs clear-cut factual answers to reasonable questions concerning procedures, timing of decisions on pending motions, schedule, and the like. Camera crews and other personnel outside the courthouse are involved. Reasonable concerns must be satisfied when possible. What the press writes is its business and not the court's, but the process flows more smoothly if purely neutral factual information can be made available to all members of the press in the same form at the same time.

Under the procedures established by the court, reporters knew they could funnel relevant questions through the liaison representative. He gathered the questions in the pressroom after each morning and afternoon session, eliminating duplicative and overlapping inquiries. The boiled-down list, usually two or three questions, was telephoned to chambers, and appropriate responses provided often immediately, but never more than an hour or two later—to be relayed to reporters in the pressroom on a non-attribution basis. On some occasions, the court believed it was necessary and useful to inform counsel of the questions received and the answers the court proposed to give.

These procedures were established as the sole means of communication between the press corps and the court. And they worked. The press knew that the court itself was involved and that there was no need individually to try to get the information from courthouse personnel or trial participants. Several times the court was able to use the liaison apparatus to relay concerns to the press about its activities, and to enlist its understanding and cooperation.

It is difficult to convey the benefits of such an arrangement unless one has experienced the massive attention one of these high visibility criminal cases can generate. The story of the trial becomes daily grist for the press, even if there is nothing to report. Without clear, fair rules and established lines of communication, the entire courthouse and the chambers of the trial judge come under siege: court personnel are distracted, and it is difficult to concentrate on the work at hand as reporters seek something to write about or talk about, running down the wildest rumors. When rules and procedures are clear the press benefits. As long as all are treated equally, matters move forward more responsibly with less confusion and greater accuracy.

In this instance the procedures worked well. My home telephone is listed, but I never received calls at home from the press. There were no newspaper personnel seeking access to chambers, and it was possible to concentrate on the judicial work at hand. Of course, designated administrative and clerical personnel and the security people were still extremely busy, but by centralizing all inquiries through the liaison representative their task was considerably lightened. Most of the problems that arose would have required the clerk of court or one of his deputies to check with the court, in any event; direct access hastened and simplified the process. Whenever inquiries touched on the evidence or the merits they were ignored. The press wrote and spoke as they chose.

Public Seating in a Notorious Trial

Article appearing in
The Los Angeles Daily Journal,
August 1, 1990.

For the Public, Attending a Trial Can Be a Trial

Whose Seats Are They?
By Terry Carter, Daily Journal Staff Reporter

When the American Civil Liberties Union intervened in the trial of Washington D.C. mayor Marion S. Barry to force the judge to allow two controversial black religious leaders into the courtroom, the public interest organization held out no hope for hundreds of others waiting in line outside.

Of the 98 seats in the courtroom, only 18 were left for the public once reporters, sketch artists—who use double spaces—and those with passes from the prosecution and defense were accommodated.

There was a similar squeeze recently in Los Angeles. Every day at the beginning of the Raymond Buckey retrial in the McMartin Pre-School molestation case, an elderly woman who had been on the panel of prospective jurors tried to be the first to the courthouse so she could get in to watch.

Few Seats for Public
And on the busiest days it wasn't easy—of 62 seats in the courtroom, only five were left for the general public. The others 57 seats went to the press, families of alleged victims and others with passes from the prosecution and defense.

Early on, because of the difficulties, the woman was given a pass by Buckey and his lawyer so she could attend without jockeying for a seat.

But for many who would like to attend high-profile trials these days, there is no such recourse.

The reason for the seating crunch has mostly to do with the news media, mathematics and architecture. The number of reporters trying to get in to cover high-profile trials has increased considerably in the past decade or so, for a variety of reasons.

Besides heightened public interest and more interest from news organizations, whatever the chicken/egg causality between the two, there also is the new technology—the ease of live remote transmission by television crews from vans parked in front of courthouses.

And many of those courthouses were built in the days when state-of-the-art news gathering encompassed little more than pencils and pads. Then, fewer reporters covered the big trials and there usually was plenty of room for regular folks, from the old courtwatchers who eschewed playing checkers on park benches in favor of real-life drama, to those interested solely in the trial at hand.

"People outside the [Barry] courtroom and courthouse came up to me and said 'Well, how about us, don't you think it's a scandal?'" says Arthur B. Spitzer, legal director of the ACLU of the National Capital Area, who represented Nation of Islam leader Louis Farrakhan and renegade Catholic priest George Augustus Stallings Jr. and got the judge to reverse himself and let them in on passes from Barry's legal team.

'It's a Real Problem'

"I do think it's a real problem," Spitzer continues. "But I told them that as a practical matter, I don't think there's anything I could do as a legal challenge. The judge has the discretion to allocate seats, and I don't think it would be overturned by an appellate court."

The irony is that during the 10 years since the U.S. Supreme Court came out with a surprisingly strong ruling in favor of criminal trials being public, the cases people are most interested in seeing have become less open to them. *Richmond Newspapers Inc. v. Virginia*, 448 U.S. 555 (1980).

While the news media and their lawyers have become more sophisticated about access to the courts, and judges have more and more recognized the media's role as surrogate for one and all, the general public has had no advocate, and its position has slipped.

Earlier this year, the National Center for State Courts began looking at problems with some of the bigger trials around the country. Its staff lawyers began interviewing judges and court administrators, including some in Los Angeles County, to put together an informative pamphlet so local, state and federal judges won't have to reinvent the wheel when a hot case lands in their court.

With the catchy title of "Managing Notorious Cases Project," and federal funding through a grant from the State Justice Institute, it will consider problems such as pretrial proceedings, jury selection and security.

Last week, the director of the NCSC's Center for Jury Studies sent a memorandum to others researching for the pamphlet, suggesting they also might look at seating for the general public during trials.

"I raised the question of how many seats do you have to have available to the public in a courtroom to make it public," says G. Thomas Munsterman. "Does one seat do it?

"I sat in on the Barry trial with a press pass, and there was a line of people out in back of the building. And of those [from the general public] who got in, once you get out of your seat and leave for the bathroom, you're done. You lose your seat."

Such pressing biological needs and logistical problems weren't addressed by former Chief Justice Warren E. Burger in writing the majority opinion in the *Richmond Newspapers* case, in which the court reversed the decision of a trial judge who ruled a criminal defendant, because prosecutors didn't object, could have his trial closed to the public. The trial judge had reasoned that because the Sixth Amendment states that in criminal cases, "the accused shall enjoy the right to a speedy and public trial . . . ," that right was the defendant's, not the public's.

The *Richmond Newspapers* decision was pegged primarily on the First Amendment, citing the "freedom of communication on matters relating to the functioning of government."

Open court proceedings in criminal matters have been an important part of Anglo-American justice since even before reliable historical records were kept, Burger noted.

"[T]he significant community therapeutic value of public trials was recognized: when a shocking crime occurs, a community reaction of outrage and public protest often follows, and thereafter the open processes of justice serve an important prophylactic purpose, providing an outlet for community concern, hostility, and emotion," he wrote.

Burger also bolstered the news media's surrogate role in representing the public interest by covering trials, and the legitimacy of privileges given them in some instances.

'Same Right of Access'

While the media "enjoy the same right of access as the public," Burger wrote, "they often are provided special seating and priority of entry so that they may report what people in attendance have seen and heard."

When a case is expected to be a big draw, judges sometimes opt for a larger courtroom when one is available, as Los Angeles Superior Court Judge William R. Pounders did in the first McMartin trial.

The bigger facility was not used in the subsequent Buckey retrial, says John E. Iverson, criminal courts coordinator for the Los Angeles Superior Court, "because there was less interest and we didn't feel like moving."

In the Barry trial, U.S. District Judge Thomas Penfield Jackson refused to move into the larger, ceremonial courtroom that is used for little more than bankruptcy discharges and naturalizations. If his courtroom was big enough for Watergate cases, said Judge Jackson when there were complaints about access, then it is big enough for Marion Barry.

An administrator at Washington's federal courthouse says acoustics are a problem in the larger courtroom and that security is a concern, too, when those in attendance might number in the hundreds.

But the judge felt the heat, as did the lawyers. In a bench conference early in the trial, Judge Jackson and the lawyers complained to each other about it.

"I've got agonizing complaints from *Time* magazine, *The Wall Street Journal*," the judge said, according to the transcript of a June 20 bench conference. He added that he'd heard "not altogether facetious conversation at lunch about moving into the sports coliseum."

One old hand at the courthouse said the regular court watchers knew better than even to try to get into the Barry trial, and moved over to the D.C. Superior Court instead for the usual murders and robberies.

Cameras in the Courtrooms

In the minds of some, greater access for cameras in the courtrooms would go a long way in ameliorating the problem of a dearth of seats for notorious trials. That has been one of the linchpins in the argument by such proponents as the First Amendment Coalition in California, an alliance of news media groups interested in court access, and more particularly the Washington-based Radio-Television News Directors Association, which has lobbied on the issue for years.

"It doesn't make sense to treat what the Constitution and the Supreme Court consider absolutely bedrock for openness as something that has to be rationed almost on a ticket basis," says Terry Francke, executive director of the First Amendment Coalition. "Something like C-SPAN or some general public-broadcasting seems in one sense the simplest way to handle that.

"At the very minimum there should be some kind of closed-circuit transmission to some other place where people can watch and hear."

For now, 44 states permit broadcast of court proceedings, but many of them put severe limitations on the what and how of doing so. The federal courts do not permit cameras, although proponents recently were encouraged when Rep. Robert W. Kastenmeier, D-Wis., chairman of the key House committee overseeing federal court administration, wrote a letter to Chief Justice William Rehnquist saying it is time for cameras in the courts and that if the courts can't bring themselves to do it, maybe Congress will.

At least four or five times a year, highly publicized trials put various courts around the country under a severe strain that makes it virtually impossible for regular citizens to see what transpires, says David Bartlett, president of the Radio-Television News Directors Association.

Besides giving those people access via broadcasts, Bartlett says, "we contend that the entirely reprehensible circus that often occurs on the steps of the courthouse, witnesses chased for comments and ad hoc news conferences by both sides and other interested parties, would be limited if the public were allowed to see [on television] witnesses in the courtroom."

Others aren't so sure cameras will alleviate the backup at the courtroom door and the theatrics on the courthouse steps.

"That's what we thought," says Justice Stephen G. Crane of the Supreme Court for the First Judicial District in New York City. "But I don't know if it's working out that way."

New York allows coverage of many court proceedings on an experimental basis.

Justice Crane is on the advisory committee for the creation of the NCSC's pamphlet on handling notorious cases and his credentials for the job are obvious: Three years ago he tried the case of Bernhard Goetz, the so-called "Subway Vigilante."

Another answer might be in the vision of the federal court clerk in the Eastern District of Wisconsin, who lately has been thinking and talking architecture more than law, as the court in Milwaukee plans for remodeling in four years.

"We have an idea for a sort of courtroom of the future," says Sofron Nedilsky, clerk of court. He wants it to be able to accommodate more defendants and more members of the public.

"I have proposed a gallery, in a two-story courtroom, an old-fashioned balcony/gallery to allow for the largest possible work space and still have visual access to the courtroom," Nedilsky explains. Though there would be more seating for the public, it would be by an entrance separate from that used by the trial principals.

"It would address security immediately," Nedilsky says. "It would separate them from the courtroom activity and for high-security cases we could easily put in bullet-proof glass and pipe in sound."

Article appearing in
The National Law Journal,
September 3, 1990.

Sometimes the Real Action Is Not in the Courtroom

As the drama of a high-profile criminal trial unfolds in a courtroom, few people following the case through newspapers and television see events that take place outside the courthouse and the ordeals of those who want a firsthand view. In the recently concluded Central Park jogger trial in New York, the logistics involved with getting inside for the main event often resembled the scene at a major sports or music event.

On most days, only a few curious citizens want to see the justice system in action. But for the seven weeks of the jogger trial, the elevators at the New York Supreme Court, the state's trial-level court, were filled to capacity.

The trial took place in a courtroom on the seventh floor, and once off the elevators, the public had to wait in a line of up to 120 people for the 40 available seats inside. Many complained about the lack of space and wanted the trial to be held in a larger room. One man waiting on line came up with a more creative tactic: He declared that it was a violation of his constitutional rights to be kept out of the trial room and drew up a petition on the spot.

"Our priority is to seat as many people as possible," says Harold Wolfe, a public information officer at the courthouse. For the press and public alike, it was first-come, first-served.

John Perno, director of court security services, says that when a large turnout is anticipated, extra officers are on reserve and extra security measures, such as the installation of a metal detector, are taken.

The jogger trial was heavily attended by a group of activists who supported the defendants, but Mr. Perno was not worried about conflicts: "Our only concern is the numbers. There have been no real problems. Things have been running very smoothly."

The District of Columbia faced similar problems with the public's interest in Mayor Marion Barry's cocaine trial. Officials there managed to eliminate some of the variables that the New York courts often must contend with. All courtrooms are the same size, and for widely publicized trials, such as Mayor Barry's, the press must apply for the limited number of passes.

Like the press, the public must follow an orderly procedure. Every morning, numbers are distributed to the first 45 people. Even a waiting room is provided. But however civilized this system may sound, it is not without its problems. While waiting for the New York jogger trial, a courtroom groupie from Virginia recalled Mayor Barry's trial: "The Barry trial is worse than a rock concert. I tried to go, but people wait outside the courthouse at 2:00 a.m. with sleeping bags."

California's Superior Court has put an interesting twist on dealing with public attendance. To accommodate the people who can't fit into the courtroom, the bailiffs assemble a closed-circuit monitor in another room so everyone can see the proceedings. Lynn Holton, the public information officer, says the clerk's office came up with the idea for the highly attended Proposition 103 hearings, an auto-insurance reform initiative, as well as the confirmation hearings for state justices.

"It's great because no one is turned away," Ms. Holton says.

Despite the best efforts of the courts, some people apparently never will be satisfied. After circulating his petition to get into the jogger trial, the author decided to test his views out on a court officer. "The Constitution guarantees the right to a speedy and public trial. Everyone who wants to see it should be able to," he said. The officer stared at the man for a moment, then answers as only a New Yorker can.

"What do you want us to do, have it in Yankee Stadium?"

Charles Phillips

Rules Concerning Electronic Media Coverage of Courts

ALASKA ADMINISTRATIVE RULES

Rule 50. Media Coverage of Court Proceedings.

(a) Media Coverage. Court proceedings may be covered by the news media under the provisions of this rule. For purposes of this rule, "media" includes the electronic media, still photographers and sketch artists. The rule applies at all times throughout state court facilities and is not limited to courtrooms or to times when court is in session. The rule does not allow media coverage of state court proceedings held in a federal court facility unless coverage is allowed by federal rule.

(b) Application for Court Approval.

(1) The media shall apply for approval of media coverage to the judge presiding over the proceeding to be covered. This application must be made at least 24 hours prior to the proceeding unless good cause is shown for a later application. A timely application will be deemed approved unless the court otherwise orders.

(2) The presiding judge and the area court administrator for each judicial district may designate for each court location a public area in which media coverage may take place without application for prior approval.

(c) Consent of Parties. All parties, including the guardian ad litem, must consent to media coverage of a divorce, dissolution of marriage, domestic violence, child custody and visitation, paternity or other family proceedings.

(d) Prohibition of Coverage. A court may prohibit or terminate media coverage only if: (1) a party does not consent to media coverage under paragraph (c); (2) prohibition of coverage is necessary to ensure the fair administration of justice in any present or future case; or (3) the media fails to comply with reasonable restrictions issued under paragraph (e).

(e) Restrictions on Coverage.

(1) A victim of a sexual offense may be not photographed, filmed, video-taped or sketched without the consent of the court and victim.

(2) Jurors may not be photographed, filmed or videotaped, except during the return of the verdict. Return of the verdict does not include polling jurors.

(3) The court may impose reasonable restrictions on the time, place or manner of media coverage in a particular case. Any restrictions must be stated on the record, and must be reasonably related and narrowly drawn by the least restrictive means to: (i) control the conduct of proceedings before the court; (ii) ensure decorum and prevent distractions; (iii) protect the reasonable privacy interests of a minor or any other person; or (iv) ensure the fair administration of justice in pending or future cases.

(4) The administrative director of the Alaska Court System may establish by administrative bulletin reasonable statewide procedures and standards for media coverage of judicial proceedings.

(f) Photographing, filming, videotaping and sketching by anyone other than news media requires a prior written determination by the presiding judge of the judicial district that the activity is not disruptive. In addition, such activity must comply with the other provisions of this rule.

(g) Challenge to Denial of Coverage.

(1) A media organization for which coverage has been denied or restricted may request in writing that the trial court reconsider its ruling. The request may be made by an officer or employee of the media organization, AS 22.20.040 notwithstanding, may be made in the form of a letter to the judge, must state the reasons why media coverage should be allowed, and must be served on all parties to the case pursuant to Civil Rule 5. The parties may submit memoranda in response to such a request only if asked to do so by the judge.

(2) If the request is denied, the media organization may petition for review pursuant to the Appellate Rules. AS 22.20.040 applies to any such petition for review.

(h) Suspension of Media Privileges. If the judge presiding at a proceeding determines that an individual or organization has violated any provision of the media plan, the judge may recommend to the administrative director that the individual's or organization's media coverage privileges be suspended for a period of up to one year. The judge shall notify the individual or organization by certified mail of the recommendation and the reasons which support it. The individual or organization has five working days from receipt of the notice to respond in writing to the administrative director. The director shall send notice to the judge and the individual or organization of the director's decision within five working days.

(Adopted by SCO 978 effective January 15, 1990; amended by SCO 1058 effective July 15, 1991.)

ALASKA COURT SYSTEM
Office of the Administrative Director
Administrative Bulletin No. 45

This administrative bulletin is adopted pursuant to Administrative Rule 50(e)
(4) and applies to any media coverage allowed under Administrative Rule 50.

1. Number of Cameras. Not more than two portable television cameras (or 16 mm sound or film cameras), operated by not more than one camera operator each, will be permitted in a courtroom or adjacent areas in any
trial court proceeding or during a recess in the proceeding. A judge may allow
only one such camera operated by one camera operator if the judge determines that the courtroom size warrants this limitation. . . . These provisions
do not apply to a courtroom which the administrative director has designated
as a media courtroom.

2. Number of Photographers. Not more than two photographers
operating not more than two still cameras each will be permitted in a courtroom or adjacent areas in any judicial proceeding or during a recess in the proceeding. These provisions do not apply to a courtroom which the administrative director has designated as a media courtroom.

3. Number of Audio Systems for Radio Broadcast. Not more than
two audio systems for radio broadcast purposes will be permitted in a courtroom or adjacent areas in any proceeding or during a recess in the proceeding
in a trial court, the court of appeals, or the supreme court. These provisions
do not apply to a courtroom which the administrative director has designated
as a media courtroom.

4. Audio Pickup. Audio pickup for all media purposes must be made
from existing audio systems present in the court facility. The court will provide audio connections for the media at microphone level output.

5. Pooling. "Pooling" arrangements among the media required by
these limitations on equipment and personnel are the sole responsibility of the
media without resort to the court or court personnel to mediate any dispute
as to the appropriate media representative or equipment authorized to cover
a particular proceeding. In the absence of media agreement on disputed
equipment or personnel issues, the court may exclude all contesting media
from a proceeding.

6.   Audio Recording. Audio recording of court proceedings are permitted in all court proceedings open to the public, unless the judge presiding at the proceeding determines that the equipment produces a distracting sound or is otherwise obtrusive.

7.   Sound and Light Criteria.

(a) *Type of Television and Audio Equipment Allowed.* Only television and audio equipment which does not produce distracting sound or light may be used to cover judicial proceedings. If the judge presiding at a proceeding determines on motion of the parties or on the judge's own motion that the equipment produces distracting sound or light, the judge may order coverage to cease until the distraction has been eliminated. No artificial lighting device of any kind may be employed in connection with a television camera, and no camera may give any indication of whether it is or is not operating, such as by use of a red light to note operational status.
(b) *Type of Photography Equipment Allowed.* Electronic flash or flashcubes, as well as motorized cameras which produce distracting sound, are prohibited from use in any proceeding.

8.   Location of Equipment and Personnel.

(a) *Television Equipment.* Television camera equipment must be positioned in a location or locations in the courtroom or adjacent areas as designated by the judge presiding at the proceeding or the judge's designee.
(b) *Still Photography.* A still camera photographer shall position himself or herself in a location in the courtroom or adjacent areas as designated by the judge presiding at the proceeding or the judge's designee, and shall take photographs only from that location. The photographer's movements while taking pictures must be unobtrusive, and he or she should not, for example, assume body positions which would be inappropriate for other spectators.
(c) *Radio Broadcast Audio Equipment.* Radio broadcast audio equipment must be positioned in a location or locations in the courtroom or adjacent areas as designated by the judge presiding at the proceeding or the judge's designee.

9.   Movement of Equipment During Proceedings. Television and audio equipment and tripod-mounted still cameras must not be placed in or removed from the courtroom except prior to commencement or after adjournment of proceedings each day, or during a recess.

10. Conference of Counsel. To protect the attorney-client privilege and the effective right to counsel, there may be no broadcast of conferences which occur in the courtroom or the court facility between attorneys and their clients, between co-counsel of a client, or between counsel and the judge held at the bench. As a further precaution, due to the sensitivity of courtroom recording equipment, the judge presiding at the proceeding may inform counsel at the outset of the proceeding that the court will entertain requests from counsel to go off record for attorney-client conferences.

11. Behavior and Dress. Media representatives are expected to present a neat appearance in keeping with the dignity of the proceedings and be sufficiently familiar with court proceedings to conduct themselves so as not to interfere with the dignity of the proceedings, or to distract counsel or the court.

12. Credentials. Media coverage under this plan is allowed only by members of the working press and other media representatives. Media representatives must present their credentials upon request. Before coverage will be allowed, media representatives shall obtain identification from the area court administrator for the judicial district or the clerk of court in which the proceeding occurs after presenting such credentials as may be requested. Identification must be worn at all times when covering judicial proceedings.

13. Procedures for Obtaining Approval.

(a) *Request to Cover a Trial Court Proceeding.* Media personnel desiring to cover a proceeding before a trial court must submit an application to the judge presiding at the proceeding on a form provided by the area court administrator's office. If no judge has been assigned to the proceeding the application must be submitted to the area court administrator and will be forwarded to the judge immediately after assignment is made. . . .

14. The judge presiding over a proceeding may alter the foregoing provisions of this bulletin for that particular proceeding upon a showing of good cause.

15. Liaison. The area court administrator shall maintain communication with the media representatives with respect to coverage of trial court proceedings to ensure smooth working relationships. The clerk of the appellate courts shall maintain this communication with respect to coverage of supreme court or court of appeals proceedings.

CALIFORNIA GENERAL RULES—ALL COURTS

Rule 980. Photographing, Recording, and Broadcasting in Court

(a) [Introduction] The judiciary is responsible for ensuring the fair and equal administration of justice. The judiciary adjudicates controversies, both civil and criminal, in accordance with established legal procedures in the calmness and solemnity of the courtroom. Photographing, recording, and broadcasting of courtroom proceedings may be permitted as circumscribed in this rule if executed in a manner that ensures that the fairness and dignity of the proceedings are not adversely affected. This rule does not create a presumption for or against granting permission to photograph, record, or broadcast court proceedings.

(b) [Definitions] For the purposes of this rule.

(1) "Media coverage" means any photographing, recording, or broadcasting of court proceedings by the media using television, radio, photographic, or recording equipment;

(2) "Media" or "media agency" means any person or organization engaging in news gathering or reporting and includes any newspaper, radio or television station or network, news service, magazine, trade paper, in-house publication, professional journal, or other news reporting or news gathering agency;

(3) "Court" means the courtroom at issue, the courthouse, and its entrances and exits;

(4) "Judge" means the judicial officer or officers assigned to or presiding at the proceeding, except as provided in subdivision (e)(1) if no judge has been assigned.

(c) [Photographing, recording, and broadcasting prohibited] Except as provided in this rule, court proceedings shall not be photographed, recorded, or broadcast. This rule does not prohibit courts from photographing or videotaping sessions for judicial education or publications and is not intended to apply to closed-circuit television broadcasts solely within the courthouse or between court facilities if the broadcasts are controlled by the court and court personnel.

(d) [Personal recording devices] The judge may permit inconspicuous personal recording devices to be used by persons in a courtroom to make sound recordings as personal notes of the proceedings. A person proposing to use a recording device shall obtain permission from the judge in advance. The recordings shall not be used for any purpose other than as personal notes.

(e) [Media coverage] Media coverage shall be permitted only on written order of the judge as provided in this subdivision. The judge in his or her discretion may refuse, limit, or terminate media coverage. This rule does not otherwise limit or restrict the right of the media to cover and report court proceedings.

(1) (*Request for order*) The media may request an order permitting media coverage on a form approved by the Judicial Council. The form shall be filed at least five court days before the portion of the proceeding to be covered unless good cause is shown. A completed, proposed order on a form approved by the Judicial Council shall be filed with the request. The judge assigned to the proceeding shall rule upon the request. If no judge has been assigned, the request shall be submitted to the judge supervising the calendar department, and thereafter be ruled upon by the judge assigned to the proceeding. The clerk shall promptly notify the parties that a request has been filed.

(2) (*Hearing*) The judge may hold a hearing on the request or rule on the request without a hearing.

(3) (*Factors to be considered by the judge*) In ruling on the request, the judge shall consider the following factors:
(i)　　　Importance of maintaining public trust and confidence in the judicial system;
(ii)　　Importance of promoting public access to the judicial system;
(iii)　　Parties' support of or opposition to the request;
(iv)　　Nature of the case;
(v)　　Privacy rights of all participants in the proceeding, including witnesses, jurors, and victims;
(vi)　　Effect on any minor who is a party, prospective witness, victim, or other participant in the proceeding;
(vii)　　Effect on the parties' ability to select a fair and unbiased jury;
(viii)　Effect on any ongoing law enforcement activity in the case;
(ix)　　Effect on any unresolved identification issues;

(x)   Effect on any subsequent proceedings in the case;
(xi)   Effect of coverage on the willingness of witnesses to cooperate, including the risk that coverage will engender threats to the health or safety of any witness;
(xii)   Effect on excluded witnesses who would have access to the televised testimony of prior witnesses;
(xiii) Scope of the coverage and whether partial coverage might unfairly influence or distract the jury;
(xiv)   Difficulty of jury selection if a mistrial is declared;
(xv)   Security and dignity of the court;
(xvi)   Undue administrative or financial burden to the court or participants;
(xvii) Interference with neighboring courtrooms;
(xviii) Maintaining orderly conduct of the proceeding;
(xix)   Any other factor the judge deems relevant.

(4) (*Order permitting media coverage*) The judge ruling on the request to permit media coverage is not required to make findings or a statement of decision. The order may incorporate any local rule or order of the presiding or supervising judge regulating media activity outside of the courtroom. The judge may condition the order permitting media coverage on the media agency's agreement to pay any increased court-incurred costs resulting from the permitted media coverage (for example, for additional court security or utility service). Each media agency shall be responsible for ensuring that all its media personnel who cover the court proceeding know and follow the provisions of the court order and this rule.
(5) (*Modified order*) The order permitting media coverage may be modified or terminated on the judge's own motion or upon application to the judge without the necessity of a prior hearing or written findings. Notice of the application and any modification or termination ordered pursuant to the application shall be given to the parties and each media agency permitted by the previous order to cover the proceeding.

(6) (*Prohibited coverage*) The judge shall not permit media coverage of the following:
(i)   Proceedings held in chambers;
(ii)   Proceedings closed to the public;
(iii) Jury selection;
(iv)   Jurors or spectators; and
(v)   Conferences between an attorney and a client, witness, or aide, between attorneys, or between counsel and the judge at the bench.

(7) (*Equipment and personnel*) The judge may require media agencies to demonstrate that proposed personnel and equipment comply with this rule. The judge may specify the placement of media personnel and equipment to permit reasonable media coverage without disruption of the proceedings.

Unless the judge in his or her discretion orders otherwise, the following rules shall apply:
(i)   One television camera and one still photographer shall be permitted.
(ii)   The equipment used shall not produce distracting sound or light. Signal lights or devices to show when equipment is operating shall not be visible.
(iii)   An order permitting or requiring modification of existing sound or lighting systems is deemed to require that the modifications be installed, maintained, and removed without public expense or disruption of proceedings. Microphones and wiring shall be unobtrusively located in places approved by the judge and shall be operated by one person.
(iv)   Operators shall not move equipment or enter or leave the courtroom while the court is in session, or otherwise cause a distraction.
(v)   Equipment or clothing shall not bear the insignia or marking of a media agency.

(8) (*Media pooling*) If two or more media agencies of the same type request media coverage of a proceeding, they shall file a statement of agreed arrangements. If they are unable to agree, the judge may deny media coverage by that type of media agency.

(f) [Sanctions] Any violation of this rule or an order made under this rule is an unlawful interference with the proceedings of the court and may be the basis for an order terminating media coverage, a citation for contempt of court, or an order imposing monetary or other sanctions as provided by law.

(Adopted. eff. July 1, 1984. As amended, eff. Jan. 1, 1997.)

NEW YORK

Rules of the Chief Administrator
Standards and Administrative Policies

Part 131. Audio-visual Coverage of Judicial Proceedings

§ 131.1 Purpose; General Provisions

(a) These rules are promulgated to comport with the legislative finding that an enhanced public understanding of the judicial system is important in maintaining a high level of public confidence in the judiciary, and with the legislative concern that cameras in the courts be compatible with the fair administration of justice.

(b) These rules shall be effective for any period when audio-visual coverage in the trial courts is authorized by law and shall apply to all counties in the State.

(c) Nothing in these rules is intended to restrict any pre-existing right of the news media to appear at and to report on judicial proceedings in accordance with law.

(d) Nothing in these rules is intended to restrict the power and discretion of the presiding trial judge to control the conduct of judicial proceedings.

(e) No judicial proceeding shall be scheduled, delayed, reenacted or continued at the request of, or for the convenience of the news media.

(f) In addition to their specific responsibilities as provided in these rules, all presiding trial judges and all administrative judges shall take whatever steps are necessary to insure that audio-visual coverage is conducted without disruption of court activities, without detracting from or interfering with the dignity or decorum of the court, courtrooms and court facilities, without compromise of the safety of persons having business before the court, and without adversely affecting the administration of justice.

§ 131.2 Definitions

For purposes of this Part:

(a) "Administrative judge" shall mean the administrative judge of each judicial district; . . .

(b) "Audio-visual coverage" or "coverage" shall mean the electronic broadcasting or other transmission to the public of radio or television signals from the courtroom, the recording of sound or light in the courtroom for later transmission or reproduction, or the taking of still or motion pictures in the courtroom by the news media.

(c) "News media" shall mean any news reporting or news gathering agency and any employee or agent associated with such agency, including television, radio, radio and television networks, news services, newspapers, magazines, trade papers, in-house publications, professional journals, or any other news reporting or news gathering agency, the function of which is to inform the public or some segment thereof.

(d) "Presiding trial judge" shall mean the justice or judge presiding over judicial proceedings at which audio-visual coverage is authorized pursuant to this Part.

(e) "Covert or undercover capacity" shall mean law enforcement activity involving criminal investigation by peace officers or police officers who usually and customarily wear no uniform, badge, or other official identification in public view.

(f) "Judicial proceedings" shall mean the proceedings of a court or a judge thereof conducted in a courtroom or any other facility being used as a courtroom.

(g) "Child" shall mean a person who has not attained the age of sixteen years.

(h) "Arraignment" shall have the same meaning as such term is defined in subdivision nine of section 1.20 of the Criminal Procedure Law.

(i) "Suppression hearing" shall mean a hearing on a motion made pursuant to the provisions of section 710.20 of the Criminal Procedure Law; a hearing on a motion to determine the admissibility of any prior criminal, vicious or immoral acts of a defendant; and any other hearing held to determine the admissibility of evidence.

(j) "Nonparty witness" shall mean any witness in a criminal trial proceeding who is not a party to such proceeding; except an expert or professional witness, a peace or police officer who acted in the course of his or her duties and was not acting in a covert or undercover capacity in connection with the instant court proceedings, or any government official acting in an official capacity, shall not be deemed to be a "nonparty witness".

(k) "Visually obscured" shall mean that the face of a participant in a criminal trial proceeding shall either not be shown or shall be rendered visually unrecognizable to the viewer of such proceeding by means of special editing by the news media.

§ 131.3 Application for Audio Visual Coverage

(a) Coverage of judicial proceedings shall be permitted only upon order of the presiding trial judge approving an application made by a representative of the news media for permission to conduct such coverage.

(b)(1) Except as provided in paragraph two of this subdivision, an application for permission to conduct coverage of a judicial proceeding shall be made to the presiding trial judge not less than seven days before the scheduled commencement of that proceeding. Where circumstances are such that an applicant cannot reasonably apply more than seven days before commencement of the proceedings, the presiding trial judge may shorten the time period. The application shall be in writing and shall specify such proceeding with sufficient particularity to assist the presiding trial judge in considering the application and shall set forth which of the types of coverage described in subdivision (b) of section 131.2 is sought, including whether live coverage is sought. Upon receipt of any application, the presiding trial judge shall cause all parties to the proceeding to be notified thereof.

(2) An application for permission to conduct coverage of an arraignment in a criminal case or of any other proceeding after it has commenced may be made to the presiding trial judge at any time and shall be otherwise subject to the provisions of paragraph one hereof.

(3) Each application shall relate to one case or proceeding only, unless the presiding trial judge permits otherwise.

(c) Where more than one representative of the news media makes an application for coverage of the same judicial proceeding, such applications shall be consolidated and treated as one.

§ 131.4 Determination of the Application

(a)   Upon receipt of an application pursuant to section 131.3, the presiding trial judge shall conduct such review as may be appropriate, including:

(1)   consultation with the news media applicant;

(2)   consultation with counsel to all parties to the proceeding of which coverage is sought, who shall be responsible for identifying any concerns or objections of the parties, prospective witnesses, and victims, if any, with respect to the proposed coverage, and advising the court thereof;

(3)   review of all statements or affidavits presented to the presiding trial judge concerning the proposed coverage.

Where the proceedings of which coverage is sought involve a child, a victim, a prospective witness, or a party, any of whom object to such coverage, and in any other appropriate instance, the presiding trial judge may hold such conferences and conduct any direct inquiry as may be fitting.

(b)(1)   Except as otherwise provided in paragraphs two and three hereof or section 131.8 of these rules, consent of the parties, prospective witnesses, victims, or other participants in judicial proceedings of which coverage is sought is not required for approval of an application for such coverage.

(2)   An application for audio-visual coverage of a trial proceeding in which a jury is sitting, made after commencement of such proceeding, shall not be approved unless counsel to all parties to such proceeding consent to such coverage; provided, however, this paragraph shall not apply where coverage is sought only of the verdict or sentencing, or both, in such proceeding.

(3)   Counsel to each party in a criminal trial proceeding shall advise each nonparty witness that he or she has the right to request that his or her image be visually obscured during said witness' testimony, and upon such request the presiding trial judge shall order the news media to visually obscure the visual image of the witness in any and all audio-visual coverage of the judicial proceeding.

(c)   In determining an application for coverage, the presiding trial judge shall consider all relevant factors, including but not limited to:

(1)   the type of case involved;

(2)   whether the coverage would cause harm to any participant;

(3)   whether the coverage would interfere with the fair administration of justice, the advancement of a fair trial, or the rights of the parties;

(4)   whether any order directing the exclusion of witnesses from the courtroom prior to their testimony could be rendered substantially inef-

fective by allowing audio-visual coverage that could be viewed by such witnesses to the detriment of any party;

(5) whether the coverage would interfere with any law enforcement activity;

(6) whether the proceedings would involve lewd or scandalous matters;

(7) the objections of any of the parties, prospective witnesses, victims, or other participants in the proceeding of which coverage is sought;

(8) the physical structure of the courtroom and the likelihood that any equipment required to conduct coverage of proceedings can be installed and operated without disturbance to those proceedings or any other proceedings in the courthouse; and

(9) the extent to which the coverage would be barred by law in the judicial proceeding of which coverage is sought.

The presiding trial judge also shall consider and give great weight to the fact that any party, prospective witness, victim, or other participant in the proceeding is a child.

(d) Following review of an application for coverage of a judicial proceeding, the presiding trial judge, as soon as practicable, shall issue an order, in writing, approving such application, in whole or in part, or denying it. Such order shall contain any restrictions imposed by the judge on the audio-visual coverage and shall contain a statement advising the parties that any violation of the order is punishable by contempt pursuant to article nineteen of the Judiciary Law. Such order shall be included in the record of such proceedings and, unless it wholly approves the application and no party, victim or prospective witness objected to coverage, it shall state the basis for its determination.

(e) Before denying an application for coverage, the presiding trial judge shall consider whether such coverage properly could be approved with the imposition of special limitations, including but not limited to:

(1) delayed broadcast of the proceedings subject to coverage, provided, however, where delayed broadcast is directed, it shall be only for the purpose of assisting the news media to comply with the restrictions on coverage provided by law or by the presiding trial judge;

(2) modification or prohibition of audio-visual coverage of individual parties, witnesses, or other trial participants, or portions of the proceedings; or

(3) modification or prohibition of video coverage of individual parties, witnesses. or other trial participants, or portions of the proceedings.

§ 131.5 Review

(a) Any order determining an application for permission to provide coverage, rendered pursuant to subdivision (d) of section 131.4 of this part, shall be subject to review by the administrative judge in such form, including telephone conference, as he or she may determine, upon the request of a person who is aggrieved thereby and who is either:
(1) a news media applicant; or
(2) a party, victim, or prospective witness who objected to coverage.

(b) Upon review of a presiding trial judge's order determining an application for permission to provide coverage, the administrative judge shall uphold such order unless it is found that the order reflects an abuse of discretion by the presiding trial judge, in which event the administrative judge may direct such modification of the presiding trial judge's order as may be deemed appropriate. Any order directing a modification or overruling a presiding trial judge's order determining an application for coverage shall be in writing.

(c) No judicial proceeding shall be delayed or continued to allow for review by an administrative judge of an order denying coverage in whole or in part.

(d) This section shall authorize review by the administrative judge only of a presiding trial judge's order pursuant to paragraph (b) of subdivision three of section 218 of the Judiciary Law determining an application for permission to provide coverage of judicial proceedings and shall not authorize review of any other orders or decisions of the presiding trial judge relating to such coverage.

§ 131.6 Mandatory Pretrial Conference

(a) Where a presiding trial judge has approved, in whole or in part, an application for coverage of any judicial proceeding, the judge, before any such coverage is to begin, shall conduct a pretrial conference for the purpose of reviewing, with counsel to all parties to the proceeding and with representatives of the news media who will provide such coverage, any objections to coverage that have been raised, the scope of coverage to be permitted, the nature and extent of the technical equipment and personnel to be deployed, and the restrictions on coverage to be observed. The court may include in the conference any other person whom it deems appropriate, including prospective witnesses and their representatives. In an appropriate case, the presiding trial judge may conduct the pretrial conference concurrently with any consultations or conferences authorized by subdivision (a) of section 131.4.

(b) Where two or more representatives of the news media are parties to an approved application for coverage, no such coverage may begin until all such representatives have agreed upon a pooling arrangement for their respective news media prior to the pretrial conference. Such pooling arrangement shall include the designation of pool operators and replacement pool operators for the electronic and motion picture media and for the still photography media, as appropriate. It also shall include procedures for the cost sharing and dissemination of audio-visual material and shall make due provision for educational users' needs for full coverage of entire proceedings. The presiding trial judge shall not be called upon to mediate or resolve any dispute as to such arrangement. Nothing herein shall prohibit a person or organization that was not party to an approved application for coverage from making appropriate arrangements with the pool operator to be given access to the audio-visual material produced by the pool.

(c) In determining the scope of coverage to be permitted, the presiding trial judge shall be guided by a consideration of all relevant factors, including those prescribed in subdivision (c) of section 131.4 of this part. Wherever necessary or appropriate, the presiding trial judge shall, at any time before or during the proceeding, proscribe coverage or modify, expand, impose, or remove special limitations on coverage, such as those prescribed in subdivision (e) of section 131.4

§ 131.7 Use and Deployment of Equipment and Personnel by the News Media
(a) Limitations Upon Use of Equipment and Personnel in the Courtroom.

(1) No more than two electronic or motion picture cameras and two camera operators shall be permitted in any proceeding.

(2) No more than one photographer to operate two still cameras, with not more than two lenses for each camera, shall be permitted in any proceeding.

(3) No more than one audio system for broadcast purposes shall be permitted in any proceeding. Audio pickup for all news media purposes shall be effectuated through existing audio systems in the court facility. If no technically suitable audio system is available, microphones and related wiring essential for media purposes shall be supplied by those persons providing coverage. Any microphones and sound wiring shall be unobtrusive and placed where designated by the presiding trial judge.

(4) Notwithstanding the provisions of paragraphs one, two, and three of this subdivision, the presiding trial judge on a finding of special circumstances may modify any restriction on the amount of equipment or number of operating personnel in the courtroom, compatible with the dignity of the court or the judicial process.

(b) Sound and Light Criteria.
(1) Only electronic and motion picture cameras, audio equipment, and still camera equipment that do not produce distracting sound or light may be employed to cover judicial proceedings. . . .
(2) Use of equipment other than that authorized . . . may be permitted by the presiding trial judge provided the judge is satisfied that the equipment sought to be utilized meets the sound and light criteria specified in paragraph one of this subdivision. A failure to obtain advance approval shall preclude use of such equipment in the coverage of the judicial proceeding.
(3) No motorized drives, moving lights, flash attachments, or sudden lighting changes shall be permitted during coverage of judicial proceedings.
(4) No light or signal visible or audible to trial participants shall be used on any equipment during coverage to indicate whether it is operating.
(5) With the concurrence of the presiding trial judge and the administrative judge, modifications and additions may be made in light sources existing in the court facility, provided such modifications or additions are installed and maintained at media expense and are not distracting or otherwise offensive.

(c) Location of Equipment and Personnel. Electronic and motion picture cameras, still cameras, and camera personnel shall be positioned in such locations as shall be designated by the presiding trial judge. The areas designated shall provide the news media with reasonable access to the persons they wish to cover while causing the least possible interference with court proceedings. Equipment that is not necessary for audiovisual coverage from inside the courtroom shall be located in an area outside the courtroom.

(d) Movement of Equipment and Media Personnel. During the proceedings, operating personnel shall not move about, nor shall there be placement, movement or removal of equipment, or the changing of film, film magazines or lenses. All such activities shall take place each day before the proceeding begins, after it ends, or during a recess.

(e) Identifying Insignia. Identifying marks, call letters, words, and symbols shall be concealed on all equipment. Persons operating such equipment shall not display any identifying insignia on their clothing.

(f) [Other Restrictions] The presiding trial judge may impose any other restrictions on the use and development of equipment and personnel as may be appropriate.

§ 131.8 Additional Restrictions on Coverage

(a) No audio pickup or audio broadcast of conferences that occur in a court facility between attorneys and their clients, between co-counsel of a client, or between counsel and the presiding trial judge, shall be permitted without the prior express consent of all participants in the conference.

(b) No conference in chambers shall be subject to coverage.

(c) No coverage of the selection of the prospective jury during voir dire shall be permitted.

(d) No coverage of the jury, or of any juror or alternate juror, while in the jury box, in the courtroom, in the jury deliberation room, or during recess, or while going to or from the deliberation room at any time, shall be permitted provided, however, that, upon consent of the foreperson of a jury, the presiding trial judge may, in his or her discretion, permit audio coverage of such foreperson delivering a verdict.

(e) No coverage shall be permitted of a witness, who as a peace officer or police officer acted in a covert or undercover capacity in connection with the proceedings being covered, without the prior written consent of such witness.

(f) No coverage shall be permitted of a witness, who as a peace officer or police officer is currently engaged in a covert or undercover capacity, without the prior written consent of such witness.

(g) No coverage shall be permitted of the victim in a prosecution for rape, sodomy, sexual abuse, or other sex offense under article one hundred thirty or section 255.25 of the Penal Law; notwithstanding the initial approval of a request for audio-visual coverage of such a proceeding, the presiding trial judge shall have discretion throughout the proceeding to limit any coverage that would identify the victim, except that said victim can request of the presiding trial judge that audio-visual coverage be permitted of his or her testimony, or in the alternative the victim can request that coverage of his or her testimony be permitted but that his or her image shall be visually obscured by the news media, and the presiding trial judge in this or her discretion shall grant the request of the victim for the coverage specified.

(h) No coverage of any participant shall be permitted if the presiding trial judge finds that such coverage is liable to endanger the safety of any person.

(i) No coverage of any judicial proceedings that are by law closed to the public, or that may be closed to the public and that have been closed by the presiding trial judge, shall be permitted.

(j) No coverage of any arraignment or suppression hearing shall be permitted, without the prior consent of counsel to all parties to the proceeding; provided, however, where a party is not yet represented by counsel, consent may not be given unless the party has been advised of his or her right to the aid of counsel pursuant to subdivision four of section 170.10 or 180.10 of the Criminal Procedure Law and the party has affirmatively elected to proceed without counsel at such proceeding.

(k) No audio-visual coverage shall be permitted which focuses on or features a family member of a victim or a party in the trial of a criminal case, except while such family member is testifying. Audio-visual coverage operators shall make all reasonable efforts to determine the identity of such persons, so that such coverage shall not occur.
The restrictions specified in subdivisions (a) through (k) may not be waived or modified except as provided herein.

§ 131.9 Supervision of Audio-Visual Coverage
(a) Coverage of judicial proceedings shall be subject to the continuing supervision of the presiding trial judge. No coverage shall take place within the courtroom, whether during recesses or at any other time, when the presiding trial judge is not present and presiding.
(b) Notwithstanding the approval of an application for permission to provide coverage of judicial proceedings, the presiding trial judge shall have discretion throughout such proceedings to revoke such approval or to limit the coverage authorized in any way. In the exercise of this discretion, the presiding trial judge shall be especially sensitive and responsive to the needs and concerns of all parties, victims, witnesses, and other par-

ticipants in such proceedings, particularly where the proceedings unnecessarily threaten the privacy or sensibilities of victims, or where they involve children or sex offenses or other matters that may be lewd or scandalous. The presiding trial judge shall be under a continuing obligation to order the discontinuation or modification of coverage where necessary to shield the identity or otherwise insure the protection of any such person, party, witness, or victim, or in order to preserve the welfare of a child.

(c) Counsel to each party in a trial proceeding that is subject to coverage shall inquire of each witness that he or she intends to call regarding any concerns or objections such witness might have with respect to coverage. Where counsel thereby is advised that a witness objects to coverage, counsel shall so notify the presiding trial judge.

§ 131.10 Cooperation with Committee

All officers and employees of the Unified Court system, and all participants in proceedings where audio-visual coverage was permitted, including judges, attorneys and jurors, shall cooperate with the committee to review audio-visual coverage of court proceedings in connection with the committee's review of the impact of audio-visual coverage on such proceedings.

§ 131.11 Appellate Courts

These rules shall not apply to coverage of proceedings in appellate courts or affect the rules governing such coverage contained in Part 29 of the Rules of the Chief Judge (22 NYCRR Part 29).

§ 131.12 Forms

The Chief Administrator will promulgate and make available forms for applications pursuant to section 131.3 and for judicial orders pursuant to section 131.4

§ 131.13 Acceptable Equipment

The following equipment shall be deemed acceptable for use in audio-visual coverage of trial court proceedings pursuant to Part 131 of the Rules of the Chief Administrator of the Courts:

(a) Video Cameras.

Sony: BVP-3, BVP-3A, BVP-3U, BVP-5, BVP-30, BVP-33Am, BVP-50J, BVP-110, BVP-150, BVP-250, BVP-300, BVU-300, BVV-1, BVV-5, DXC-3000, M-3

Ikegami: HL-79, HL-79D, HL-79E, HL-83, HL-95, ITC-170, SP-3A, 75-D, 79-E, 95, 730, 730a, 730ap

JVC: KY–1900, KY–2000, KY–2700, BY–110
RCA: TK–76
Thompson: 501, 601
NEC: SP–3A
Sharp: XC–800
Panasonic: X–100 (the recam system in a camera/recorder combination)
Ampex: Betacam

(b) Still Cameras.
Leica: M
Nikon: FE, F–3, FM–2, 2000
Canon: F–1, T–90

(c) Any other audio or video equipment may be used with the permission of the presiding trial judge.

Media Advisories

MEDIA ADVISORY
McMartin Trial

Taking Verdicts in the McMartin Trial

Place:

1 — Verdicts will be taken in Department 101, 9th Floor
[NOTE: NO ONE WILL BE PERMITTED TO LEAVE UNTIL ALL VERDICTS HAVE BEEN RECEIVED;
NOTE: MOST OF THE SEATING IS RESERVED FOR PARTICIPANTS AND MEDIA]
2 — Taking of verdicts can be seen on a monitor in the courtroom across the hall, Department 105.
[ENTRY AND EXIT WILL BE PERMITTED AT ANY TIME.]

Procedure:

1 — Courtroom opens for reserved seating and then general seating
2 — Session begins with the court outlining final procedures
3 — JURY ENTERS; court inquires whether all verdicts have been reached
4 — If the jury is deadlocked on any count, determine whether further deliberations are necessary
5 — ACCEPTING THE VERDICTS: As to those verdicts which have been reached
a — Court determines the validity of the forms and confers with counsel on any errors
b — Clerk reads the verdicts, using a "block form" announcement system (if all verdicts as to either defendant are the same, they will be read as a group)
c — Jurors are polled as to verdicts
[EXIT FROM DEPARTMENT 101 IS PERMITTED AT THIS TIME ONLY]
6 — Jurors are thanked for their service and encouraged to remain for interviews
7 — Final legal proceedings are concluded as required by law

8 — INTERVIEWS ARE HELD

a — Jurors meet with attorneys in jury room while Department 101 is set up for video interviews

b — During this time interviews of spectators will be permitted in Department 101

c — Attorneys may be interviewed upon leaving the jury room in Department 101

d — Jurors willing to be photographed will be interviewed in Department 101 at counsel table

e — Jurors *not willing* to be photographed during the interviews will be escorted to Department 105 across the hall for media interviews (cameras prohibited)

f — Jurors unwilling to be interviewed by the media will be invited to meet with the judge in Chambers

MEDIA ADVISORY REGARDING ANNOUNCEMENT OF BUCKEY JURY VERDICT

1. The jury in the Raymond Buckey retrial will announce its verdict at _____ on _____ in the courtroom of Los Angeles Superior Court Judge Stanley Weisberg, Dept. 111, on the 11th floor of the Criminal Courts Building, 210 W. Temple St., in downtown Los Angeles.

2. A list of news organizations allowed to have a representative inside the courtroom has previously been compiled. A bailiff will be stationed outside the courtroom and will require each reporter to state the name of the news organization with which he/she is affiliated before they can enter the courtroom.

3. KNBC-TV will provide pooled TV coverage of the verdict announcement. Only one TV camera will be allowed inside the courtroom when the verdict announcement is read.

4. A photographer from Associated Press (AP) and a photographer from the *Los Angeles Times* will be the only photographers allowed inside the courtroom during the verdict announcement and any subsequent news conference.

5. With the exception of the photographers and TV camera operators all other representatives of news organizations must remain seated at all times during the jury announcement and subsequent courtroom news conference.

6. Following the verdict announcement the courtroom will be cleared and the judge will ask jurors if they wish to take part in a news conference. Following this discussion reporters will be allowed to reenter the courtroom to question jurors who have consented to be interviewed and photographed. Before this news conference begins a second TV camera from KCBS-TV will

be allowed inside the courtroom to enable camera operators to film the reporters asking questions as well as the jurors. During the news conference reporters who wish to ask questions will raise their hands and be recognized to address a specific juror or the jurors generally.

7. Jurors taking part in the news conference will be the only persons who will be allowed to grant interviews inside the courtroom. Interviews with lawyers and others involved in the case must be conducted outside of the courtroom.

8. Following the verdict announcement reporters will be allowed to conduct interviews on the 11th floor of the Criminal Courts Building. However, reporters conducting hallway interviews must comply with bailiffs' security and crowd control procedures.

9. Following the verdict announcement prosecutors in the case and other representatives of the District Attorney's Office will be available for interviews in the District Attorney's Office on the 18th floor of the Criminal Courts Building.

Media Advisory Regarding Buckey Retrial

The jury in the Raymond Buckey retrial is set to begin deliberating on Monday, July 9.

When the jury announces its verdict, space in the courtroom will be extremely limited. To ensure that all news organizations that wish to cover the announcement will have access to the courtroom, only one reporter from each organization will be allowed inside the courtroom when the verdict is read.

A bailiff stationed outside the courtroom will have a list of news organizations that will be allowed inside, and any organization that is not listed will be denied entry.

The list is being compiled now. If your organization wants to be included, you must contact Rebecca Kuzins, Los Angeles Superior Court Public Information Officer, at 213-974-5565, *no later than 5 p.m. Wed. July 11.*

Juror Prescreening Questionnaire and Judge's Instructions

VOIR DIRE

United States v. Barry, Cr. No. 90-0068

Ladies and Gentlemen:

We are about to select a jury for the trial of the case of *United States v. Marion S. Barry, Jr.* As you may know, 12 of you will be selected as the jury, and several of you will be asked to serve as alternates in the event a member of the jury should have to be excused before the jury retires to deliberate.

To assist counsel in the selection process, I shall ask the courtroom deputy clerk to call the roll of the panel. As your name is called, please stand and announce yourself as "present."

(ROLL CALL)

This is a criminal case. The defendant is Marion S. Barry, Jr. (Barry stands). The case is being prosecuted by Assistant United States Attorneys Judith Retchin and Richard Roberts. (AUSAs stand). Mr. Barry is being defended by R. Kenneth Mundy and Robert W. Mance. (Mundy and Mance stand.)

You have previously been advised that the jury, once selected, will be "sequestered," that is, it will be kept together and housed at public expense, but isolated from the news media and the public generally to insure that it will not be improperly influenced. This jury will not, however, be "anonymous." In other words, the identities of the jurors will be known to the press and the public.

The trial itself is expected to take approximately one month.

The process we are about to engage in is called *voir dire*. Its purpose is to assure that the jury ultimately empaneled to hear this case is comprised of people who are unbiased and unprejudiced, who can fairly and impartially decide the facts of the case based solely upon the evidence presented in this courtroom, and who will then follow my instructions as to the law applicable to those facts.

The process is going to require that you disclose publicly a certain amount of personal information about yourselves and your families that you might otherwise want to keep to yourself. It is, unfortunately, necessary. In special circumstances exceptions may sometimes be made to insure the privacy of your answers. You will have to ask me at the appropriate time if you think you have a valid reason to ask for an exception.

We will proceed as follows:

The U.S. Marshals will hand out questionnaires which I will ask you to fill out. Please take your time and answer all questions as completely and accurately as you can. When you have completed and signed your questionnaire, return it to a Marshal who will turn them all over to me. You will then be excused to return to the Jurors' Lounge. You should advise the person in charge that you have completed your questionnaire, and you will then be excused for the remainder of the day.

Panel members whose last names begin with the letters "A" through "C" should report back to the Jurors' Lounge tomorrow morning at 9:15 a.m. Other panel members will be given instructions as to when they should report back.

When you report back, you will be brought down in small groups from the Jurors' Lounge, or from a nearby courtroom, by a U.S. Marshal to the jury room immediately behind this courtroom and, one by one, brought out into the courtroom to take the witness stand and answer certain further questions which your answers on the questionnaire may suggest to the lawyers and to me to be appropriate. Then, once again, you will be excused to return to the Jurors' Lounge for further instructions.

After all prospective jurors brought in that day have been questioned individually, at the end of each day the lawyers and I will confer to decide if any should be excused for "cause," that is, for any legally sufficient reason. If I rule that any prospective juror is to be excused for "cause," that particular panel member will be told and released from further service in this case.

After all prospective jurors have been questioned individually, the lawyers will be permitted to exercise their "peremptory" challenges upon those remaining on the panel. Once the "peremptory" challenges have been exhausted, a jury of 12 persons and six alternates will be seated. The jurors will be numbered "one" through "eighteen," and will not be told until the conclusion of the trial which of them are the 12 primary jurors and which are the six alternates.

The process will take some time, as you can see. You will simply have to be patient while we are concerned with matters that don't involve you personally. I suggest you bring something to read while you wait.

It is estimated by the lawyers that it will take about four weeks to try the case once the jury has been selected. You should all have received a letter asking you to request to be excused in advance if a case of that length would cause you any extraordinary personal hardship. Those who responded that it would, and whose reasons were found to be sufficient, have already been excused. If any of you has a reason now to believe that you would suffer some exceptional hardship, other than the inconvenience jury service causes everyone, to sit on a case of this duration and under sequestration, please give specific reasons in your response to the pertinent question on the questionnaire.

This case, and many of the events that preceded it, have received a substantial amount of publicity in the newspapers, magazines, and on radio and television. That you are aware of the publicity does not, by itself, disqualify you. If, however, that publicity has caused you to form some opinions about the case already, and you think you might be unable to put those opinions aside entirely and listen to the evidence with an open mind, please be candid about it in your answers to the relevant questions on the questionnaire and in open court.

After the trial starts it is absolutely essential that the jurors who are chosen for the case learn nothing whatsoever about it from any source other than the evidence presented in this courtroom. The jury will be obliged, to that end, not to read, listen to, or watch any news accounts of the trial, nor to talk, or let anyone else, including one another, talk to them, about any aspect of the case until it is over.

I also instruct you that, for so long as we are engaged in the process of jury selection, you are not to read, listen to, or watch any news accounts of the case or of these proceedings, nor to talk, or let any else talk to you, about any aspect of the case. This includes each other. As we conduct the *voir dire* over the next several days, you will naturally be meeting each other and talking among yourselves. It is extremely important, however, that you do not discuss this case, including the *voir dire*. Do not share anything you may know, or any opinions or impressions you may have, with any other prospective juror. Do not talk about your individual answers to the questionnaire, or to any questions you are asked in open court.

Both the government and Mr. Barry are entitled to have a completely fair, open-minded and impartial jury sit in judgment upon this case. You will be asked many questions intended to enable me and the lawyers to draw some inferences about your attitudes. As you answer the questions, I ask you to ask yourself directly: do I have any reason to question my own impartiality; to suspect that I might be prejudiced for or against the government or the defendant for any reason? In other words, are you aware of anything which might prevent you from rendering a fair and impartial verdict based solely upon the evidence to be presented in this courtroom and the instructions I will give you at the end of the trial as to the law applicable to the case? If so, please be truthful in making that known to us.

(DISTRIBUTE QUESTIONNAIRES)

United States District Court
for the District of Columbia

UNITED STATES OF AMERICA

v.

MARION S. BARRY, JR.

Criminal Case No. 90-0068
(TPJ)

Prospective Juror Questionnaire
Instructions

You are now a prospective juror in a criminal case known as *United States v. Marion S. Barry, Jr.* The trial is expected to begin immediately after selection of a jury.

The purpose of this questionnaire is to assist the Court and attorneys to select a fair and impartial jury to hear and decide this case. The defendant, Marion S. Barry, Jr., has been charged with violating certain federal laws relating to possession of a controlled substance, cocaine, and making false statements to the grand jury while under oath. Mr. Barry has denied the charges and entered a plea of not guilty.

Please answer each question below as completely and accurately as you can. Complete candor is expected of you. Truthful and non-evasive answers are necessary to ensure that both the government and the defense have a meaningful opportunity to satisfy themselves that a fair and impartial jury has been seated. Your answers should enable the Court and the lawyers to determine whether you will be able to act as an objective and unbiased decision-maker. By fully answering each question you will save a great deal of time later on for the Court and the attorneys, as well as yourself and fellow prospective jurors.

You are required to sign your questionnaire, and your answers are considered to be statements given to the Court under oath. If the space provided for you is not sufficient for a full answer to any question, you may simply continue that answer on one of the blank pages at the end. Be sure to write the question number next to the remainder of your answer to make clear which question you are continuing to answer. Please write legibly.

You will be asked follow-up questions in open court regarding your answers on this questionnaire at the time you are separately examined outside of the presence of other prospective jurors. If there is any deeply personal or confidential information called for by these questions that you believe you have a legitimate reason to keep out of the public domain, and you wish to discuss those matters privately with the Court and counsel, you may be per-

mitted to do so, but you must make a request for privacy known to the Court
in your answer to Question No. 69 or at the time you are being questioned
individually.

Now that you are a prospective juror it is important that, except as part of
these proceedings, you are not exposed to any outside information about this
case. For this reason, you are not to read, watch or listen to press reports relating to this case or the trial. You are also instructed not to discuss the case with
anyone, including another juror, or to let anyone talk to you about the case.

Thomas Penfield Jackson
U.S. District Judge

United States District Court
for the District of Columbia

UNITED STATES OF AMERICA

v.

MARION S. BARRY, JR.

Criminal Case No. 90-0068
(TPJ)

QUESTIONNAIRE
Part I

Juror No. _____

1. Full Name: _____
2. Place and date of birth: _____
3. Citizenship: _____
4. Present Address: _____

      _____

      _____

5. Do you have any difficulty in reading, speaking, or understanding the written or spoken English language? _____. If "yes," please explain briefly.

6. Do you have any significant problems with your hearing or your eyesight? _____. If "yes," please explain briefly.
7. How long have you lived at your present address? _____
8. How long have you lived in the District of Columbia? _____
9. Are you a registered voter? _____. If so, where are you registered? _____. How are you registered (i.e., Democrat, Republican, Independent, or other)?
10. Are you presently married? _____. If "yes," what is the full name of your spouse? _____. How long have you been married? _____

11. If your spouse is employed or has been employed, who is (or was) his or her employer? _____
12. If previously married, please state the full names and occupations of all former spouses. _____

      _____

      _____

13. If you have children, please state their full names and ages, and occupations (if working).

Child's name	Age	Occupation
_____	_____	_____
_____	_____	_____
_____	_____	_____

14. If you are presently employed, by whom and where are you employed?

_____

_____ .

What is (or was) your principal occupation? _____ .
What is (or was) the nature of your work? _____ .
List all places at which you have worked full-time for as long as three consecutive years (including military service).

_____ .

_____ .

_____ .

_____ .

If you are not currently working, are you temporarily unemployed? _____ retired? _____ other?_____

15. How many years of formal education have you had? _____ .
What is the name of the last full-time school you attended?

_____ .

When did you last attend school? _____ .

16. Do you have any chronic or major health problem[s]? _____ . If "yes," please explain briefly.

17. Does any member of your household have any chronic or major health problem[s]? _____ . If "yes," please explain briefly.

18. You have been advised that the jury will be sequestered once trial begins, and that the trial is expected to take approximately one month. Is there any reason that has not previously been ruled on by the Court why you would suffer exceptional personal hardship if selected to sit as a juror in this case? _____ . If "yes," please explain briefly.

Part II

19. Do you, to your knowledge, have any personal or family connection of any sort with the defendant Marion S. Barry, Jr.? _____. With the United States Attorney for the District of Columbia, Jay P. Stephens, or his staff, including Assistant United States Attorneys Judith Retchin and Richard Roberts? _____. With defense attorneys R. Kenneth Mundy, Reginald L. Holt, Robert W. Mance, or Karen McDonald? _____. If any answer is "yes," please explain briefly.

20. The following is a partial list of people who *may* be called as witnesses in this case. Do you, to your knowledge, have any personal, family, or business connection of any sort with any of them? If " yes," please *circle the numbers* of each of those with whom you may have such a connection.

1.	Albert Arrington	25.	David Meyerson
2.	Samad Arshadi	26.	Arthur J. Mitchell
3.	Maandria Askia	27.	Hassan Mohammadi
4.	Maria Barba	28.	Lloyd Moore
5.	Albert Benjamin	29.	Mary Moore
6.	Orlando Berrios	30.	Mertine Moore
7.	Johnann Coleman	31.	Rasheeda Moore
8.	Doris Crenshaw	32.	Sherle Moore
9.	Carthur Drake	33.	John Olsen
10.	Fred Gaskins	34.	James Pawlik
11.	Marcia Griffin	35.	Lydia Pearson
12.	Ronald Harvey	36.	Edward Prichard
13.	Dixie Hedrington	37.	Marshall Reel
14.	Tivia Hoppenstein	38.	Robin Ridgeway
15.	Carole Jackson	39.	Darrel Sabbs
16.	Wanda King	40.	Sukhjit Singh
17.	Charles Lewis	41.	Bettye Smith
18.	Thomas Lynch	42.	Theresa Southerland
19.	Roger Martz	43.	Wanda Stansbury
20.	Charles Mason	44.	James Stays
21.	Zenna Mathis	45.	Frank Steele
22.	Linda Maynard	46.	Jonetta Vincent
23.	Rose M. McCarthy	47.	Clifton West
24.	James McWilliams	48.	Peter Wubbenhorst

21. Do you have any first-hand knowledge of the facts of this case?_____. If "yes," please explain briefly.

22. As you may be aware, this case, and certain events leading up to it, have received considerable publicity, both before and after the indictment was filed. Are you aware of the publicity? _____ . If "yes," please describe briefly what you remember about it.

23. Have you formed any personal opinions based upon the publicity? _____. If "yes," please explain briefly.

24. Specifically, have you formed any opinions whatsoever, based on information from any source, of Mr. Barry's guilt or innocence of anything? _____. If "yes," please explain briefly.

25. The jury will be instructed that the defendant is presumed to be innocent throughout the trial, and that he cannot be found guilty of any offense until the government has proven each element of that offense beyond a reasonable doubt. Would you find it difficult for any reason to follow that instruction? _____. If "yes," please explain briefly.

26. The jury will be instructed not to read, watch, or listen to any news accounts of this trial whatsoever until it is over, and not to talk to anyone about the case, not even to one another, until it retires to deliberate upon its verdict. Would you find it difficult to follow such an instruction for any reasons? _____. If "yes," please explain briefly.

27. What TV or radio news programs do you watch or listen to fairly regularly?

28. What newspapers or magazines do you read fairly regularly?

Part III

29. Did you vote in the national elections in 1988? _____. 1984? _____.
    1980?_____.

30. Did you vote in the local elections in 1986? _____. 1982? _____.
    1978?_____

31. Other than as a voter, are you active politically? _____. If "yes," please
    explain briefly.

32. Have you been active in the campaign of any candidate(s) for elective
    office in the District of Columbia? _____. If "yes," please explain briefly.

33. Have you ever held elected or appointed office in the District of
    Columbia government? _____. If "yes," please explain briefly.

34. Have you ever held elected or appointed office in the federal government
    or any other state or local government? _____. If "yes," please explain
    briefly.

35. Have you ever been employed by the District of Columbia government?
    _____. If "yes," please explain briefly (including each position you have
    held, the inclusive dates of your employment in that position, and the
    department[s] or agency[ies] for which you have worked).

36. Have you had any contracts to supply goods or services to the District of
    Columbia government in the past four years? _____. If "yes," please
    explain briefly.

37. Have you received any benefits or services not given to the public-at-large
    from the District of Columbia government in the past four years?_____.
    If "yes," please explain briefly.

38. Have you ever contributed money or property to any candidate(s) for elective office in the District of Columbia? _____. If "yes," please explain briefly (including the identity[ies] of the candidate[s] and the election year[s]).

39. Have you, or any member of your family, contributed to any fund for the benefit of Marion Barry or his family since January 18, 1990? _____. If "yes," please explain briefly.

40. Have you, or any member of your family, attended any fundraisers, rallies, receptions, or other functions in support or in honor of Marion Barry since January 18, 1990? _____. If "yes," please explain briefly.

41. Have you had any major disputes or litigation with the United States government or District of Columbia government in the past four years? _____. If "yes," please explain briefly.

42. Other than what you have stated in answer to a previous question, or the relationships we all have in common with the government, do you, or does any relative or close friend, have any special connection with the District of Columbia government? _____. If "yes," please explain briefly.

Part IV

43. Have you, any member of your immediate family, or a close personal friend ever been employed by any local, state or federal law enforcement agency? _____. If "yes," please explain briefly.

44. Have you, or has any member of your family, ever contributed to an organization sponsored by, or for the benefit of, law enforcement officers (e.g., the Metropolitan Police Boys and Girls Club, the Fraternal Order of Police, etc.)? _____. If "yes," please explain briefly.

45. Have you or any member of your immediate family ever studied law, practiced law, or been employed by a lawyer or law firm?_____. If "yes," please explain briefly.

46. Have you ever served on a grand jury? _____. If "yes," please explain briefly.

47. Have you ever served on a trial jury? _____ . If "yes," were the case(s) criminal? _____ . civil?_____. other?_____. Please state where and when you have so served.

Part V

48. Do you attend church or synagogue on a regular basis? _____. If "yes," please explain briefly.

49. Have you, or has any relative or close friend, ever had a drinking problem or suffered from alcoholism? _____ . If "yes," please explain briefly.

50. Do you hold any personal opinions about alcoholism? _____. If "yes," please explain briefly.

51. Have you, or has any relative or close friend, ever been addicted to any drug? _____. If "yes," please explain briefly.

52. Have you had any other personal or family experience with substance abuse? _____. If "yes," please explain briefly.

53. Do you have any opinion as to whether certain drugs that are now illegal should be legalized? _____. If "yes," please explain briefly.

54. Do you have any opinion as to whether a person is ever justified in lying after having taken an oath to tell the truth?_____. If "yes," please explain briefly.

55. Do you hold any personal opinions about the use of undercover, or "sting," operations by law enforcement agencies, in which, for example, friends or associates of a subject co-operate in monitoring the subject's activities? _____ . If "yes," please check the response below which most accurately reflects your opinion.

_____ I am opposed to such methods.

_____ I favor the use of such methods.

_____ I have some reservations about the use of such methods, but realize they are sometimes necessary.

Please explain briefly, if you wish.

56. Do you have an opinion about the fairness of law enforcement agencies using concealed video and audio recording devices during the course of an undercover investigation? _____ . If "yes," please check the response below which most accurately reflects your opinion.

_____ I am opposed to the use of concealed recording devices.

_____ I favor the use of concealed recording devices.

_____ I have some reservations about the use of concealed recording devices, but realize they are sometimes necessary.

Please explain briefly, if you wish.

57. Do you hold any personal opinions about persons engaged in the fields of law or law enforcement (e.g. the Metropolitan Police Department, the FBI, or the Drug Enforcement Administration)?_____. If "yes," please explain briefly.

58. Do you hold any personal opinions about politicians or high government officials in general? _____. If "yes," please explain briefly.

59. Do you hold any opinions about the District of Columbia's form of government? _____. If "yes," please explain briefly.

60. Do you have an opinion as to whether race or politics played any part in the charges against Mr. Barry? _____. If "yes," please explain briefly.

61. Have you ever believed yourself to be a victim of prejudice of any sort? _____. If so, explain briefly.

Part VI

62. Have you, or has any relative or close friend, ever been a victim of a crime? _____ . Charged with a crime?_____. A witness to a crime? _____ . If any answer is "yes," please explain briefly.

63. Have you, or has any relative or close friend, ever been falsely accused of a crime? _____. If "yes," please explain briefly.

64. Have you, or has any relative or close friend, ever participated in a criminal trial in any other capacity (e.g., party, lawyer, witness, juror, investigator, etc.)? _____. If "yes," please explain briefly.

Part VII

65. If, during the course of jury deliberations, a fellow juror should suggest that you disregard the law or the evidence, and decide the case on other grounds, would you, as a juror, be able to reject the suggestion and abide by your oath to this Court to decide the case solely on the evidence and the law as the Court has instructed you, without regard to sympathy, bias or prejudice? _____. If "no," please explain briefly.

66. Do you hold any religious or philosophical beliefs that forbid your rendering judgment upon the innocence or guilt of another person? _____. If "yes," please explain briefly.

67. Would a defendant's religious beliefs, or the fact that a defendant had asked for Divine forgiveness, affect your judgment upon his innocence or guilt of a criminal charge in any way? _____. If "yes," please explain briefly.

68. Is there anything, or any reason at all, however personal or private, that makes you feel you should not serve as a juror on this case, or could not be a fair and impartial juror? _____. If "yes," please explain briefly.

69. Do any of the foregoing questions touch upon matters that you regard as deeply personal and would like to keep private, that is, not released to the press or public generally? _____. If "yes," please identify those questions *by question number alone.*

I declare under penalty of perjury that the foregoing answers to each question are true and correct, to the best of my knowledge and belief.

_____

Signature

_____

Date

Security Orders

Security Order

In the Circuit Court of the State of Oregon
For the County of Multnomah

ENGEDAW BERHANU, on
behalf of the Estate and heirs of
Mulegeta Scrawl Deceased,
      Plaintiff,

        vs.

TOM METZGER, WHITE
ARYAN RESISTANCE,

JOHN METZGER, KENNETH
MIESKE and KYLE BREWSTER,

      Defendants.

A8911-07007

ORDER ALLOWING USE

OF METAL DETECTOR
AND HAND SEARCH

IT IS HEREBY ORDERED that all persons entering the Multnomah County Courthouse commencing on Monday, October 8, 1990, after hours and on weekends until trial is finished will submit to a metal detector search of their person, and a hand search of all bags, briefcases, valises, and hand-carried clothing by any representative of the Multnomah County Sheriff's Office, pursuant to the authority provided in ORS 206.010(5).

IT IS HEREBY FURTHER ORDERED that any representative of the Multnomah County Sheriff's Office shall have the authority to require any person who enters the Courthouse to leave any bags, briefcases, or valises at the Information Desk in the Courthouse.

DATED this 5th day of October, 1990.

DONALD H. LONDER, Judge

Security Order

Superior Court of the State of California
For the County of Los Angeles

THE PEOPLE OF THE STATE
OF CALIFORNIA
          Plaintiff,   Case No. A-750900

          vs.   ORDER RE SECURITY

RAYMOND BUCKEY,
          Defendant.

    It is the opinion of this Court based upon information derived from investigative and public sources that the potential exists for disruption of orderly proceedings in this case.

    IT IS THE ORDER OF THIS COURT that the Sheriff of Los Angeles County shall place into effect the following security measures immediately and until rescinded by further order of this court, in and around designated security areas in the Central District Department 101 and the 9th floor of the Los Angeles Superior Court.

    1. All persons desiring to enter the courtroom shall be searched for weapons at the discretion of the Sheriff, including their person, briefcases, packages, and containers of all description, prior to being admitted into the courtroom. Failure to submit to search shall result in denial of entry into the courtroom.

    2. Bags, packages, or containers of unreasonable size shall be excluded from the courtroom.

    3. All persons desiring entry into the courtroom during proceedings shall produce valid and satisfactory identification upon demand by the Sheriff. Failure to produce such identification upon demand shall result in denial of entry into the courtroom.

    4. The Sheriff shall provide such adequate numbers of personnel as will ensure that a proper level of security is effected within the security areas.

DATED: January 29, 1990

_____

                         Judge, William R. Pounders

Trial Security Plan

Interior Courthouse Security
Tom Metzger Trial
Monday, October 8, 1990
Lt. Gerry Nyberg

Situation:

On Monday, October 8, 1990, a civil trial involving Tom and John Metzger as defendants shall commence at the Multnomah County Courthouse. It is estimated that the trial could last for as long as a month. A potential for the disturbances, and/or violence exists within the courthouse and within the courtroom. The trial is expected to be the focus of concentrated media attention both locally and nationally. Large demonstrations are anticipated.

A. Potential Threats:

The judge, litigants, and several witnesses are considered to be high risk targets for assault or even assassination. Several have already received threats. The potential exists for violence to erupt in the court room or elsewhere in the courthouse.

The opposing parties in this proceeding are extremely hostile toward each other. Fringe elements sympathetic to both sides are considered capable of carrying out acts of violence or terrorism. Both sides have put out a call to associates nationwide to congregate in Portland for the trial.

Past dealings by police with elements from both sides have erupted into violence directed at officers. On Monday, September 24, 1990, Portland Police Bureau officers clashed with similar groups during a vice presidential visit, resulting in 51 arrests. Assaults upon officers and random acts of violence were experienced throughout the demonstration in the downtown area.

Mission:

The Multnomah County Sheriff's office (MCSO) has responsibility for security and maintenance of order within the courthouse, and within the courtroom. The Portland Police Bureau shall assist MCSO by providing a reaction team located on the same floor as the courtroom. A Police Bureau Lieutenant shall act as a liaison with MCSO in their command post.

Central Precinct shall be responsible for maintenance of order outside of the courthouse. They shall also be prepared to respond to requests for assistance from inside the courthouse.

Execution:
A. Concept of Operation: (Courthouse Interior Detail)
An MCSO command post shall be located in room #430 of the courthouse, and shall become operational at 0700 hours on Monday, October 8, 1990. It shall remain operational during the hours that the trial is in session.

The trial shall be held in room #546 serving as Judge Haggerty's chambers. MCSO shall control access to the entire north side of the 5th floor, from room #534 to room #546. They shall electronically search everyone entering the perimeter.

The Police Bureau reaction team of one uniformed Sergeant and six uniformed officers shall be located in room #540. They shall respond as needed to the court room or to the hallway behind the MCSO perimeter. They shall not be used at the MCSO fixed posts. They shall not respond to problems outside the perimeter.

Fifth Floor Posts:
Posts 1 and 2:
> Shall be MCSO deputies attired in green blazers. They shall be located inside of room #544 in positions allowing them to respond immediately to situations inside the court room.

Posts 3 and 4:
> Shall be unarmed MCSO FSO's attired in green blazers. They shall be located at a checkpoint containing a magnetometer located in the north hall of the 5th floor between room #546 and room #548. They shall electronically and/or physically search every person entering the secure area.

Posts 5 and 6:
> Shall be MCSO deputies in uniform. They shall be located at a check point containing a magnetometer located in the north hall of the 5th floor between room #546 and room #548. They shall prevent unauthorized persons from entering the secure area, and assist posts 3 and 4 in adequately searching persons authorized to enter the secure area.

Posts 7 and 8:
> Shall be MCSO deputies in uniform. They shall be located at a barricade located in the west hall of the 5th floor, between room #530 and room #534. No unescorted persons shall pass this position into the secure area. *All* escorted persons shall pass through a magnetometer at this post.

Post 9:

Shall be a MCSO deputy in uniform. This post is located in the jail elevator corridor in the west hall. This post is responsible for controlling the jail elevator, coordinating prisoner movement with the arrival and departure of our protectees.

Post 10:

Shall he a MCSO deputy in uniform. This post shall be used to relieve posts 1 through 9, and to occasionally monitor the activity on the first floor.

Post 11: (MCSO Reaction Team)

Shall consist of a MCSO sergeant and three deputies in uniform located in room #828. The team shall act as a first responder to incidents elsewhere in the courthouse. The team shall be dispatched via the MCSO command post (call #160).

Task to Subordinates:

At a meeting with Judge Londer and Judge Haggerty, it was agreed that the following rules shall be followed to ensure an orderly trial and the security of the participants:

1. All officers assigned within the perimeter, including those inside the Court room shall be armed. Armed officers in plainclothes shall be so identified.

2. All persons who enter the perimeter shall be searched electronically. Parcels and baggage shall be hand searched.

3. No unescorted persons shall enter or exit the secure area except by the checkpoint located on the northeast corner.

4. Protectees, to include the judge and jury, shall be escorted to the secure area via the jail elevator located within the perimeter, across from Room #534. Protectee movements shall be coordinated with MCSO prisoner transports and the protection teams commanded by Lt. Greg Clark. Evacuation of the protectees in the event of an incident shall be accomplished in cooperation with Lt. Clark's teams.

5. Prior to 0700 hours each day, bomb sweeps shall be conducted within the perimeter, and in designated areas on the fourth and sixth floors. The sweeps shall be conducted by the POP bomb dog and PPB EDU teams commanded by Lt. Mark Paresi. MCSO shall post the fixed perimeter positions immediately after the sweeps and maintain the posting until the conclusion of the court day.

In the event of a threat, or the detection of an actual device, MCSO's procedures regarding threats and/or evacuation of the Courthouse shall be followed (see attached). PPB shall provide assistance as requested in these circumstances.

6. The roof of the Courthouse and/or adjacent buildings shall be posted with PPB SERT spotter/anti-sniper teams under the command of Lt. Mark Paresi.

7. PPB officers assigned to the detail shall remain on the floor while the perimeter is in place. MCSO shall provide meals for all officers assigned to the Courthouse interior detail.

8. The curtains in Rooms #542, #544, and #546 shall remain closed for the duration of the trial.

9. The hallway windows across from Room #544 shall be covered to obscure vision for the duration of the trial.

10. The Fifth floor stairwell adjacent to the jail elevator shall remain locked and the windows covered for the duration of the trial.

11. The men's restroom across from Room #550 shall remain locked for the duration of the trial.

12. Barriers shall be placed behind the checkpoints at either end of the hall to obscure vision into the secure area.

13. On Monday, October 8, the jury panel shall be seated in Room #602 for preliminary instructions by Judge Haggerty. MCSO shall post two Deputies at the door to control access. Admittance shall be limited to those persons presenting authorization, a letter from the Court. Judge Haggerty's protection team shall be present inside the room.

Potential jurors shall be brought to Room #544 in groups of 12 to 15, via the west stairwell accessed through Room #600. The perimeter on the fifth floor shall be maintained throughout the jury selection process.

14. Media relations/rules during the duration of the trial shall be the responsibility of PPB PIO Det. Dave Simpson and MCSO Sergeant Judy Taylor. Questions/conflicts shall be referred to them for resolution.

Media seating in the Courtroom shall be limited to two benches. (Approximately 14 persons.) Admittance shall be on a first come, first seated basis via the magnetometer checkpoint. Proper media credentials shall be required. All media persons shall be searched prior to entering the perimeter.

Media persons leaving the Courtroom shall lose their seat to the next person in line. No media persons shall be allowed in the hallway within the perimeter.

Media persons shall not have direct access to the judge, jury, or protectees within the perimeter. Requests for interviews, etc. shall be arranged privately between the parties involved.

15. Public access to the Courtroom shall be controlled by MCSO. Conflicts or questions shall be referred to either Sgt. Judy Taylor or Lt. Bud Johnson for resolution.

Public seating in the Courtroom shall be limited to those seats not pre-reserved by Judge Haggerty.

Admittance shall be on a first come first seated basis via the magnetometer checkpoint. All persons shall be searched prior to entering the perimeter.

Persons leaving the Courtroom shall lose their seat to the next person in line. No persons shall be allowed in the hallway within the perimeter.

16. Police Officers and other employees wishing to be spectators shall be admitted with the public via the magnetometer on a first come first seated basis. Officers not assigned to the detail *shall not* be armed within the perimeter. This information shall be relayed to PPB and MCSO officers via roll call.

17. The Courthouse shall be locked down from approximately 1730 hours to 0700 hours each weekday. MCSO shall be responsible for controlling access during these hours to persons with legitimate business. Persons admitted during non-business hours shall pass through a magnetometer inside the fourth street doors.

18. PPB Central Precinct district officers shall be instructed to make regular inspections of the outside of the Courthouse and other Downtown governmental buildings during the course of their shifts.

Coordinating Instructions

Direct contact shall be maintained between the PPB Command Post in the Justice Center and MCSO command post in the courthouse via radio and telephone. PPB Lt. Nyberg shall be present in the MCSO Command Post when court is in session to assist in coordinating activities between the agencies.

Movement of the judge, jury, and protectees shall be coordinated between the Court, Lt. Nyberg, Lt. Clark, and MCSO Corrections Commanders.

Bomb sweeps and the handling of any suspected devices shall be coordinated between MCSO, Lt. Nyberg and Lt. Paresi.

PPB Courthouse Interior Detail
Commander—Lt. Gerry Nyberg, BPST #1762
Detail Supervisor
Sgt. Garland Snowden, PST #2235

Officer Tom Peavey, BPST #4578
Officer Neal Schmitt, BPST #14534
Officer Jason Saunders, BPST #23691
Officer Terry Kruger, BPST #21778
Officer Charlie Brown, BPST #11925
Officer Harry Jackson, BPST #9556

UNIFORM AND EQUIPMENT:
Short sleeve uniform shirt—no tie
Uniform trousers
PR-24
Helmet
One North Precinct packset (Sergeant only)

Instructions:

Report to Central Precinct roll call room each day at 0700 hours.

City vehicles shall be parked in the public parking structure located at S.W. 1st and Jefferson Street. A sign-up sheet shall be provided at the entrance. No special provision has been made for privately owned vehicles.

MCSO shall provide noontime meals at the courthouse. Detail officers shall not leave the building during the noon break.

Tips for Coping after Jury Duty

The techniques in this brochure may be helpful in understanding your experience as a juror.

Superior Court of Arizona
In Maricopa County
101 W. Jefferson
Phoenix, AZ 85003

The Jury Duty Experience

Thank you for serving your community. Being on a jury is a rewarding experience which in some cases may be quite demanding. You were asked to listen to testimony and to examine facts and evidence. Coming to decisions is often not easy, but your participation is appreciated.

Serving on a jury is not a common experience and may cause some jurors to have temporary symptoms of distress.

This booklet reviews ways to cope with symptoms of distress. Not everyone feels anxiety or increased stress after jury duty. However, it may be helpful to be aware of the symptoms if they arise.

Some temporary signs of distress following jury duty include: anxiety, sleep or appetite changes, moodiness, physical problems, (e.g. headaches, stomach aches, no energy, and the like), second guessing your verdict, feeling guilty, fear, trouble dealing with issues or topics related to the case, a desire to be by yourself, or decreased concentration or memory problems.

Symptoms may come and go, but will eventually go away. To help yourself, it is important to admit any symptoms you may have and deal with any unpleasant reactions.

Coping Techniques After Serving on a Jury

- Talk to family members and friends. One of the best ways to put your jury experience in perspective is to discuss your feelings and reactions with loved ones and friends. You may also want to talk with your family physician or a member of the clergy.
- Stick to your normal, daily routines. It is important to return to your normal schedule. Don't isolate yourself.

- Before you leave the court, you may wish to get the names and numbers of at least two of your fellow jurors. Sometimes it is helpful to talk to people who went through the experience with you. This can help you to remember that you were part of a group (jury) and are not alone.
- Remember that you are having normal responses to an unusual experience. You can deal with signs of distress by cutting down on alcohol, caffeine, and nicotine. These substances can increase anxiety, fatigue and make sleep problems worse.
- Relax with deep breathing.
  Breathe in slowly through your nose.
  Breathe out through your mouth.
  Slow your thoughts down and think about a relaxing scene.
  Continue deep breathing until you feel more relaxed.
  Cope with sleep problems.
- Increase your daily exercise, but do not exercise just before bedtime.
  Decrease your caffeine consumption, especially in the afternoon or evening.
  Do "boring" activities before bedtime.
  Listen to relaxation tapes or relaxing music before bedtime.

Final Thoughts
- Remember that jury service is the responsibility of good citizens.
- Resist negative thoughts about the verdict.
- No matter what others think about the verdict, your opinion is the only one that matters.
- You don't have to prove yourself to anyone.
- Sometimes it takes a lot of courage to serve on a jury. Some cases are very violent and brutal and hard to deal with. The case is now over and it is important for you to get on with your life.
- If you are fearful of retaliation or if you are threatened after the trial, tell the court and/or law enforcement immediately.

If signs of distress persist for two weeks after jury service has ended, you may wish to contact your primary care physician, a counselor, or one of the following agencies for a referral.

Mental Health Association of Arizona: 602-994-4407 • 800-642-9277
Arizona Psychiatric Society: 602-898-3314
Arizona Psychological Association: 602-675-9477

Acknowledgments

The development and publication of this manual reflects the efforts and support of a wide variety of persons and entities. The project was funded by the State Justice Institute. We are particularly indebted to Kathy Schwartz, the Deputy Chief of the Program Division of the State Justice Institute, who has been the grant monitor throughout the project. From the project's inception to the arduous drafting and editing of the manual, Kathy Schwartz has been generous with her time, sympathetic to our problems, and unwavering in her support.

The project staff owes a major debt of gratitude to the project advisory committee, whose members made themselves readily available for guidance and assistance throughout the project. The advisory committee consisted of:

Honorable Roger W. Boren
Court of Appeal
Second Appellate District
Los Angeles, California

Ms. Carol Ivy
KGO TV News
San Francisco, California

Honorable Stephen Crane
Justice of the Supreme Court
New York, New York

Mr. R. William Linden, Jr.
State Court Administrator
Salem, Oregon

Mr. Joseph Fallin
Assistant to the Executive Officer
Los Angeles Superior Court
Los Angeles, California

Mr. Donald I. Pollock
Director of the Legal Division
Administrative Office of Courts
Dade County, Florida

This advisory committee contributed remarkable talents, insight, and expertise, which was particularly useful in developing and refining the data collection instrument and during the final review and editing process of this manual.

The project staff is especially indebted to Justice Steve Crane, who supervised the arrangements for a judges' forum held in Manhattan. Moreover, his willingness to undertake the grim task of microscopically editing the footnotes of this manual while commuting to work on a crowded Manhattan subway train in the middle of July was certainly service above and beyond the call of duty and reflects a degree of devotion rarely found in the annals of advisory committee service. Similarly, Don Pollock's legal expertise has been a steady source of insight and guidance as we raised repeated questions of law and legal precedent with him throughout the project. We certainly appreciated both of their contributions, and the contributions of each of the advisory committee members.

The success of a project of this type depends on the degree of cooperation and access granted by judges and court officials. This project relied for its ideas, insights, recommendations, and occasional inspiration on the cooperation and assistance of judges, court administrators, court staff, television and newspaper reporters, attorneys, and former judges. Without their gracious willingness to take time from their demanding schedules to be interviewed by the project staff and share their thoughts and recommendations, this project could not have gone forward. Because this project relied so heavily on the insights and expertise of those with whom we spoke, we want to acknowledge prominently their contribution. The following are the sites we visited and people with whom the project staff spoke during the course of the project and upon whom we have relied for much of the material contained in this manual:

Los Angeles County Superior Court, Los Angeles, California
People v. Virginia McMartin, et al.
People v. Raymond Buckey
Buchwald v. Paramount Pictures

Judge Richard Byrne
Judge David Horowitz
Judge William R. Pounders
Judge Harvey A. Schneider
Judge Stanley M. Weisberg
Frank Zolin, Executive Officer and County Clerk
Raymond Arce, Jury Manager
Juanita Blankenship, Office of Jury Commissioner
Judy Rivituso, Office of Jury Commissioner
Edward Breckke, Assistant Director, Criminal Division
John Iverson, Criminal Courts Coordinator
Joseph Fallin, Assistant to the Executive Officer
Roger Gunson, Deputy District Attorney
Pamela Ferrero, Deputy District Attorney
James Gilpin, Deputy Sheriff and Bailiff
Joseph Hellmond, Sergeant, Los Angeles County Sheriff
Kenneth Johnson, Lieutenant, Los Angeles County Sheriff
Rebecca Kuzins, Public Information Officer, Los Angeles Superior Court
Sandi Gibbons, Public Information Officer, District Attorney's Office

Dawn Webber, *Valley Daily News*
Daniel G. Davis, Attorney for Raymond Buckey

Multnomah County Circuit Court, Portland, Oregon
Engedaw Berhanu v. Tom Metzger, White Aryan Resistance, et al.

Judge Ancer L. Haggerty
Dan Wood, Administrative Services Director
Janice Hall, Jury Room Coordinator
Judy Taylor, Sergeant, Multnomah County Sheriff
Dave Simpson, Detective, Portland Police Bureau

Connecticut Superior Court, Bridgeport, Connecticut
Julius Gold v. Paul Newman, et al.

Judge George N. Thim
Edwin S. Mak, Sheriff, Fairfield County
Anthony Pelegrino, Lieutenant, Fairfield County Sheriff
Warren Tingley, Lieutenant, Fairfield County Sheriff
Walter Olbrys, Special Deputy Sheriff, Fairfield County Sheriff
Don Mastrony, Chief Court Clerk
Bruce Olcott, Reporter, WVIT television
Richard L. Albrecht, Attorney for Julius Gold
W. Patrick Ryan, Attorney for Paul Newman

Orange County Superior Court, Santa Ana, California
Anna Johnson v. Mark and Crispina Calvert

Judge Richard N. Parslow, Jr.
Alan Slater, Court Administrator
Marci Dambert, Courtroom Clerk
Jim Springer, Deputy Sheriff and Bailiff
Tricia Takasugi, Orange County News Channel
William Vogeler, Reporter, Los Angeles Daily Journal
Robert Walmsley, Attorney for Mark and Crispina Calvert
Harold LaFlamme, Attorney and Guardian ad litem for child

Twenty-ninth Judicial Circuit, Talladega, Alabama
State v. Daniel L. Siebert
State v. Judy Haney
State v. John Peoples

Judge William C. Sullivan
Judge Jerry L. Fielding
Judge George N. Simms
Robert L. Rumsey, District Attorney
John Dyson, Court Bailiff
Mike Anderson, Reporter, *Talladega Daily Home*

New York State Supreme Court, White Plains, New York
People v. Jean Harris
People v. Kathy Boudin and Sam Brown

Justice David Ritter
Russell Leggett, Retired Justice of the Supreme Court
Nicholas Federici, Senior Administrative Assistant to the Administrative
Judge

Court of Common Pleas, Pittsburgh, Pennsylvania
Abortion Protesters Trespass Trial

Judge Robert E. Dauer
Charles H. Starrett, Jr., Allegheny County Court Administrator

Judges' Forum, New York, New York
People v. Robert Chambers
People v. Bernhard Goetz
People v. Antron McCray
      v. Yusef Salaam
      v. Raymond Santana
People v. John Gotti
People v. Joel Steinberg
U.S. v. Bess Meyerson
U.S. v. Imelda Marcos
U.S. v. Gaetano Badalamienti
Westmoreland v. CBS

Justice Howard E. Bell
Justice Stephen G. Crane
Justice Thomas Galligan
Justice Edward J. McLaughlin
Justice Harold Rothwax
Judge John F. Keenan
Judge Pierre N. Leval

United States District Court for the District of Columbia
U.S. v. Oliver L. North
U.S. v. Marion S. Barry, Jr.
Judge Gerhard Gesell
Judge Thomas Penfield Jackson
LeeAnn Flynn Hall, Administrative Assistant to the Chief Judge
Nancy Mayer-Whittington, Clerk, U.S. District Court
Carl Stern, Law Correspondent, NBC News

The project staff was also assisted in a variety of important ways by National Center staff. Dr. Geoff Gallas, Vice President for Research and Technical Services of the National Center for State Courts, was a ready source of encouragement and assistance, as were Charles Ferrell and Alexander Aikman, Vice Presidents of the National Center's Southeastern and Western regional offices, respectively. Michael Haas and William Brousseau assisted in the early site visit and data collection. Mary Louise Clifford was instrumental in imposing some order on the prose and format of the final manuscript. Andrea Amy was particularly helpful checking and verifying cites in the legal section of the document. The painstaking efforts of Angela Lewis and Suzanne Dassel in typing, editing, retyping, and reformatting the final manuscript were particularly noteworthy as were the efforts of Cathy Grandison, Karin Higa, Antigone Foreman, and Helen Ogata who assisted in the typing and editing tasks at the National Center's Western Regional Office.

This publication reflects the generous assistance and dedicated efforts of many persons who have reviewed, edited, commented upon, and thereby enhanced this final product. To all of those who have assisted and supported in the production and publication of this manual, we express our sincere appreciation and gratitude.

Genevra Kay Loveland   G. Thomas Munsterman   Timothy R. Murphy
December 1991

Index

with sequestered juries, 91
Emotional stress, of jurors, 97-98, 207-208
Encryption, of closed-circuit television
    transmission, 52
Equipment, audiovisual. See also *Cameras,*
    in courtroom; Television coverage.
    costs of in change-of-venue cases, 138
    court accommodation of, 53-54
    New York court rules on, 177-178
    pretrial decisions about, 26
    rules governing use in courtroom, 54,
        161, 166, 173-174, 177-178
    security considerations with, 105
Escorts, security, of jurors, judges, and
    parties, 59, 108
    in Tom Metzger trial, 203
Evacuation procedures, in courtroom and
    courthouse, 103
Evidence, media access to, 48-49, 113. See
    also *Media access.*
    pretrial planning for, 27
Executive officer. See *Court administrator.*
Exhibits, media access to, media liaison
    handling of, 146-147
    pretrial planning for, 27
    restrictions on, 115, 117
Extortion threats, media restrictions with,
    118
Extrajudicial communications. See also
    Attorneys, extrajudicial statements of.
    restraints on, legal background materi-
        als on, 120-127

F

Family members, of victims or parties,
        courtroom seating of, 44-45, 146
    prohibition of media coverage of, 176
Farrakhan, Louis, 150
Favoritism, avoidance of, in dealing with
        media, 41-42
Ferguson, Colin, 18
Filings, clerk's, Internet access to, 49
    media access to, 48-49
    media liaison handling of, 48-49,
        146-147
    pretrial planning for, 27
Firearms, courtroom policy on, 102
First Amendment, attorney speech and, 123
    gag orders and, 58, 120-121
    public seating and, 151
    right of access to judicial proceedings,
        legal background materials on,
        113-119
    right to commercial speech and,
        court's restriction of, 126
First Amendment Coalition, 152
Florida, right of access for television
    cameras, 116

Fourteenth Amendment, violation of,
    pretrial publicity and, 115
Fourth Amendment, right-of-access
    restrictions and, 116-117
Francke, Terry, 152
Fully Informed Jury Association (FIJA),
    protection of jurors from, 57

G

Gacy, John Wayne, 22
Gag orders, alternatives to, 15
    on attorney speech, 12, 14-15
    enforcement of, 15
    "indirect," 121
    "limited," 121
    on media, 15
        legal background materials on,
            120-122
    persons affected by, 14, 14n.
    recent success of, 14, 58
    requirements for, 14
    for shielding jury, 58-59
Gentile v. State Bar of Nevada, 12-13,
    122-125
Gesell, Judge Gerhard A., 42, 145-148
Globe Newspaper Co. v. Superior Court, 118
Goetz, Bernhard, 88, 153
Grant, Cary, 9

H

Ham v. South Carolina, 129
Hand searches, for courtroom entry,
    105, 117
    security orders for, 199-200
Hearings, ex parte, 43
    handling of, in dealing with media,
        42-43
    on motions to close judicial proceed-
        ings or seal records, 43, 113
    preliminary, right of access to, 113
    pretrial planning for, 28
    suppression, 168
        right of access to, 113, 176
Helicopters, 110
Hinckley, John, 71
Holton, Lynn, 155

I

Identification, for courtroom access,
    security considerations and, 105
In camera proceedings, media access to, 43,
    56-57
    in California, 165
    in New York, 175
    restrictions on, 118-119
    in voir dire, 80, 81
        background legal materials on,
            132-133

About the Authors

Timothy R. Murphy is an attorney with the Hampton County (Virginia) Commonwealth Attorney's Office. He has served as a senior staff attorney with the National Center for State Courts and is one of the coauthors of *A Manual for Managing Notorious Cases* (first edition, 1992).

Paula L. Hannaford is an attorney and senior research analyst for the National Center for State Courts' Research Division. She has contributed to several NCSC publications, including *Jury Trial Innovations, Resolving Disputes Over Life-sustaining Treatment: A Health Care Provider's Guide*, and *A Manual for Cooperation Between State and Federal Courts*. Her areas of expertise include jury system management and trial procedure; legal and judicial ethics and discipline; state-federal jurisdiction; and probate court procedure. Ms. Hannaford received a J.D. from the Marshall-Wythe School of Law of the College of William and Mary and an M.P.P from the Thomas Jefferson Program in Public Policy of the College of William and Mary.

Genevra Kay Loveland is senior attorney/producer-writer for the Federal Judicial Center in Washington, D.C. She is currently producing *Perspectives on Probation and Pretrial Services*, a video magazine program for the Federal Judicial Television Network. She served as a senior staff attorney with the National Center for State Courts and is one of the coauthors of *A Manual for Managing Notorious Cases* (first edition 1992). Ms. Loveland has a J.D. (Order of the Coif) from the University of Texas Law School and served as a law clerk on the U.S. Court of Appeals for the Ninth Circuit.

G. Thomas Munsterman is director and cofounder of the Center for Jury Studies of the National Center for State Courts. He is coauthor of *A Guide to Jury System Management* (1975) and *A Manual for Managing Notorious Cases* (first edition, 1992), author of *Jury System Management* (1996), and a contributor to *Jury Trial Innovations* (1997). Mr. Munsterman has worked with the ABA/JAD Committee on Jury Standards since its inception in 1982 in the development, implementation, and revision of trial court jury standards. He has testified as the court's witness in cases concerning jury representativeness and jury management and has testified before state legislative committees. In 1993 he was part of a team sent to Russia to provide technical assistance for the reintroduction of the right to trial by jury. He holds a BSEE from Northwestern University and a MSE from George Washington University.

About the National Center for State Courts

The nation's state chief justices founded the National Center for State Courts (NCSC) in 1971 with the support of Chief Justice Warren E. Burger. NCSC is a nonprofit organization dedicated to improving the administration of justice in our state courts by providing both leadership and service to the state courts through direct technical assistance and consulting, research and technology, information and education, government relations and association management, and international exchange and cooperation.

For More Information, Contact:
Headquarters
300 Newport Avenue (23185)
P.O. Box 8798
Williamsburg, VA 23187-8798
(800) 877-1233
fax: (757) 220-0449

Court Services Division
1331 Seventeenth Street, Suite 402
Denver, CO 80202-1554
(800) 466-3063
fax: (303) 296-9007

Office of Government Relations
1700 North Moore Street, Suite 1710
Arlington, VA 22209
(703) 841-0200
fax: (703) 841-0206

We invite you to visit NCSC's Website. Set your browser to http://www.ncsc.dni.us/.